MW01343182

Gunsmoke in Lincoln County

Philip J. Rasch

Gunsmoke in Lincoln County

By Philip J. Rasch

Introduction by Frederick Nolan

Edited by Robert K. DeArment

Outlaw-Lawman Research Series
Volume II
Limited to 1,000 Copies

National Association for Outlaw and Lawman
History, Inc.

In affiliation with the
University of Wyoming
Laramie, Wyoming

Rasch, Philip J.

Gunsmoke in Lincoln County / by Philip J. Rasch: introduction by Frederick Nolan; edited by Robert K. DeArment.

p. cm.—(Outlaw-lawman research series; v.2)

Includes bibliographical reference and index.

ISBN 0-935269-24-X

1. Lincoln County (N.M.)—History. 2. Violence—New Mexico-Lincoln County—History—19th century. 3. Frontier and pioneer life—New Mexico—Lincoln County. I. DeArment, Robert K., 1925- . II. Title. III. Series.

F802.L7R37 1996 96-44659

9778.9'6404—dc20 CIP

Cover design by Marcus Huff.

Cover painting by Gary Zaboly.

ISBN 0–935269–24–X

Distributed by Western Publications, PO Box 2107, Stillwater, Oklahoma 74076, 1-800-749-3369.

Manufactured in the United States of America. First edition.

CONTENTS

Editor's Note

This volume is the second book-length collection of articles authored by Philip J. Rasch and published by The National Association for Outlaw and Lawman History, Inc. (NOLA). The first, *Trailing Billy the Kid*, with articles written by Dr. Rasch over a period of thirty-five years and focusing on the forever fascinating New Mexico outlaw, Henry McCarty, a.k.a. William Bonney, appeared in 1995.

Gunsmoke in Lincoln County contains twenty-one chapters which first appeared as what Rasch always called "papers," all dealing with his primary interest, the violent history of Lincoln County, New Mexico, and published between 1949 and 1970. The chapters have not been arranged in their order of appearance, but in accordance with the chronology of the events they describe. The pieces first appeared in publications ranging from scholarly historical quarterlies to Brand Books and Newsletters of Westerners groups from Los Angeles to England and popular Western magazines.

While these articles deal primarily with events in New Mexico's turbulent frontier past, a planned third volume will focus on individuals, other than Billy the Kid, who played important roles in that drama.

Sadly, Phil Rasch did not survive to see his lifetime work appear in book form, but it is the hope of this editor that these volumes will serve as a kind of monument to the memory of this tireless research pioneer and chronicler of the history of the American Wild West. William D. "Bill" Reynolds, whose untiring efforts to hunt down and collect the complete works of Phil Rasch made these volumes possible, has also passed over the divide since we began this project. Like Phil Rasch he will be sorely missed by those of us who were privileged to know him.

Robert K. DeArment
May, 1996

INTRODUCTION

Treasure the articles you are about to read. Each of them could be considered a benchmark, the minimum required entry level for anyone professing to be or wishing to become a researcher into the history of the Old West. Philip J. Rasch, the man who wrote them, was—no other word will do—a phenomenon. Writing about him—*inter alia* Honorary President of the English Westerners Society, NOLA Lifetime Achievement Award winner, recipient of the Ralph Emerson Twitchell Award for his contribution to history—is a little bit like writing about a Jim Bridger, a Kit Carson, a Jedediah Smith. For nearly half a century he was out there in front, blazing completely new trails, and becoming something of a legend in the process.

In these days of computerized records it is easy to forget that when Phil began researching the Lincoln County War, information retrieval was in its infancy, and the best "authorities" most of us had to work with were of the Burns and Raine variety. Looking back on the sheer volume of his work now it is hard to remember a time when he wasn't there, writing prodigious numbers of letters, finding what always seemed to me then—stranded as I then was in England, for I did not even set foot in the United States until 1971—totally, remarkably unfindable material. I unhesitatingly confess to having shamelessly emulated his technique and his preference for doing research by mail. The astonishing range of his published work—and the bulky files of research out of which it grew—testify how enormously successful he was at it.

My first encounter with Phil came about, as did so many of my early contacts with American researchers into the history of the Lincoln County Follies, through Robert N. Mullin. I remember at that time Bob professed to me and to others that he was using Phil as a sort of legman, but I suspect even then he knew he had a tiger by the tail. Phil played neither Uriah Heep nor errand boy to anyone. He belonged to the publish-and-be-damned school and if that rubbed some of the old fuddy-duddies up the wrong way, well, maybe that was what the old fuddy-duddies needed.

Soon after we started up the English Corral of the Westerners in 1954, Phil became a member; although I take some pride in it now, I doubt we realized, when we published his article "Finis for Red Weaver" in the January, 1956, *Brand Book*, exactly what we were beginning. I was already corresponding with him—I recall he was working on an article about the "Horrell War" (which remained the landmark work on the subject for almost thirty years) and I on the efforts of the Tunstall family to obtain recompense from the United States Government for the murder of their son and the loss of their property. His letters were always full of a lively curiosity and down-to-earth assessments of new books or articles. Over the years we often differed, and argued hotly and furiously over half a hundred topics—the personality of John Tunstall, for instance, or Phil's opinion that Alexander McSween was "as crooked as a dog's hind leg"—but our arguments were always academic, never personal.

Reading through these articles again rekindles my sense of wonder at Phil's remarkable ability not only to get at the facts but to synthesize and simplify the complexities of his subjects. There was no highflown rhetoric, there were no frills. Like Jack Webb's Sergeant Friday in that old fifties TV show *Dragnet*, he was interested in only one thing: "The facts, ma'am. Just give me the facts." As for content, it is a lasting tribute to their author that not only do they constitute a concise history of the Lincoln County War, but forty years after they first appeared, it is still difficult to find significant errors in any of them.

His style was the man: blunt, unadorned, direct. If an inaccurate piece on some aspect of western history which interested him—and there were few that did not—came to his notice, you could be sure a sharply worded letter from Phil would appear setting its misguided author right. Both as an authority on the Lincoln County Wars and as a book reviewer under the pseudonym "Quago" he went mercilessly for the jugular whenever he encountered what he deemed sloppy work.

If he was interested in a topic, a person, or some phase of the West's history and learned you might have information he needed, he expected you to share it. He made no attempt to conceal his scorn for those "historians" (and in those days they were many) who would not immediately and unquestioningly make their findings or their documentation available to him. His judgments on those who refused were devastatingly final. I remember once when he was researching the background of the men who had fought for the Dolan faction and a relative of one of them, who had better remain nameless, told him she would send him the information about her father for $200. The idea of anyone asking for *money* when the pursuit of truth was involved was to him both astonishing and insulting.

The correspondence we began in 1952 continued almost to the end of Phil's life, although it was vastly curtailed following the stroke he suffered early in 1988. It was typical of the man, I think, that his note in painfully cramped writing announcing that event consisted of two lines, one thanking me for material I had sent him, the other saying simply, "I have had a stroke and cannot correspond yet. Sorry." No self-pity, no regret. It was just something he was dealing with. He told me I would be able to judge his condition from his signature; if it was smooth and flowing he was in good shape, if small and cramped, bad. The last letter he wrote me was to praise, with characteristic generosity, my book on the Lincoln County War. "I'm glad I'm not competing with you," he joked. As if I, or anyone who has ever studied the subject seriously, could have written such a book without the groundbreaking work Phil had first done.

Erudite, intelligent, dynamic, he was always the best of correspondents and the most sagacious of devil's advocates, but he wasn't always easy to get along with. He had very set ideas on certain things—he once asked me, as if it were my personal responsibility, just what the *hell* the British were doing in Northern Ireland?

Phil always played it as it laid: he was a patriot and a staunch Republican. Politicians he felt were selling his country short got the roughest edge of what sometimes could be a very rough tongue. Come to think of it, he gave God pretty short shrift.

His name is so well known to researchers into the life and legend of Billy the Kid that his "other" career sometimes gets overlooked, but it was a highly successful one. He held the rank of lieutenant commander in the United States Navy. He had a Ph.D., master's degrees in education and physical education, a bachelor's in anthropology. He was one-time chief of the Physiology Division of the Naval Field Medical Research Lab, and physiologist for the Marine Corps Physical Fitness Academy at Quantico. He had associate editorships and fellowships and honorary life memberships without number. He was a brilliant scientific academician, a qualified archaeologist, a distinguished and hugely successful technical author.

Philip J. Rasch died on October 3, 1995, just a few weeks too soon to see a lifetime ambition realized—his work being published in book form. It would have meant so much to him to see his articles made permanent between hard-covers, and it is a matter of continuing sadness to all his friends that he is not here to enjoy it. These papers (as he always called them) are, in a sense, a life work, and in them, as in his Billy the Kid pieces, it is possible to observe his understanding of events growing, his range widening. Taken together, this collection of articles and the earlier ones published in *Trailing Billy the Kid* constitute not only one of the most trenchant and credible overviews of the Lincoln County War, but also provide future researchers with the most complete and reliable guide to the available sources extant.

One last personal story: a few years ago, after a dauntingly long search, I finally tracked down a delightful old lady in Iowa who was a descendant of New Mexico badman John Kinney. What a triumph, I thought. What a coup! That same day I excitedly telephoned her. After we had talked a while the conversation turned to the matter of photographs, and I asked her whether, by any chance, she had any photographs of her great-uncle. "You know," she said, "you're the second person to ask me that."

"Oh, yes," I said, my heart sinking down to my boots. "And who was the first?"

"Why, that nice Mr. Rasch in California," she said brightly. "In 1954."

Forty years: that's how far ahead of the rest of us Phil Rasch was.

FREDERICK NOLAN
SOMERSET, ENGLAND

Gunsmoke in Lincoln County

1.
The Rise of the House of Murphy

Brand Book of the Denver Westerners, 1956

On October 20, 1878, Lawrence Gustave Murphy, retired merchant, ex-soldier, former Indian trader, quondam political and economic dictator of Lincoln County, New Mexico, died in Santa Fe. His obituary gave the cause of his death as "general debility"[1]; if so, it seems likely that it resulted from a combination of despair and alcohol. Only a few months earlier, this broken man had been one of the most powerful and ruthless individuals in the territory of New Mexico. The story of his rise and fall and the consequences of each is largely the history of Lincoln County during the period immediately following the War Between the States.

Almost nothing is known of his early years. His obituary stated that he was born in County Wexford, Ireland, about 1831; that he graduated from Maynooth College; that he had served in the Army of the United States for several years as a sergeant major. The records in County Wexford date back only to 1864. No one of this name has ever been listed among the students of St. Patrick's College at Maynooth.[2] His name is not to be found in the lists of the Army of the United States.[3] Yet on various occasions, Murphy claimed to have had sixteen years of service in the Army. Possibly at some stage of his career, he found it advisable to change his name. There is a tradition in Lincoln that he had come from Canada and had studied for the priesthood in the Episcopalian church, but there seems to be no tangible evidence to substantiate this version.

The historical account begins on July 27, 1861, when he was mustered into service at Fort Union, New Mexico, as a 1st lieutenant and quartermaster of the 1st Regiment New Mexico Infantry. He was transferred to Company G, 1st Regiment New Mexico Cavalry, on September 27, 1862. Here he served under Kit Carson in the campaign against the Navajos. Carson's report from Fort Canby contains these words:

> I am especially indebted to the zeal and intelligence of my acting assistant adjutant general, Lieut. Lawrence G. Murphy, First Cavalry, New Mexico Volunteers, and I particularly recommend him to the notice of the general commanding as a most efficient and energetic officer.[4]

His recommendation did not go unheeded. On October 27, 1865, General James H. Carleton nominated Murphy to be brevet major of volunteers for faithful and meritorious service in the Navajo Wars and in controlling the Mescalero Apaches at Bosque Redondo. Simultaneously, he brevetted two other officers, whose careers were to be inextricably entwined with those of Murphy: William Brady, for gallantry against the Navajos, July 1, 1865, and Emil Fritz, for gallantry against the Kiowas and Comanches at the battle of the Adobe Fort,[5] November 15, 1864. As in the case of Murphy, little is known of the early life of these two individuals. Brady, said to have been born in Covan, Ireland, in 1825, served in the 1st Regiment New Mexico Cavalry. Fritz, born in Ludwigsburg, Germany, on March 3, 1832, had enrolled in the 1st Regiment of California Cavalry at Camp Merchant, California, on August 16, 1861. All three men were mustered out of service in 1866.

In 1861, Fort Stanton, nine miles west of Lincoln, the capital of Lincoln County, had been destroyed by Confederate troops from Texas. The post was rebuilt in 1868 and a survey was made in September of that year which established a military reservation eight miles long and two miles wide, with the post in the center. At the eastern edge of the reservation, a brewery and store was erected by Murphy and Fritz, under the firm name of L.G. Murphy & Co. Murphy shortly became probate judge in Lincoln.

Lieutenant A.G. Hennisee commenced negotiations to induce the Mescalero Apaches to return to the reservation, but he was relieved in February, 1870. Robert S. Clark was appointed to succeed him, but never took charge. When Agent A.J. Curtis, a protege of the

American Unitarian Association, arrived in March of 1871, he found only a petty chief, Jose de la Paz, and twenty-seven of his band on the reservation. Curtis reported that,

> I take pleasure in mentioning, in this connection, that the fact of these Indians being now in and at peace is mainly, if not entirely, the result of efforts put forth by Judge Murphy and Colonel Fritz in command of a company of troops at Fort acquainted with Cadetta and the principal men of the tribe, Judge Murphy having been their agent at the Bosque Redondo, and Colonel Fritz in command of a company of troops at Fort Sumner at that time. They have several times, at their own expense, sent out clothing and other presents with messengers to communicate with the tribe, and on one occasion sent a team and wagon laden with presents into the Comanche country, to induce them if possible, to come in and make peace. These efforts were at last crowned with success, and the Government not only, but the people of this county as well, are largely indebted to these gentlemen for the important results obtained by their efforts.[6]

An agency was established on the premises of Murphy & Co. and the concern became self-appointed Indian traders. Curtis quickly learned that their influence with the Indians enabled them to exercise the authority which legally belonged to the Agent.

Murphy assumed the position of post trader and successfully resisted all attempts to dislodge him. In the summer of 1870, a new survey was made, which took in an area twelve miles square, with the post in the center, and on October 14, 1870, the secretary of war appointed A.M. Stephens as post trader. Murphy and Fritz made a trip to Washington and petitioned for permission to retain their holdings and to carry on their business. The secretary replied that he could do nothing for them except to permit them to remain in possession of their property, and advised them to petition Congress for a confirmation of their land title.

Stephens was removed on April 1, 1871, and Bliss & Lombard were appointed in his stead. Frank T. Bliss promptly requested that Murphy & Co. be ordered off the reservation, in accordance with the provisions of a circular of June 7, 1871, which provided that the legal post trader should have exclusive privileges to erect buildings and trade upon the grounds of the post. The commanding officer of Fort Stanton, Lieutenant Colonel August V. Kautz, 15th Infantry, advised that he did not feel authorized to remove anyone having a claim prior to the making of the second survey, and that he considered that the removal of Murphy & Co. would create difficulties with the Indian Department. He further urged that competition between the two traders would work for the benefit of the troops. Apparently, Murphy & Co. then bought Bliss out. When this became known in Washington, the appointment of Bliss & Lombard was revoked. C.F. Tracy was appointed March 12, 1872, but his appointment was revoked August 12, 1872. He made arrangements to "farm out" the business to Murphy & Co. for $125 a month and returned to Washington.

Through all of this, Murphy & Co. were careful to maintain friendly relations with the officers of the fort. Money was available to them if they needed a loan; advice if they were having difficulties with their duties; warnings if anyone else attempted to perpetrate a fraud upon them; guides if they had to go out on a scout. The result was that the Murphy store became a place of resort of officers and men alike—and the company gained almost a monopoly of the highly lucrative government business. Since it had the hay and corn contracts, it could make or break the local farmers. Underbid on one occasion, it purchased all the hay in the area, so that the successful bidder was unable to fulfill his commitment and his bondsmen were forced to make good the difference in price which the Army had to pay to obtain hay from Murphy & Co.

On the 14th of December, 1872, a new superintendent of Indian Affairs, Colonel L. Edwin Dudley, took up his duties. His opinion of the condition of affairs at the Mescalero Apache Agency has been preserved in a report to the commissioner of Indian Affairs:

> I found that affairs at this agency required the presence of some officer determined to protect the interests of the Government. The firm which held the appointment of Indian traders, and acted as military traders, seemed to have taken possession of Indian affairs at that place. The agent appeared to have very little business except to approve vouchers made for him by these men. The Government had no building, and there were none in the neighborhood that could be rented. The agent was, in consequence, compelled to accept such hospitalities as they felt inclined to bestow on the Government and its officers.[7]

Under the Curtis regime the number of Indians allegedly being fed had risen to an unbelievable 2,679. He was replaced as agent by Samuel B. Bushnell. Murphy merely shrugged. "It don't make any difference who the Government sends here as agent," he remarked. "We control these Indians."[8]

This happy state of affairs was too good to last. Dudley wrote to the commissioner of Indian Affairs complaining that,

> I have the honor to request that you will invite the attention of the War Department to the fact that the post trader at Fort Stanton, Mr. Dayton by name, appointed several months since, has never opened his store, and from what I can learn has probably sold out to the firm of L.G. Murphy & Co., who seem to have been able to annul in fact the appointment of post trader at this point.
>
> The Indian Department is interested in this from the fact that no other store exists there, and these men are also in fact the Indian traders. What I desire is that some man friendly to the Administration, and of good character and reputation should be appointed as post trader, who shall have sufficient capital and will open a business of his own, and that I can also appoint an Indian trader.[9]

L.L. Higgins was appointed Dayton's successor, but does not seem to have ever actually taken up the position.

Bushnell was anxious to set up his own agency, where he would be out from under Murphy's domination. On the 18th of May, he invited Captain James F. Randlett, 8th Cavalry, to ride out with him and a Mr. Reilly to select a place for a new location for an agency. On their return, Reilly remarked that he was at outs with Murphy & Co. and had no place to stay. Randlett invited him to stay at his quarters. The officer then went off to dine with Captain Chambers McKibbin, 15th Infantry, commanding officer of Fort Stanton. Returning to his house that evening, he found James Dolan,[10] a clerk for Murphy & Co., abusing Reilly and threatening to kill him unless he retracted certain statements he was said to have made. That night, Randlett and Reilly went to church together. Murphy and Dolan also attended the services. As the officer and his friend left, Dolan commenced insulting Reilly. Randlett finally called the sergeant of the guard, whereupon Dolan snarled, "Damn you, I'll kill you then right here," drew a revolver, and discharged one shot at Randlett.[11] The captain grappled with him and the guard took

Dolan into custody. Murphy then attempted to rescue Dolan from the soldiers, whereupon he too was arrested.

Dolan was released the next morning on a writ of habeas corpus and turned over to the civil authorities. McKibbin ordered him to remain away from the post, but revoked his edict when Fritz, who was ill and needed Dolan's aid in arranging his affairs, asked that as a personal favor the clerk be allowed to remain, and personally guaranteed that he would not create any further trouble on the reservation. Randlett, Bushnell, 2nd Lieutenant John W. Wilkinson, 8th Cavalry, and a civilian employee of the agency appeared in court at Lincoln and testified in regard to the incident, but Dolan was released and a warrant was issued commanding Sheriff L.J. [Jacob Lewis] Gylam to arrest Randlett on charges of assault.

Randlett retaliated with a letter to the adjutant general, in which he stated:

> I came to this Post with my Troop in April 1872. I found the tradership of the Post in the hands of L.G. Murphy & Co. (Indian traders) and their prices for goods sold to enlisted men extortionate almost to robbery. These parties have also been engaged in supplying the Indians supposed to be on this Reservation; I soon became convinced that they were swindling the Government in the matter outrageously. As a Troop's Captain I complained of the prices for goods sold to my men. As an officer of the Government, if no higher motives impelled me I have spoken freely my condemnation of which I have every reason to believe of the dishonesty of their transactions connected with the supplies furnished to the Indians and I believe it is generally understood that I have no better opinion of their place than that it is a den of infamy and its toleration a disgrace to the Public Service.
>
> In assuming the position with its risks the War Department will understand the situation when it is considered that one officer of the Army has told me that Murphy has said he would kill me, another that so mighty was the power of the firm that they could get false testimony enough to deprive me of my Commission as an officer. Murphy I am told on what I believe good authority has said that if he could not have his way in feeding the Indians he would put them on the Warpath and corral me and my command here in the Post, and one of their employees "Dolan" I believe said that he would put on a breech cloth and lead the Apaches against me.[12]

Captain McKibbin took the attitude that this was a purely personal matter in which he had no right to interfere. Secretary of War William W. Belknap was of a different mind. He inquired whether there were any traders appointed by the Indian Office on the reservation. On being assured by the Office of Indian Affairs that there were no licensed traders at Fort Stanton, he issued the following order:

> The Secretary also directs that you remove from the Post Murphy, Fritz and every man who is in any way in their employ, and keep them *off the reservation*;[13] and further, if the new trader who is to come to Fort Stanton, has, or attains, any interest whatever with Fritz or Murphy, that you remove *him* also.[14]

During the summer, forces under Major William Redwood Price, 8th Cavalry, were sent on a scout through southern New Mexico. In his report, the major stated that Murphy had called the Indians together and told them many things that were injudicious. Bushnell had complained to him that he had been unable to get possession of their building, which had been purchased for agency quarters by the government in May at a price of $8,000; that all goods for the agency were invoiced to Murphy; and that the company controlled all issues. He said that he was the agent only in name—Murphy was the agent in fact. He had not even been able to learn the number of Indians on the reservation. Murphy claimed that there were between 2,000 and 2,500, but Bushnell did not believe that there were more than 800. Price himself estimated their number at not more than 500.[15]

The major refused to consult with Murphy, taking the stand that his business was only with the agent. At this, Murphy, who had been drinking heavily, became highly incensed and threatened to send the Apaches to the mountains. Price informed General Vandever and Superintendent Dudley of what had occurred and recommended that Murphy & Co. be required to vacate the building immediately. What followed may be reported in Dudley's own words:

> The new agent, Mr. S.B. Bushnell, reported for duty on the 29th of March, and at once undertook to assume charge of the affairs of his agency; he, however, found so much opposition on the part of those

> who had formerly managed affairs there, that he only secured full charge of his agency when I visited there on the 2d of September. Although the buildings had been purchased by the Government, the former owners had upon one pretext and another retained possession of the buildings and Agent Bushnell had very little more to say about the conduct of Indian affairs there than had Agent Curtis at the time of my first visit. I at once demanded possession, and promised to take the trouble of vacating the premises myself unless the agent received possession within twenty-four hours. The buildings were vacated.[16]

Paul Dowlin[17] was finally appointed post trader. He bought the stock of his predecessors and rented part of their former building from Bushnell.

Bowing to the inevitable, Murphy & Co. moved to Lincoln, a plaza of about 40 houses, and set up business in temporary quarters[18] while awaiting construction of the building which was to become known as "The House." Meanwhile, Murphy did everything in his power to impede Price's movements. Gylam,[19] who had contracted to supply feed for Price's horses, failed to appear with it. The major learned that he had been arrested in Lincoln and jailed on some trumped-up charge. The only other source of supply was Dow & Co. However, the post quartermaster, Lieutenant C.H. Conrad, 15th Infantry, who had earlier made difficulties over Murphy & Co. being barred from the post, refused to buy from Dow. The result was that Price was forced to withdraw his troops from the Black River area. He wrote,

> I think that the influence of Murphy & Co. is the most pernicious to the interests of the Government. I think that their power should be as much decreased as possible by the officers of the Government that other individuals might have an opportunity of doing some business here.[20]

Conrad, he suggested, should be relieved for the good of the service.

Colonel J. Irvin Gregg, 8th Cavalry, commanding the District of New Mexico, recommended a favorable consideration of Price's suggestions. General John Pope, commanding the Department of the Missouri, concurred. In his endorsement, he stated,

> As long as Murphy & Co. Can control all the crops, etc. etc., the supply of the post with forage, etc. must depend on him. I have several times recommended the abandonment of Stanton for these and kindred reasons, but it has not been approved by higher authority.[21]

Bushnell wrote Price that since his visit, there had been a great change in the bearing and deportment of the Indians at Fort Stanton. To Superintendent Dudley, he made the remarkable boast that "all are now of the opinion that I have broken the backbone of the Indian ring in New Mexico, and the most formidable anti-administration party in the Territory."[22] He crowed too soon. Murphy had suffered a setback, but he had not lost the war. The dominant political power in New Mexico at this time was the Santa Fe Ring, led by Thomas B. Catron, U.S. district attorney and president of the First National Bank of Santa Fe. Practically all the members of this Ring were Masons. District Attorney William L. Rynerson, Lieutenant Colonel N.A.M. Dudley, Emil Fritz, the Spiegelberg brothers, John Riley, John Kinney, and Morris J. Bernstein were lodge members. Catron, Murphy, Dolan, and Brady were among those who organized the first Grand Lodge in New Mexico. Joined in fraternal brotherhood in addition to a common desire for power, the members of the Ring had little trouble disposing of Bushnell. On December 15, Price protested that,

> I understand that Dr. Bushnell Agent of the Mescaleros has been removed from his position. If such is the case he has fallen a victim to the machinations of the Murphy ring whose ramifications must reach to the office of the Superintendent at Santa Fe. The only fault they could find with him is that he is too honest. I would like to remonstrate against his removal, through the War to the Indian Department.[23]

Although Price was unable to help Bushnell, the Santa Fe Ring proved equally powerless to reinstate Murphy on the reservation. Murphy himself did everything possible to fight the expulsion order. In a long, sarcastic letter to the secretary of war, he ridiculed Randlett's charges and accused him of slander and defamation of character. He submitted a number of letters from officers previously stationed at Fort Stanton and prominent local citizens testifying to the good character, fair dealing, and high reputation of Murphy and Fritz. All of this was in vain. Secretary Belknap was more impressed by the reports from the officers in the field than he was by Murphy's pleadings. The ouster order remained in effect.

Murphy had scarcely settled in the plaza before he became involved in the Horrell War.[24] What role he played in it is not clear. He is said to have financed two of the family in the purchase of ranches, but at a mass meeting in Lincoln, Murphy, Brady, and Jose Montaño were chosen a committee to preserve the peace. Before giving up the conflict and leaving the area, the Horrell party made a trip to Lincoln specifically to kill Murphy and Dolan, but at least some of their property ended up in Murphy's hands. Juan Patrón drily commented that, "There are people who say this was one of the ends Murphy was working for."[25] In due course, one of their former ranches was sold to Richard M. Brewer,[26] a Murphy-Dolan employee to whom The House loaned $2,000.

In the aftermath of the Horrell War, Murphy saw an opportunity for revenge on Randlett. In October, 1874, that officer found himself charged with murder and accessory to murder in the cases of Ysidro Padia [Isidro Padilla], Davio Balisan [Mario Balazan], Pedro Patrón, and Jose Candelaria.[27] Details of the charges made against him cannot be located. Catron, as U.S. district attorney, was ordered to defend the soldier. On his advice, Randlett employed D.B. Rea and L. Baca to assist. A change of venue to Socorro was obtained and on November 10, 1874, the jury returned a verdict of "not guilty" without leaving their seats. Robert Casey, the staunch friend of the Horrells, who had been indicted at the same time on four charges[28] growing out of the same affair, had also retained Rea. After Randlett was discharged, the prosecutor entered a *nol pros* in all the cases against Casey. Rea and Baca submitted bills for $50.00 each to Randlett, which the officer paid and passed to the War Department for reimbursement. When the secretary of war forwarded these to the attorney general, the latter wrote:

> Under the law I am not authorized to approve accounts of this character and must decline doing so.
>
> The U.S. Attorney for New Mexico had been allowed a liberal fee for his services in defending Capt. Randlett, and in a conversation with me this morning he agreed to refund Capt. Randlett out of his fee the amount he paid to Messrs. Rea and Baca.[29]

Meanwhile, Fritz, whose health had not improved, decided to return to Germany to visit his parents. In Trinidad, Colorado, he met his sister, Mrs. Emilie Scholand, who was on her way to visit him. He returned with her to the post, saw her comfortably settled at the sutler's store and hotel, and arranged for the appointment of her husband as postmaster. A month or so later, he resumed his trip, stopping in St. Louis to purchase a grand piano[30] for his sister and to take out a $10,000 life insurance policy with the Merchants Mutual Insurance Company of the City and State of New York. During his absence, Dolan bought into the business, becoming a partner in the concern on April 1, 1874, although no change was made in the firm's name.

Once entrenched in Lincoln, Murphy lost little time in tightening his political and economic control over the county. In the absence of any effective competition, the local farmers were forced to pay The House's prices for their supplies and to accept whatever was offered for their own produce. If the farmers became discouraged and moved away, The House promptly seized their land "to settle debts owing to the Company." Undeterred by the absence of legal title resulting from such tactics, the farms were promptly resold to the next immigrants and the vicious circle started all over again. Directly or indirectly, L.G. Murphy & Co. managed to control most of the profitable government contracts for supplying Fort Stanton and the Mescalero Apaches. Their enemies charged that the beef contracts with the government were filled with cattle stolen by a band of rustlers known as The Boys, led by Jessie J. Evans. Allegedly, The House paid only $5.00 a head for these cattle, whereas they cost $15.00 a head from honest stockmen.[31]

Politically, Murphy was a Democrat, and usually managed to carry the county for that party. On one occasion, he stormed into a political convention which proposed to select candidates opposed to him, overthrew the table, destroyed the stationery, and warned, "You might as well try to stop the waves of the ocean with a fork as to try and oppose me."[32]

Bushnell was succeeded as agent for the Apaches by W.D. Crothers on April 1, 1874. To get the Indians away from Dowlin, whose sale of whisky to them created constant difficulties, Crothers moved the agency to the Copeland ranch. In the course of time, it was moved to South Fork, about forty miles from Fort Stanton, where both the agency and the agent's home were established in a house leased from Dr. Joseph Hoy Blazer. Here, The House opened a branch store under the charge of Mike Harkins, later succeeded by John [Frank] Regan. When Murphy was unable to influence Crothers to his own advantage, the agent was indicted (October 1, 1874) on a trumped-up charge of operating a hotel without a license. The case was finally dropped by the district attorney, but the secretary of war charged Crothers with dereliction of duty and he finally resigned in 1876. He was followed in the post by Frederick C. Godfroy, a protege of the Presbyterian Board of Missions.

That same October, William Burns, a clerk at The House, killed Deputy Sheriff Lyon Philliporske [Phillipowski]. Philliporske, very much intoxicated, entered the store late in the evening of the 21st and started insulting the clerk. When the deputy drew his gun and threatened to kill Burns, the latter procured a pistol and mortally wounded his annoyer. The coroner's inquest found the killing justifiable.

About November, Wortley's Hotel was the scene of a killing when Jose Domingo Valencia shot Daniel Fisher. Valencia was sentenced to seven-year imprisonment. Since there was no county jail in Lincoln County, he was placed in the guard house at Fort Stanton. When it was ruled that no civilian could be held there after sentence, Valencia had to be turned loose. Eventually, George W. Peppin contracted to build a jail, at, it was asserted, a price far in excess of its actual cost. It was alleged that the entire amount ended up in Murphy's pocket; that Peppin was deeply in his debt and the construction of the jail was primarily an expedient designed to enable Murphy to recoup a potentially bad debt.

Early in 1875, the Santa Fe *New Mexican* began to complain that Lincoln County had made no returns on its tax assessment rolls and had not paid any monies into the territorial treasury during the past two years. It pointed out that the law held the collector (the sheriff) to a strict accountability, that the probate judge (Murphy) was required to look after the finances of the county and its relations to the treasury, and that it was the duty of the district attorney (John Bail) to see that collection was enforced. At the April term of court held in Lincoln by Judge Warren Bristol, the grand jury congratulated the people of the county on the small amount of actual crime that it was called upon to investigate, but Bail instituted criminal proceedings against seventy citizens for non-payment of taxes. In due course, these individuals paid about $6,000 into the treasury and the proceedings were dropped. However, the sheriff, the county clerk, the treasurer, and the justice of the peace were indicted and Murphy submitted his resignation. One of his last official acts was to offer a reward of $250 by the county and an equal sum made up by his firm and other business men for the apprehension of the murderers of a young soldier of Company H, 8th Cavalry, who had been shot between Lincoln and Fort Stanton.

That spring, a promising young bad man, Josiah G. "Doc" Scurlock, succeeded in getting his name in the papers by stealing three horses, two saddles, and a gun and making off to Arizona with them. Unfortunately for the peace of the community, he returned the following year and seems to have made something of a career of carrying deadly weapons, threatening the citizens, obstructing the laws, and generally making a nuisance of himself.[33]

The fall of the year proved to be a bit more exciting than the spring had been. On the 1st of August, Robert Casey was murdered by a man named William Wilson, whom Casey had discharged because of his horse stealing proclivities. Wilson contended that Casey still owed him $8.00 in wages and shot him to prove it. A Charles Myrick was held as an accessory. On December 10, the murderer was executed by Sheriff Saturnino Baca in what is said to have been the first legal hanging in the territory of New Mexico.[34]

Only a few days after the death of Casey, Jesus Mes, Pas Mes, Tomas Madril, and Jermain [Jermin] Aguirre, thieves and murderers belonging to a large gang making their headquarters at Boquilla, a small settlement about forty-five miles below Fort Stanton, had a personal experience with New Mexican non-legal justice. They stole thirty animals and made their way to San Ignacio, Mexico, pursued by Jim McDaniels and four men. Three of the outlaws, Jesus being the fortunate fourth, were seized by the Mexican officials and turned over to McDaniels. He arrived safely at the San Augustin [Agustin] ranch with the prisoners, but on the night of August 8, a party of masked men took the thieves out and shot them.

On September 11, John H. Riley, bookkeeper for The House, shot Juan B. Patrón. He claimed that Patrón followed him around, became abusive, and finally pulled out a pistol, whereupon Riley employed his rifle in self-defense. What he never did explain was how it happened that his bullet entered Patrón's back. [Patrón survived this shooting, only to be murdered later. See Chapter 21, ed.]

Next of the Murphy clique to become involved in a gun fight was Steve Stanley, a teamster, who was said to have killed at least four men in New Mexico. On February 18, 1876, S.W. Lloyd challenged him to a duel over the ownership of some ranch property. As soon as Lloyd stepped off the distance, Stanley fired, seriously wounding his opponent. Stanley defied Sheriff Baca to arrest him, but the sheriff, with the aid of Thomas Cochran [Cochrane], George Clark, and John L. Williams, forced his way into Stanley's house and effected the arrest. The prisoner was examined before Justice of the Peace John B. Wilson and promptly acquitted.

A few days before this shooting, a detachment from Fort Stanton raided Boquilla, capturing Juan Chaves and three other well known horse thieves. Even this failed to settle the situation. Haley,[35] apparently basing his account on interviews with Frank Coe, has described the sad fate of some members of the Mes family who failed to profit from the experience of their namesakes and became troublesome. Pancho, Cruz, and Roman Mes were pursued by Frank Freeman, Charles Woolsey, John Mosley, Jessie J. Evans, and others to a spot across the border from Isleta. There they were captured, along with a cousin, Tomas Cuerele, brought back to the east of the pass across the Organ Mountains, and liquidated.

Through all of this, The House continued to grow and prosper. In April, it purchased the forty acres of land attached to the establishment, thus continuing to extend its domain. The partners may have felt some uneasiness, however, at a resurgence of strength in the local Republican party. Led by a local lawyer, Alexander A. McSween, as secretary, and including in its ranks such prominent citizens as Juan Patrón, Jose Montaño, and Probate Judge Florencio Gonzales, the organization clearly was dominated by men unfriendly to the Murphy-Dolan interests. Yet it seems doubtful that the party could have mustered enough strength to have presented any serious threat to the *status quo*.

On the surface, affairs in Lincoln County appear to have remained generally quiet until October, when John H. Slaughter killed Barney Gallagher, a cattle dealer, at South Spring. A Juan

Gonzales was also shot, although it is not clear whether he was involved in the Slaughter-Gallagher fracas. On the lighter side, Justice Wilson created some amusement by trying W.W. Campbell for the killing of Thomas King, acquitting him, and then ordering the arrest of L.S. Tesson as Campbell's accomplice in the murder! Appearances, however, were deceptive. This was the proverbial calm before the storm. Underneath the apparent quiet, forces were gathering which were to erupt into the most famous of frontier clashes—The Lincoln County War.

On June 26, 1874, Fritz had died from dropsy in Stuttgart, Germany. No steps were taken to administer his estate until April 20, 1875, when Probate Judge Murphy appointed William Brady, one of his employees, as administrator. Brady, in turn, employed McSween to make collections for the estate. Murphy, however, alleging that the Fritz estate owed the partnership $76,000, turned the policy over to Levi Spiegelberg, of New York, for collection, instructing him to place the money received to the credit of Murphy & Co. with Spiegelberg & Bros., of Santa Fe, to whom The House was deeply indebted. Unexpected difficulties arose in the collection of the insurance. The company contended that Fritz had actually died of tuberculosis, which voided the policy, but finally offered to adjust the claim for $6,500. Spiegelberg asked to be appointed an administrator in order to have a free hand in dealing with the company. Unwilling to become involved in this, Brady resigned as administrator in September, 1876, and letters of administration were issued to Charles Fritz, Emil's brother, and to Emilie Scholand, his sister.

Friction developed between everyone concerned, but that fall, the administrators agreed to give McSween a power of attorney and to send him to New York to investigate the situation, promising to give him 10 percent of the face value of the policy if he were successful in collecting the full amount. Arriving in St. Louis, McSween decided that he needed legal help and employed a firm there to assist him, offering them $2,800 for their aid. In New York, he paid Spiegelberg $700 for his services and dismissed him from the case, the St. Louis parties having recommended the retention of Donnell, Lawson & Co. in his stead. After two months of work on the case, McSween returned home, leaving his confreres to continue the battle. Fritz had become seriously disturbed over McSween's activities, but the lawyer wrote him a soothing letter, assuring him of his good faith and promising to place the money to his credit in the First National Bank of Santa Fe just as soon as he received it.[36]

During McSween's absence, an important change had occurred: in the month of November, Riley had been taken into Murphy & Co., allegedly investing a $6,000 inheritance in the firm. About the middle of the following month, Murphy was elected president of the Lincoln County Farmers Club, with Brady as vice-president, Morris J. Bernstein as secretary, and Fritz as treasurer. On March 14, 1877, Murphy retired from the business, leaving it to be continued by Dolan and Riley under the firm name of James J. Dolan & Co. Local gossip, however, insisted that he actually remained as a silent partner and whatever orders he gave were promptly obeyed.[37]

It is probable that Murphy's resignation—real or alleged—created comparatively little attention, as it came while the county was in the throes of the Pecos War.[38] It is still less likely that many of the local citizenry gave heed to the fact that a psychopathic young rustler name Henry McCarty,[39] alias William Antrim, alias Bill Bonney, alias Billy Kidd, alias Billy the Kid, had arrived in Lincoln County from Arizona, where he was wanted for the murder of F.P. Cahill. Only one gifted with the ability to foresee the future could have known that he was destined to play a leading role in the explosion which was about the engulf the House of Murphy and bring it crashing down upon its proprietors.

ACKNOWLEDGMENTS

The writer is indebted to Mrs. Bessie Dolan Chester, Mrs. Carrie Dolan Vorwark, and Miss Genevieve Riley for both pictures and information. Much of the information on Fritz was obtained through the courtesy of Herr Ernst Schmid and Dr. Herbert Schiller, of the Culture Office of the City of Stuttgart, Germany. Personnel of the National Archives have been extremely helpful. Miss Gertrude Hill, Miss Ruth E. Rambo, and Mrs. Edith O. McManmon, of the Library of the Museum of New Mexico, have aided in many ways and on many occasions. Mr. and Mrs. John Boylan, curator-custodians, Old Lincoln County Memorial Commission, made their files freely available to the writer.

NOTES

[1] Santa Fe *New Mexican*, October 26, 1878.

[2] Monsignor Edward J. Kissane to Philip J. Rasch, October 27, 1952.

[3] Adjutant General Wm. E. Bergin to P.J. Rasch, July 3, 1953.

[4] *War of the Rebellion*, XXXIV:75. Washington, D.C.: Government Printing Office, 1891.

[5] For an account of this battle, see George H. Pettis, *Personal Narratives of the Battles of the Rebellion*, "Kit Carson's Fight with the Comanches and Kiowa Indians." Historical Society of New Mexico Publication No. 12. Santa Fe: The New Mexico Printing Co., 1908.

[6] A.J. Curtis to Nathaniel Pope, September 18, 1871. In *Report of the Commissioner of Indian Affairs to the Secretary of the Interior for the Year 1871*. Washington, D.C.: Government Printing Office, 1872, p. 401.

[7] L. Edwin Dudley to E.P. Smith, April 10, 1873. In Records in *Annual Report of the Commissioner of Indian Affairs to the Secretary of the Interior for the Year 1873*. Washington, D.C.: Government Printing Office, 1874, p. 263.

[8] Quoted in Frank D. Reeve, "The Federal Indian Policy in New Mexico," *New Mexico Historical Review*, XIII:261–313, July, 1938.

[9] L. Edwin Dudley to E.P. Smith, April 10, 1873. In Records of the War Department (R.G. 94), 3211-AGO-1873. In National Archives.

[10] James Joseph Dolan was born at Laughrea, County Galway, Ireland, on May 2, 1848. When he was 5 years old, his parents emigrated to this country. After serving in the New York Zouaves during the Civil War, he enlisted in the 37th Regiment, U.S. Infantry. He was discharged at Fort Stanton on April 3, 1869. Dolan died at his Feliz Ranch, February 26, 1898.

[11] James F. Randlett to Adjutant General, U.S.A., July 22, 1873. 3211-AGO-1873.

[12] Ibid.

[13] Walter Noble Burns in *The Saga of Billy the Kid* stated that Murphy sold out at the suggestion of Major Glendenning, "who expressed disapprobation of his business methods." Presumably, he had reference to Major David R. Clendenin, 8th Cavalry. Clendenin commanded Fort Stanton from January, 1874, to July, 1875. In 1873, however, he was in command of Fort Seldon, New Mexico, and, of course, had nothing to do with Murphy's removal.

[14] E.D. Townsend to C. McKibbin, September 30, 1873. 3211-AGO-1873.

[15] Wm. Redwood Price to Thos. Blair, November 25, 1873. 3211-AGO-

1873.

[16] L. Edwin Dudley to Edward P. Smith, op. cit., p. 264.

[17] Dowlin was killed by Jere Dillon in May, 1877. See the Santa Fe *New Mexican*, May 8 and 15, 1877.

[18] The exact location of these premises is a matter of dispute. One story is that they were turned into a mess for employees. This was operated by Sam Wortley and became known as the Wortley Hotel. Another version is that the Tunstall store was built around the original Murphy quarters. A third is that the McSween house was an enlargement of this building. It is said that the Murphy mess was directly north of the old courthouse. R.N. Mullin to John Boylan, undated letter. (Written in August, 1955.)

[19] Gylam was killed in Lincoln on December 1, 1873, in the fight which touched off the Horrell War.

[20] Wm. Redwood Price to J.P. Willard, November 25, 1873. 3211-AGO-1873.

[21] John Pope to R.C. Drum, December 19, 1873. 3211-AGO-1873.

[22] Reeve, "The Federal Indian Policy in New Mexico," op. cit.

[23] Wm. Redwood Price to J.P. Willard, December 15, 1873. 3211-AGO-1873.

[24] For details of this affair, see P.J. Rasch, "The Horrell War," *New Mexico Historical Review*, XXXI:223–231, July, 1956. [See Chapter 2.]

[25] Juan B. Patrón, Unpublished Affidavit, June 6, 1878. In Frank W. Angel, "Report to the Department of Justice in the Matter of the Cause and Circumstances of the Death of John H. Tunstall, a British Subject." In National Archives.

[26] According to R.N. Mullin, Brewer was born in St. Albans, Vermont, in 1852. After his death, his parents deeded his ranch to Mrs. McSween in part payment of the note he had given McSween to secure him for paying the money owing Dolan & Co. Later, the ranch became the property of Frank Coe, and then of Coe's daughter, Mrs. Bonnell. It is located at the Glencoe Post Office, on Highway 70, between San Patricio and Greentree.

[27] See Causes No. 73, 79, 80, Lincoln County; No. 22, 23, 25, 26, Socorro County.

[28] See Causes No. 48, 63, 80, Lincoln County; No. 19, 20, 25, 26, Socorro County.

[29] G. Williams to W.W. Belknap, January 6, 1875. 3211-AGO-1873.

[30] This piano was later purchased by Mrs. McSween. Burns was in error in crediting her with having brought it out from St. Louis.

[31] Cimarron *News and Press*, April 11, 1878.

[32] Juan B. Patrón, Unpublished Affidavit, June 6, 1878, op. cit.

[33] See Causes 213, 220, 223, 226, 230, Lincoln County. Scurlock was born in Alabama about 1850. He is described as "between five feet eight or ten

inches high, light hair, light complexion, front teeth out, writes a very good hand, quick spoken, and usually makes a good impression on first acquaintaince." *Arizona Citizen*, quoted in Silver City *The Herald*, May 9, 1875.

[34] Philip J. Rasch, "The Gun and the Rope." *West Texas Historical Association Year Book*, October, 1957.

[35] J. Evetts Haley, "Horse Thieves." *Southwest Review*. 15:317–332, Spring, 1930.

[36] A.A. McSween to Charles Fritz, December 14, 1876. In collection at Old Lincoln County Memorial Commission.

[37] Stephen Stanley, Unpublished Affidavit, 28 May 1878. With report of E.C. Watkins, June 27, 1878, in Records of the Bureau of Indian Affairs, M-319, L-147, and M-320, Record Group 75. In National Archives.

[38] Philip J. Rasch, "The Pecos War." *Panhandle-Plains Historical Review*. XXIX:101–111, 1956. [See Chapter 3.]

[39] Studies of the background of this individual have been reported in Philip J. Rasch and R.N. Mullin, "New Light on the Legend of Billy the Kid," *New Mexico Folklore Record,* VII:1–5, 1952–53; Rasch and Mullin, "Dim Trails—The Pursuit of the McCarty Family," op. cit., VIII:6–11, 1953–54; Rasch, "The Twenty-One Men He Put Bullets Through," op. cit., IX:8–14, 1954–55; Rasch, "A Man Named Antrim," Los Angeles Westerners *Brand Book*, 6:48–54, 1956; Rasch, "More on the McCartys," The English Westerners *Brand Book*, 3:3–9, April, 1957. [All of these articles appear in *Trailing Billy the Kid*, Volume I of NOLA's Outlaw and Lawman Series, published in 1995.]

2.
The Horrell War

New Mexico Historical Review, July 1956

While L.G. Murphy & Company were consolidating their economic and political control over Lincoln County in 1873, events were taking place in Texas which were to eventuate in the Horrell War of New Mexico.

Residing in the vicinity of Lampasas were the five Horrell brothers—Ben, Martin, Merritt, Sam, and Thomas. The family originated in Arkansas, but had lived at one time in Lincoln County itself. A contemporary newspaper[1] mentions that several members of the family had been killed by Indians in San Augustin [Agustin] Pass,[2] and Gillette[3] recalled that another brother, John, was slain in a gun fight in Las Cruces.

However, at least some of the family were in Lampasas County during the census of 1870. So ferocious were the Indian raids at this time that the county was specifically exempted from the provisions of the law of April 13, 1871, entitled "An Act to Regulate the Keeping and Bearing of Deadly Weapons." A company of Minute Men was organized and the state furnished rifles to the members, among them Ben Horrell and his brother-in-law, Ben Turner.

Unfortunately, there are few records of that time and place. The courthouse files were destroyed in a fire in 1872 and no run of the Lampasas *Dispatch* has been preserved. However, there can be little doubt but that the Horrells were leading spirits among the fun-loving cowboys who regularly shot up the town. Favorite targets were the knot-holes in the front and sides of the business buildings. The office of White & Gibson alone had twenty or thirty bullets fired through it, and the editor of the *Dispatch* finally gave up trying to keep glass in his windows. What else the brothers might have been doing is suggested in a report from Adjutant General and Chief of State Police F.L. Britton to Governor Edmund J. Davis charging that Thomas, Martin, Merritt, and Ben Horrell, Ben Turner, Joe Bolden, Allen Whitcraft, James Grizzell, Jerry Scott, Bill Bowen, Billy Gray, G.W. Short, Mark Short, Jim Jenkins, Sam Sneed, and Billy Sneed were members of a gang "whose occupation was the branding, killing, and skinning of other people's cattle."[4]

On January 14, 1873, affairs suddenly became serious. During the noon recess of the district court, G.W. Short became disorderly in Schoot's saloon. When Sheriff Shadrach T. Denson attempted to arrest the disturber of the peace, Mark Short stepped between them and grappled with the officer. G.W. then drew his pistol and shot the sheriff. When Judge Turner heard Denson's calls for help, he ordered Thomas Sparks and several other men to arrest the brothers. At this, Ben, Thomas, and Martin Horrell, Patrick Ginnity, and a number of their companions among the Minute Men interfered. Drawing their guns, they warned the posse that the Shorts were their friends and that they would protect them. So determined was their attitude that the posse only watched helplessly as the Shorts rode out of town.

In desperation, five justices of the peace, members of the Lampasas County court, submitted a petition to Governor Davis requesting that certain of the law-abiding citizens be appointed to the State Police and that a reward of $250 be offered for each of the Shorts. The governor then extended the provisions of the act regulating the bearing of arms to include Lampasas County, and Britton dispatched a squad of State Police under Sergeant J. M. Redmon to enforce it. Simultaneously, the Minute Men were reorganized.

Redmon[5] soon reported that shooting was continuing at night, but that the citizens were afraid to swear out warrants so that he could make arrests. He advised that the situation could be remedied only by having about twenty-five policemen present to patrol the streets or by declaring martial law. Lack of funds soon made it necessary to withdraw the troopers, although the sheriff begged that they be returned as soon as possible.

His fears proved well founded. The disorders promptly became worse than ever, and Britton finally sent seven policemen under Captain Thomas G. Williams to enforce the law against bearing arms. En route, Williams stopped Tilford [Telford] Bean, a Lampasas freighter, to ask for directions. It is alleged that he had been drinking and told Bean that he was going to clean up the Horrell boys.[6] The police reached town about 1 p.m. on March 14 and halted in front of Jerry Scott's saloon. In the bar room were ten or fifteen of the Horrell party, including Thomas, Martin, and Merritt Horrell, Turner, Bolden, Whitcraft, Grizzell, Gray, and Jenkins. They had had some difficulty with the Minute Men that morning, but most of the latter and practically everybody else in town were attending a trial being held some distance away. As the police watched, Bill Bowen, Merritt's brother-in-law, entered the saloon, a pistol hanging from his hip. Accompanied by Privates Wesley Cherry, T.M. Daniels, and Andrew Melville, Williams followed Bowen inside, notified him that he was under arrest, and demanded the revolver.

"Bill," interrupted Martin, "you haven't done any wrong. You don't have to be arrested."

The officer then made a mistake. He tried to take the pistol from Bowen by force. In the gunplay that followed, Williams, Daniels, and Cherry were killed. Melville, fatally wounded by a bullet through the left lung, died in the Huling Hotel a few days later. When the Horrell party carried the fight to the four policemen outside, Policeman Eddie shot Tom just below the shoulder blade and Martin was shot in the neck. The troopers then gave up the battle and rode frantically for Austin. Martin was carried to his mother's home, about 200 yards from the saloon, and the rest of the party left the town.

Britton, with an escort of twelve State Police, arrived at Lampasas on the 17th. He addressed a mass meeting of the citizens and they adopted a set of resolutions pledging their aid in enforcing the law and arresting the fugitives. With the aid of the Lampasas Minute Company, the Burnet Minute Company, the State Police, and a posse of citizens, Britton scoured five counties and finally succeeded in arresting Scott, Martin Horrell, Whitcraft, Jenkins, and Grizzell and lodging them in the Travis County jail.

Within two weeks, Horrell and Scott were transferred to Georgetown on a writ of habeas corpus. Mrs. Horrell was permitted to stay at the jail to nurse her husband. About eleven o'clock on the night of May 2, a body of thirty-five men, led by one of the brothers, rode into town. They warned the citizens that they did not want to injure any of them, but that they meant to free the prisoners at any cost. Shots were exchanged until the five guards in the jail ran out of ammunition, one of them, a young lawyer named A.S. Fisher, receiving serious wounds in the side and leg. The assailants were then able to get up the stairs and Bowen broke in the door with a sledge hammer. Two prisoners under indictment for horse-stealing, Berry and Whittington, were also freed.

The Horrells rounded up their cattle, selling the remnant to Cooksey and Clayton, and set out for New Mexico. With supreme recklessness, they notified the sheriff when they would pass through Russell Gap, but that gentleman made no effort to halt them.

On arriving in Lincoln County, the Horrells bought a homestead from Frank Reagan and Heiskell Jones in the Ruidoso Valley, near present day Hondo, and the rest of the clan located in the same vicinity. Hough[7] says that two of the family were financed by Murphy. On December 1, 1873, Ben Horrell, accompanied by Dave C. Warner, E. Scott, Zacharias Crompton, and the ex-sheriff of Lincoln County, L.J. [Jacob Lewis] Gylam, went to Lincoln on business. The party drank heavily, became boisterous, and began firing off their guns. Constable Juan Martinez [Martín] demanded that they surrender their weapons. This was done, but about an hour later, the men secured other arms, congregated at a local house of ill repute, and resumed their spree. The constable then summoned four or five of the Police Guard to restore order, taking with them a Mr. Warwick [William Warnick] as interpreter. While Warwick was explaining the object of the party, Warner suddenly shot the constable, killing him instantly. Warner was killed in the return fire, but Gylam and Horrell broke out of the house and ran across the acequia. They were pursued and wounded. Apparently, both of them surrendered, gave up their arms, and were then shot in cold blood. The Silver City *Mining Life*[8] suggested that the murders might have been an outgrowth of the ill feeling resulting from the shooting of a couple of Mexican horse thieves by Riley and Copeland a year or so earlier.

The Horrells went to Lincoln and demanded the arrest and trial of the murderers. This was refused, the Mexicans claiming that the

Police Guard had simply been doing its duty. Three days later, Seferino [Severiano] Trujillo and another Mexican were found dead on the Horrell ranch. A posse of about 40 men, led by Sheriff Ham Mills, descended on the Horrells on December 5 and demanded their surrender. Their women and children had been placed in Robert Casey's[9] grist mill and the ranch house prepared for a siege, but the Horrells offered to go with any military or civil authorities who would guarantee them protection while under arrest. When the sheriff refused to make this guarantee, the Horrells refused to be arrested.

In response to a letter from Justice of the Peace Manuel Gutierrez requesting the aid of troops in preventing a renewal of the riot in Lincoln, Major John S. Mason, commanding Fort Stanton, had advised that the military could be used only for protection against the Indians. However, he now ordered a detachment under Captain Chambers McKibbin to camp on Eagle Creek in the vicinity of the Horrell ranch and to investigate the circumstances. They were not to participate in any way in the quarrel, but were to notify him immediately if the Mexicans should make an attack. Shots were exchanged between the posse and the Horrells throughout the day, without casualities to either side. That evening, the sheriff withdrew his force, possibly because of uncertainty regarding action which might be taken by the troops.

On the night of December 20, the Texans struck back. While a wedding was being celebrated in Lincoln, they raided the party. Their promiscuous shooting resulted in the killing of Isidro Patrón,[10] Dario Balizan [Mario Balazan], Isidro Padia [Padilla], and Jose Candelaria. Apolonia Garcia, Pilar Candelaria, and a young man were dangerously wounded. The citizens of Lincoln now petitioned Governor Marsh Giddings for protection. Murphy wrote that the civil officials were unable to meet the situation and requested that arrangements be made for the use of troops from Fort Stanton. Associate Justice Warren Bristol advised that it was out of the question to find impartial juries and that only the military could quiet the disturbances. Mason sent troops from Fort Stanton to camp on the outskirts of the plaza in hope that their presence would be a moral deterrent to further outbreaks of violence.

However, a letter written by Captain James F. Randlett[11] gives good reason to question whether the citizens of the plaza were as peaceable and law-abiding as they would have liked the governor to believe:

> The civil law is powerless and has no active execution except a lawless posse led by one Juan Gonzales[12] a noted murderer and horse thief. This man Gonzales pretends to act as (and I believe is actually) a deputy Sheriff.
>
> No white citizens would surrender to this Villian [sic] and his posse with a show for anything but a barbarous death.
>
> The Mexican population have nothing to fear from Gonzales and can commit crime with impunity unless some action is taken by authority sufficient to control the elements at work.

Governor Giddings wrote Secretary of the Interior C. Delano requesting that he arrange for the use of soldiers to assist the civil authorities, but Secretary of War William W. Belknap informed Delano that Lincoln was an organized county and that there was no authority for troops to interfere in the affairs of the citizens. If they did so, they would be subject to indictment by civil authorities. The assistant general of the Department of the Missouri then issued a general order specifically forbidding the troops to act except on the orders of the President of the United States.

Another clash seems to have taken place in the village of San Patricio on January 4, 1874. Three days later, Governor Giddings[13] signed a proclamation offering $100 each for the apprehension of Crompton, Scott, and "three other persons, brothers, by the name of Harrold, whose first names are unknown." Nevertheless, about the end of that month, another raid was made on Lincoln, during which Deputy Sheriff Joseph Haskins was taken out of his bed and murdered, allegedly by Edward "Little" Hart, Thomas Keenan, and C.W. King, for no other reason than that he had a Mexican wife. The Horrells declared their intention of killing L.G. Murphy and J.J. Dolan, but were unable to find them. First reports stated that Dave Stanley was killed; later, it was announced that this was a mistake and that Mr. and Mrs. Steve Stanley had been killed by a wild shot while in their bed. Since a Steve Stanley, a Murphy & Co. teamster, fought a duel with S.W. Lloyd in Lincoln on February 24, 1876, it seems likely that there may have been an error in this report as well.

This was the Texans' parting gesture. Apparently, they had already decided to return to Lampasas and had sent their families ahead of them to Roswell, leaving their ranch property in the hands of Murphy. Later, Juan B. Patrón[14] significantly commented, "There are people who say that this was one of the ends Murphy was working for." It suggests that the Texans represented a force which Murphy felt that he could not control and which he therefore determined to drive out.

On the way to Roswell, Ben Turner was killed by a shot fired from ambush by, it has been said, a man named Martin Chaves. The party started back to Lincoln to wipe out the town, got as far as the Casey Ranch, were unable to agree on a course of action, and finally headed back to Roswell. About fifteen miles west of the town, they met a party of five Mexican freighters and killed them all. At some stage of all this fighting, Reymundo and Ceberiano [Severiano] Aguilar, Pablo Romero, Severiano Apadaca [Apodaca], Juan Silva, Ramondo Apadaca [Reymundo Apodaca], Leverian Apadaca [Apodaca], and Juan Lyban lost their lives. The total number of persons killed was no doubt considerably in excess of those whom it has been possible to name here. The Santa Fe *Daily New Mexican* for December 29, 1873, had noted that up to that time, thirteen individuals had been murdered.

Warrants were issued charging Frank H. Ricker, Zacharias Crompton, John D. Scott, John Walker, James [Jerry?] Scott, Merritt Horrell, James McLaine, Charles Powell, William Williams, Thomas Bowen, Samuel Horrell, Thomas Horrell, Martin Horrell, William Applegate, James Wilson, William Little [Lyttle], Robert Honeycutt, C.W. King, W.A. Jacoby, Robert Casey, Edward Hart, Thomas Keenan, Rufus Overstreet, Captain James Randlett, and two men identified only as Woods and Jones with murder or complicity in murder. Randlett and Casey obtained changes of venue to Socorro County, where Randlett was found not guilty by a jury which did not even leave their seats and the charges against Casey were dismissed. Randlett asserted that the charge was made simply in revenge for his actions which had resulted in the removal of Murphy as Indian trader at Fort Stanton. Charges against the others were later dismissed because they had left the country and the warrants could not be served.

The Texans did not leave empty handed. Ricker had stolen four horses from Stanley. Crompton, Applegate, Hart, and a man named Still rustled some horses and mules belonging to Aaron O. Wilburn, of Roswell. Some of the other members of the party met Robert W. Beckwith on the public road and robbed him of horse, saddle, and pistol. All of the stock was driven off Sheriff Mills' ranch. Beckwith lost eight horses and mules. Wilburn and his brother Frank raised a posse and pursued the thieves to the Hueco Tanks, east of El Paso, where Crompton and Still were killed. Wilburn returned to Roswell, but, fearing the vengeance of the Horrells, fled to Las Vegas.

According to Sonnichsen,[15] when the Horrells reached home, they told their friends, "We fought them all the way to Fort Davis." Unhappily, Lampasas proved no haven of refuge. Word of their coming had preceded them and the sheriff had assembled a posse of fifty men. As the Horrells' wagons rolled into town on the 5th of March, the posse opened fire. Jerry Scott and Rufus Overstreet were captured. Scott was shot through the lung, and one Johnny Green, the proverbial innocent bystander, received a serious wound in the abdomen from a shot aimed at Overstreet. Mart Horrell was slightly wounded.

That the Horrells hoped to make a new start in life is shown by the fact that the Lampasas *Dispatch*[16] reported that "The Horrell party didn't fire a shot at the posse during the engagement." Their new attitude of "peaceful coexistence" was further confirmed in September, when the Horrells surrendered to stand trial for the Williams affair, finally being acquitted in October, 1876.

At this point, a mystery arises. About the end of November, 1874, the Las Cruces *Borderer*[17] noted that "The Harold boys have returned to Lincoln County and trouble is feared." Who it was that returned, and on what business, the writer has been unable to learn. Diligent search of contemporary newspapers reveals no further reports of troubles with the Horrells in New Mexico.

ACKNOWLEDGMENTS

The writer takes pleasure in acknowledging the assistance of the following in collecting material for this paper: Dr. C.L. Sonnichsen, Texas Western College; Dr. Seymour V. Connor and Mrs. B. Brandt, Texas State Archives; Dr. Llerena Friend, Barker Texas History Center; Mr. Michael T. Brimble, Library of the University of Texas; Miss Elizabeth McCollister, San Antonio Public Library; Mr.

George R. Rawley, librarian, Southwestern University; Mr. Glenn Turner and Lieutenant Robert Dykstra, U.S.A. Also Miss Gertrude Hill, Miss Ruth E. Rambo, and Mrs. Edith G. McManmon of the Library of the Museum of New Mexico.

NOTES

[1] Silver City *Mining Life*, December 20, 1873.

[2] It seems likely that the killing of a Mr. Howell at Shedd's San Agustin ranch reported in the Santa Fe *Weekly New Mexican* January 26, 1869, actually refers to Samuel Horrell, Sr. Some of the Lampasas newspaper reports also give the name as Howell instead of Horrell.

[3] James B. Gillette, *Six Years With the Texas Rangers*. Chicago: R.R. Donnelley & Sons., Co., 1943, p. 107.

[4] F.L. Britton to Edmund J. Davis, March 24, 1873. In *Journal of the Senate of Texas*, March 25, 1873, p. 352.

[5] J.M. Redmon to F.L. Britton, February 17, 1873, and J.M. Redmon to F.L. Britton, February 28, 1873.

[6] C.L. Sonnichsen, *I'll Die Before I'll Run*. New York: Harper & Brothers, 1951, p. 98.

[7] Emerson Hough, *The Story of the Outlaw*. New York: Grosset & Dunlap, 1907, p. 201.

[8] December 20, 1873.

[9] Casey had come to New Mexico in 1867 from Mason County, Texas. He had purchased a ranch from Leopold Chene located about two miles from Picacho on the Rio Hondo.

[10] Some of the records give the name as Pedro Patrón. He was Juan B. Patrón's father.

[11] James F. Randlett to Adjutant General, District of New Mexico, January 5, 1874.

[12] In October, 1876, Frank Coe and Ab Saunders ambushed Juan Gonzales at his house in Lincoln. Saunders succeeded in wounding him slightly, but he escaped to Albuquerque, where he was later killed while trying to rob a house. See Haley, "Horse Thieves," op. cit.

[13] Santa Fe Daily *New Mexican*, January 9, 1874.

[14] Juan B. Patrón, Unpublished affidavit. Patrón had been raised by Archbishop Lamy and educated at Notre Dame. He was murdered by M.E. Maney at Puerto de Luna on April 9, 1884. The killing appears to have been the senseless act of a drunken cowboy, but some of the contemporary newspapers suggested that it was an outgrowth of the Horrell War.

[15] Sonnichsen, op. cit., p. 103.

[16] Lampasas *Dispatch*, March 19, 1874, quoted in Dallas *Daily Herald*, March 25, 1874.

[17] Las Cruces *The Borderer*, quoted in Santa Fe *Daily New Mexican*, December 7, 1874.

3.
The Pecos War

Panhandle Plains Historical Review, 1956

Unfortunately for the peace-loving citizens—if any—of Lincoln County, New Mexico, the departure of the Horrell clan for Texas in 1874[1] failed to introduce an era of brotherly love and sweet reasonableness. Guns continued to roar and cattle and horses continued to disappear with almost monotonous regularity. To even list all such incidents here would be a profitless undertaking; the writer shall do no more than to mention a few of the more important encounters.

On October 21, 1874, William Burns, a clerk in the employ of L.G. Murphy & Co., shot Deputy Sheriff Lyon Phillipowski when the latter drunkenly threatened his life.

In December, Jose Domingo Valencia killed Daniel Fisher in the dining room of Sam Wortley's hotel.

In May, 1875, a promising young badman named Josiah G. "Dock" Scurlock got his name in the papers by stealing three horses, two saddles, and a gun and lighting out of Arizona.

On the 1st of August, Robert Casey, the Horrell's staunch friend, was murdered by a man named William Wilson, whom Casey had discharged because of his horse stealing proclivities. Wilson contended that Casey still owed him $8.00 in wages and shot him to prove it. A Charles Myrick was held as an accessory. In due course, the murderer was executed by Sheriff Saturnino Baca in what is said to have been the first legal hanging in the territory of New Mexico.

Only a few days later, Jesus Mes, Pas Mes, Tomas Madril, and Jermin Aguirre, thieves and murderers making their headquarters at

Boquilla, had a personal experience with New Mexican non-legal justice. They stole thirty animals and made their way to San Ignacio, pursued by Jim McDaniels and four men. Three of the outlaws, Jesus being the fortunate fourth, were seized by the Mexican officials and turned over to McDaniels. He arrived safely at the San Augustin [Agustin] ranch with the prisoners, but on the night of August 8, a party of masked men took the thieves out and shot them.

On September 11, John Riley shot Juan B. Patrón. He claimed that Patrón followed him around, became abusive, and finally pulled out a pistol, whereupon he employed his rifle in self-defense. Riley never did explain how it was that his bullet entered Patrón's back [Patrón survived this shooting. See Chapter 21, ed.].

In February, 1876, Steve Stanley,[2] a teamster for L.G. Murphy & Co., fought a duel with S.W. Lloyd over the ownership of the Stanley ranch. Lloyd was seriously wounded. Stanley defied Sheriff Baca to arrest him, but surrendered when the sheriff obtained the aid of Thomas Corcoran [Cochrane], George Clark, and John L. Williams. Stanley was examined before Justice John B. Wilson and promptly acquitted.

Haley,[3] apparently basing his account on interviews with Frank Coe, has described the sad fate of some of the Mes family who failed to profit from the experience of their namesakes and became troublesome in 1876. Pancho, Cruz, and Roman Mes were pursued by Frank Freeman, Charles Woolsey, John Mosley, Jessie J. Evans, and others. At a spot across the border from Isleta, they were captured, along with a cousin, Tomas Cuerele, brought back to the east of the pass across the Organs, and there shot.

In October, John H. Slaughter killed a cattle dealer named Gallagher at South Spring.

These bloody incidents were but curtain raisers preceding the main event, known to history as the Pecos War. John Simpson Chisum had come to New Mexico from Texas in the late fall of 1866. By right of preemption, his range extended along the Pecos River from Fort Sumner to Seven Rivers, a distance of about 150 miles, with the home ranch at Bosque Grande, fifty miles below Fort Sumner. In 1877, he was credited with possessing 80,000 head of cattle and was known as "the cattle king of New Mexico." Almost inevitably, his regal ambitions brought him into conflict with the small ranchmen who dwelt on the frontiers of his domain. Unfortunately, there were few newspapers in existence in the area at that time and still fewer have been preserved. As a result, the story of the Pecos War is incomplete and contradictory, nor is it likely that the full details will ever be known.

The principal evidence on the subject consists of a long letter dated June 15, 1877, which Deputy Sheriff Andrew J. Boyle,[4] anything but an impartial witness, wrote to U.S. Attorney Thomas B. Catron. According to Boyle, Chisum and an ally, Robert K. Wylie, attempted to extend their range fifty miles south, to Pope's Crossing. Chisum's version would probably have been that he was determined to wipe out the rustlers who were preying on his Long Rail brand. Fulton[5] has noted that it was a current saying that "No one can live at Seven Rivers who does not steal from Chisum's range," and Billie Wilson[6] later wrote Governor Lew Wallace that "The Beckwith family made their boasts that they come to Seven Rivers a little over four years ago with one Milch cow borrowed from John Chisum they had when I was there year ago one thousand six hundred head of cattle."

One of the first reports of trouble on the range was contained in a letter from Ash Upson, postmaster at Roswell, published in the Santa Fe *New Mexican* on February 8, 1877. It related that about six weeks earlier, a man named Yopp, who was in charge of Wylie's cattle camp some eighty miles south of Roswell, became enraged at one of the employees, William [Thomas] B. "Buck" Powell. Yopp drew his revolver and fired three shots, but missed. Powell seized a Winchester and shot Yopp in the mouth. Yopp fell insensible. Recovering consciousness, he again fired at Powell, and again missed. Wrestling the gun away from him, Powell shot him through the heart.

On March 28, James M. Highsaw, a Chisum employee, accused Richard Smith, Wylie's foreman, of being in league with the thieves. In the ensuing altercation at Loving's Bend of the Pecos River, Smith was killed. According to Boyle, when the news reached Chisum he remarked that the war had commenced and that there were six more Seven Rivers thieves to be killed: Louis Paxton, Underwood, Charles M. Woltz, Robert W. Beckwith, William H. Johnson, and Powell.

On April 10, James J. Dolan and a party of men from Lincoln

rode down to Paxton and Underwood's camp to purchase some beef for the use of the troops at Fort Stanton. Near Wylie's camp, six Chisum and Wylie employees laid an ambush for them, but were sighted by a party led by Underwood. After a few shots were exchanged without effect, the Chisum-Wylie force withdrew. Chisum demanded help from the commanding officer at Fort Stanton, but was refused. He then appealed to Sheriff William Brady, of Lincoln County, who reminded him that the scene of the trouble was in Doña Ana County, which was not under his jurisdiction.

Chisum returned home determined to take the law into his own hands. On April 20, Chisum, Wylie, and about thirty men surrounded Hugh Beckwith's house, cut off his water supply, and seized the horses and mules which were grazing nearby. During the night, Woltz and Powell slipped through their lines and rode to Mesilla, the county seat, to obtain warrants for the arrest of Chisum, Wylie, and Highsaw for the murder of Smith. The next morning, Chisum sent a Mr. and Mrs. Gray to the Beckwith house to urge the women and children to leave. These, consisting of Mrs. Stafford, Miss Helen Beckwith, and two younger Beckwith children, retorted that they felt that they were safer within the walls of their home than they would be with the besiegers. The following morning, shots were exchanged. Apparently, there were no casualties, but Chisum's men began to rebel, saying that they had been hired to herd cattle, not to fight, and did not propose to get killed for $30.00 a month.

Chisum now sent for Johnson, offering to effect a compromise. The Beckwith forces, however, proved unexpectedly obdurate. They claimed that Chisum owed money to some of them and they wanted the cash before any compromise was agreed upon. Chisum then withdrew his forces.

Powell returned from Mesilla with the warrants on May 7, and Boyle led a posse of fourteen men to arrest the accused. At the Chisum camp, near present day Carlsbad, they found only the cattle king himself, too sick with smallpox to be moved. Three days later, the posse surrounded his South Spring River Ranche, four miles south of Roswell. Wylie sent Charlie Moore out to talk with them, warning that if they attacked, innocent persons might be killed, and offering to make a satisfactory settlement. During the negotiations, Highsaw slipped out the back way and made his escape.

That not all of Chisum's warriors were satisfied with the outcome of this affair is shown by a letter written to Boyle by Charles H. Brady:

> Dear Sir, you red headed —— of — b——— if you do not bring them horses back you stole you shall hear the gentle report of my needle gun; that is the kind of a hair pin I am, this thing of being on a sheriff's posse for a band of horse thieves may do in some places but, it has got too thin with me, yours, on the first dark stormy night.[7]

At the June term of court, the Grand Jury issued indictments against Chisum, Wyley, Highsaw, Hendricks, Brady, Thomas Easton, Cicero Knight, Edward Jackson, "and divers other persons whose names are unknown" for unlawfully assembling to assault the Beckwith house and to cut his water ditch. Other causes cited Chisum, Wylie, and Highsaw for riot and larceny, Highsaw for murder, and Robert W. Beckwith, Louis Paxton, Buck Powell, and George Hindman for various offenses.[8]

While the war had raged on the range, an important change had taken place in Lincoln. On March 14, 1877, L.G. Murphy & Co. was dissolved. The business was continued by James J. Dolan and John H. Riley[9] under the name of James J. Dolan & Co. Dolan promptly demonstrated that the new firm would carry on in the tradition of its predecessor by killing Hiraldo Jaramillo early in May. Since the Mexican was busily wielding a knife at the time, it was deemed a routine case of self-defense. A day or two later, the community suffered a more serious loss when Paul Dowlin was murdered in cold blood at his mill near Fort Stanton by one Jere Dillon, who escaped to Texas.

Haley relates that during the summer of 1877, Frank Coe and his brother-in-law, Ab Saunders, lost five valuable horses to thieves led by Nica [Nicas] Meras. With Charles Bowdre, Dock Scurlock, John Jones, a negro named Joe Howard, a halfbreed Cherokee-Mexican called Chihuahua, and a Mexican, they pursued the rustlers to Coyote Springs, twenty miles below Puerto de Luna. Here, the tables were turned. The outlaws captured the halfbreed, the Mexican, and all their pursuers' horses. Early the next morning, Jesús Largo offered to return the horses and the breed if the posse would leave the country. On their return home, the negro killed Chihuahua, whom they felt had betrayed them.

In August, Largo was captured. Sheriff Baca set out for Fort Stanton with the prisoner in a buggy. Frank Coe, Scurlock, Bowdre, Saunders, and another man stopped the sheriff six miles above Lincoln and lynched the prisoner. Later, Ab Saunders and another man captured Meras and killed him in what is now known as Meras Canyon when he attempted to escape.

Early in August, Chisum and George Hogg visited the McSweens at their residence in Lincoln. Unexpectedly, an attempt was made to assassinate Chisum. About a year previously, Frank Freeman, who was from Alabama, had killed a negro sergeant in Lincoln when the latter took a seat beside him at the dinner table. Freeman fled to Texas, but returned in company with a man named Armstrong. Freeman and Bowdre came to Lincoln on Sunday, August 5, and forced Jose Montaño to open his store and provide them with liquor. Freeman shot and wounded another sergeant, and then paraded the streets shouting that his "name was Frank Freeman, and no twenty men could arrest him," and that he intended "to kill every man in town that he didn't like."[10] After the novelty of this wore off, the two men went up to the McSween house and shouted that "If John Chisum or his corpse was not turned over to them, they would burned the d——d house down," meanwhile firing promiscuously into the building. A Mexican servant returned the fire, slightly wounding Freeman, whereupon the desperadoes retired to the store of Dolan & Co.

Meanwhile, Sheriff Brady had collected a posse and attempted to arrest the two disturbers of the peace. They resisted, knocked the sheriff down, and probably would have killed him had not Dolan, Riley, and Jacob B. Mathews gone to his aid. The two gunmen were arrested, but Freeman escaped while being taken to Fort Stanton and Bowdre was able to raise $500 bail.

About a week afterward, Armstrong came to town, bragging that he was going to join Freeman and his gang and they would come in and burn the town. When he commenced emphasizing his remarks by firing his gun, Deputy Sheriff Francisco Romero y Valencia and a posse attempted to arrest him. Armstrong fired at the deputy and then fled toward the Rio Bonito. The posse returned the fire and killed the gunman. According to a letter to the Mesilla *Independent*, "Nelson from the Gila" boasted that he would help burn the town, but apparently he failed to carry out his threat.[11]

Brady now raised a posse to arrest Freeman. Reinforced by troops furnished by Captain George A. Purington, commanding Fort Stanton, the party proceeded to the Bowdre ranch about August 15. Freeman ran out of the house and was killed as he tried to escape by wading down the bed of the stream. The troops were under the command of Lieutenant Smith and this would seem to be the affair whose sequel is described by Coe,[12] although the incident is dated March, 1878, in that highly inaccurate work.

Little is known concerning the antecedents of Scurlock and Bowdre, but these two have a rather extensive record in the Lincoln criminal files. Charges of carrying deadly weapons, threatening a citizen, assault, and disguising themselves to obstruct the laws are to be found.[13] Apparently, no serious penalty was incurred in the present instance.

Chisum started a herd of 4,000 cattle to Sulphur Springs, Arizona, about this time, but the Long Rail riders' troubles were not over. As the herd passed Dowlin's mill about August 23, some of the boys obtained a supply of whiskey. The first casualty was Johnny Evers [Ewer], who shot himself in the leg and had to be taken to the hospital at Fort Stanton. Next, a halfbreed Comanche named Ramon Garcia, alias Capitan, alias Tegua, became crazy drunk, shot J.M. Franklin, one of Chisum's best men, in the back, and killed his own horse. Garcia was captured by some men from Mesilla. Hogg explained what had happened and the prisoner was started for the guard house at Fort Stanton. There seems to be no indication that he ever arrived there. About the 18th or 19th of September, the trail herd arrived at its destination, although a large number of cattle had been lost due to a great scarcity of water and grass and extremely hot and dry weather.

In publishing the Boyle letter, the Silver City *The Herald*[14] had advised its readers to await the Chisum and Wylie version before coming to a conclusion in the matter. Chisum never made a direct reply to Boyle's charges. What was evidently intended to be his *apologia pro su vita* now appeared in the form of a letter from Jacob Harris, George Harris, and Ezra Lee, "representing twenty-four persons living in the immediate vicinity of John S. Chisum's ranche." These Mormon immigrants branded Boyle's intimation that Chisum was attempting to monopolize two hundred miles of the Pecos River a base slander. They cited their own experience as an instance of Chisum's true nature. Upon their arrival at his South Spring River Ranche about the middle of March, 1877, out of money and provisions, Chisum had encouraged them to put in a crop in the vicinity of the Bottomless Lakes to supply provisions for the following year. He had furnished land, water, and supplies, and had moved his hogs to Bosque Grande so that they would not bother the crops. Heiskell Jones, who kept the only store at Roswell, and Martin Sanchez [Sanches] endorsed the letter with a testimonial of their own to Chisum's good character.

As might have been anticipated, horse and cattle thieves were quick to take advantage of the disordered conditions. The most prominent gang, known as "The Boys," was led by Jessie Evans and included George Davis, alias Tom Jones, said to be his brother, Tom Hill, an alias for Tom Childron [Chelson], and Frank Baker, all from Texas, Bill Allen, Nicolas [Nicholas] Provencio, Bob Martin, Ponciano [Ponciacho?], and George W. "Buffalo Bill" Spawn. Henry McCarty, later to become famous as "Billy the Kid," apparently did not join The Boys until that fall. Their headquarters were at Shedd's San Augustin [Agustin] ranch and Chisum was their principal target. It was charged that The Boys operated under the direction of the Murphy-Dolan-Riley combine, the cattle which they rustled being used to fill the latter's government beef contracts.

The gang raided through Lincoln County in August and September of 1877, in the process stealing horses and mules belonging to Richard M. Brewer, Robert A. Widenmann, Alexander A. McSween, John H. Tunstall, and others. Brewer, Scurlock, and Bowdre trailed the rustlers to the San Augustin [Agustin] ranch, but were unable to effect the return of the animals. On the 17th of October, Sheriff Brady, acting under heavy pressure from Tunstall, arrested Evans, Baker, Hill, and Davis at the Beckwith ranch and placed them in jail at Lincoln.

About the first week in November, Katarino [Catarino] Romero, confined for the murder of Prudencia Garcia, made his escape. When safely away, he wrote Juan B. Patrón that tools had come into the possession of The Boys, with which they had filed their shackles and sawed through the logs composing the wall of their cell. Brady investigated, found affairs as described, but took no action in the matter. When Patrón refused to continue acting as jailor, the sheriff appointed Lueilla Archuletta [Diego Archuleta] to the post, but failed to swear him in or turn the keys over to him.

As a result, on the night of November 16, there was no guard at the jail and the doors were unlocked. The prisoners simply walked out. Horses furnished by Boyle and other friends waiting in the nearby hills took them to Brewer's ranch, where they re-equipped themselves from horses, saddles, and arms belonging to Tunstall and Brewer. McSween claimed that the tools had been furnished by Panteleon {Pantaleon] Gallegos, a Dolan & Co. employee; Sheriff Brady accused Tunstall of having arranged the escape in exchange for the return of his horses and those of his friends and refused to rearrest them. The sole result was an intensification of the already existing bitterness between Dolan-Riley and Tunstall-McSween.

The hatreds engendered by the Pecos War were to bear bitter fruit. A few years afterward, when Governor Lew Wallace was asked about the origins of the Lincoln County War, he gave the following account:

> For many years previous to that time New Mexico had been occupied by hundreds of herders of cattle, who were regulated by no especial laws except a common understanding, but who lived in tolerable peace. About four years ago, a rich stock raiser from Texas came up in New Mexico and in a short time he had about $300,000 worth of cattle. He settled on the Pecos River, and in a short time he had succeeded in driving almost all the small grazers away. To get even, they began stealing from him. Now, they don't steal in that country like they do here, but they drive off droves of cattle—sometimes 500 at a time. To protect himself the Texan went down into his native State and recruited about seventy men, murderers, thieves and dangerous men of all classes, together with a number of sharpshooters and buffalo hunters. His enemies, seeing these warlike proceedings, banded together in common defense, and the result was open war.[15]

He might have added that Wilson told him that

> The Beckwith family were attending to their own business when this war (Lincoln County War) started but G.W. Peppin told them that this was John Chisums war and so they took a hand thinking they would loose their cattle in case that the Chisum won the fight.

Much the same thing appears to have been true of Boyle, Powell, Johnson, and others. While the murder of John Tunstall early the following year provided the spark that ignited the explosion, some of the underlying causes of the Lincoln County War dated back to the trouble between John S. Chisum and the small ranchers at the time of the Pecos War.

NOTES

[1] See Philip J. Rasch, "The Horrell War," op. cit. [See Chapter 2.]

[2] "This man Stanley is a hard case in every respect. It is said and generally believed that he has killed at least four men in this Ty. one of whom was a Zuni Indian." E.C. Watkins to Commissioner of Indian Affairs, June 27, 1878. Stanley afterwards quarrelled with Dolan and Riley and testified against them and Frederick C. Godfroy, agent at the Mescalero Apache Reservation, at the April, 1878, term of the grand jury in Lincoln. He left the county the end of May or early in June, 1878, so took no part in the Lincoln County War.

[3] Haley, "Horse Thieves," op. cit.

[4] Mesilla Valley *Independent*, June 23, 1877; reprinted with minor changes in Silver City *The Herald*, June 30, 1877.

[5] Maurice G. Fulton, "Roswell in its Early Years," Roswell *Daily Record*, October 7, 1937.

[6] From a letter in the Wallace Collection, William Henry Smith Memorial Library of Indiana Historical Society. Quoted by permission.

[7] Silver City *Grant County Herald*, August 24, 1878.

[8] See Causes 368, 369, 370, 371, 372, 416, 448, 449, and 451, Dona Ana County. Most of the actual records are missing.

[9] John Henry Riley was born on the Island of Valencia, off the southern tip of Ireland, on May 12, 1850. He came to the U.S. when he was about 12 years old. He died in Colorado Springs, Colorado, of pneumonia on February 10, 1916, and is buried in Mount Olivet Cemetery there.

[10] Mesilla Valley *Independent*, September 8, 1877.

[11] Ibid., August 25, 1877.

[12] George W. Coe, *Frontier Fighter* (New York: Houghton Mifflin Company, 1934), 49–56.

[13] See Causes 213, 215, 220, 224, 226, 230, 231, 239 *et cetera* in Lincoln County.

[14] Mesilla Valley *Independent*, September 22, 1877.

[15] Unidentified newspaper clipping in the Wallace Collection.

4.
How the Lincoln County War Started

True West, March-April 1962

On February 18, 1878, a young Englishman named John Henry Tunstall was murdered in Lincoln County, Territory of New Mexico. The immediate result of that killing was the Lincoln County War and a controversy which threatened to embitter the relationship between the United States and Great Britain.

Argument over this murder and its aftermath continues to this day. Some of the details will never be known, but the main outline of the story has become clear since the War Department removed certain pertinent documents from classified status. To understand what happened and why it happened, one must understand the backgrounds of the men involved and the situation into which the inexperienced Tunstall unwittingly blundered.

At the time of Tunstall's entrance on the scene, two parties were locked in a ruthless struggle for control of Lincoln County. On one side were three merchants: Lawrence G. Murphy, James J. Dolan, and John H. Riley. On the other were a lawyer, Alexander A. McSween, and a large rancher, John S. Chisum. Supporting the merchants were their employees, the small farmers in the vicinity of Seven Rivers, a gang of cattle thieves led by Jessie J. Evans and known as "The Boys," and the influence of the shadowy Santa Fe Ring, a predominantly Masonic organization which was the political ruler of the territory.

Behind the McSween-Chisum combine stood the Chisum cowhands, the majority of the citizens of Lincoln, some of the small ranchers in the vicinity of the plaza, and many of the local Mexicans.

Lawrence Gustave Murphy's origin is shrouded in mystery. The obituary published in the Santa Fe *New Mexican* on October 26, 1878, stated that he was born in County Wexford, Ireland, circa 1831, that he had been educated at Maynooth College, and that he had served several years in the regular army of the United States as a sergeant major.

However, County Wexford possesses no birth records for that time; the president of the college at Maynooth states that no student by that name ever matriculated there, and the adjutant general of the United States Army has no record of a soldier by that name. For what it is worth, there is a Lincoln tradition that he had studied for the Episcopalian priesthood and had emigrated to New Mexico from Canada.

The first known historical record of this individual is dated July 27, 1861, when he was commissioned first lieutenant in the First Regiment of the New Mexico Infantry. Shortly thereafter, he transferred to the First Regiment, New Mexico Cavalry, and accompanied Kit Carson on his campaign against the Navajos. He did not, therefore, come to New Mexico with the California Column, as has so often been written.

Murphy was an excellent officer; Carson personally called his services to the attention of Brigadier General James H. Carleton and eventually Murphy, by then a captain, was brevetted a major for meritorious service in the Navajo Wars and in controlling the Apaches at Bosque Redondo.

Murphy was mustered out of service in 1866. About 1868, in partnership with Lieutenant Colonel Emil Fritz, late First Regiment California Cavalry, he established a brewery on the eastern edge of the Fort Stanton reservation. In the summer of 1870, the reservation boundaries were enlarged and L.G. Murphy and Company became a privately owned island in the midst of government property.

The partners made the most of their opportunity. In effect, they became both sutlers and Indian traders, although they did not hold a license in either capacity. Men lawfully appointed and sent out by the authorities in Washington were bought out or run off. Murphy was elected probate judge of the county, a position which enabled him to wield a considerable amount of power.

Taking good care to ingratiate themselves with the officers stationed at the fort, Murphy and Fritz gained almost a monopoly of government business in the area. The Indian agent himself had his quarters in their building and had little to do other than to approve the vouchers which they made out for his signature.

James Joseph Dolan, from Laughrea, County Galway, Ireland, went to work for this company after receiving his discharge from the Thirty-seventh Regiment, United States Infantry, in 1869. A short, powerful youngster who feared neither man nor devil, Dolan was thoroughly dangerous when aroused or when he had been drinking. He became a particular favorite of the Apaches and was able to exert considerable influence in their councils. Some said that he became Murphy's adopted son.

Later, another lad from the Old Country joined the firm. John Henry Riley, born on the Island of Valencia off the southern coast of Ireland, became bookkeeper. Riley was no fighting man, but possessed a calculating turn of mind.

L.G. Murphy and Company prospered and waxed fat, but with prosperity came arrogance. Underbid on a hay contract on one occasion, the company purchased all of the hay in the neighborhood. As a result, the successful bidder was unable to fulfill his commitment and his bondsmen were forced to make good the difference when the Army had to pay a premium price to Murphy and Company for forage.

The local farmers had little choice but to sell their produce to the company and to purchase supplies from it, both at prices set by the firm. Whenever one of them went bankrupt and left the county, L.G. Murphy and Company seized his property for "debts owed the company." Undeterred by the lack of a good title, they promptly sold the land to the next comer.

In May, 1873, Captain James F. Randlett, Eighth Cavalry, had as his house guest a man named Reilly. Returning to his quarters one evening, he found Dolan threatening to kill Reilly unless the latter retracted certain statements he had made.

Randlett ejected Dolan, but that evening the Irishman renewed the quarrel. When Randlett interfered and called the guard, Dolan drew his pistol and fired at the officer. The guard seized Dolan and Murphy intervened; Randlett promptly placed both men under arrest. At court in Lincoln, the two merchants were released and a warrant was issued charging the captain with assault.

When the commanding officer of the post, Captain Chambers

McKibbin, Fifteenth Infantry, took the position that this was a personal quarrel in which he had no right to interfere, the irate Randlett wrote the adjutant general, giving a full description of the affair and complaining that L.G. Murphy and Company were unmercifully swindling the government. Secretary of War William W. Belknap immediately ordered Murphy, Fritz, and every man in their employ off the reservation.

With the help of Post Quartermaster Lieutenant C.H. Conrad, Fifteenth Infantry, and other friends, Murphy and Company procrastinated in obeying the fiat, but that summer Murphy clashed with Major William Redwood Price, Eighth Cavalry, who insisted that he would deal only with the legally appointed Indian agent. Price referred the matter to his superiors and on September 24, Superintendent L. Edwin Dudley told the partners to leave within twenty-four hours.

Bowing to the inevitable, the firm moved to Lincoln and set up temporary headquarters while busying themselves with the construction of a new store and with plans for revenge. Price suddenly found himself unable to secure feed for his horses, as the contractor, L.J. [Jacob Lewis] Gylam, had been jailed in Lincoln on a trumped-up charge. Conrad refused to buy from the only other source of supply, and was forced to withdraw his troops from the area. Randlett's turn came the following year, when he was charged with murder and accessory to murder in connection with the killing of four men during the Horrell War.

Meanwhile, Fritz's health had failed and he had decided to return to Germany to visit his parents. Stopping in St. Louis, he took out an insurance policy for $10,000 in favor of his brother, Charles Fritz, and his sister, Emilie Scholand. On July 26, 1874, Fritz died of dropsy in Stuttgart, Germany. A Lincoln lawyer, Alexander A. McSween, was employed to make collections for the estate, but Probate Judge Murphy refused to surrender the policy, alleging that Fritz was indebted to L.G. Murphy and Company for far more than its value.

Unexpected complications arose, however, when the insurance company was reluctant about paying off, alleging that Fritz had actually died of tuberculosis, which voided the policy.

Friction developed between everyone concerned, but eventually McSween was given power of attorney and sent to New York to investigate the situation. For his work, he was to receive ten percent of the face value of the policy if he succeeded in collecting the full amount.

Very little is known about McSween. He is variously said to have come from Scotland, Prince Edward Island, and Nova Scotia, but there is no definite record of him until 1873, at which time he was a lawyer in Eureka, Kansas. He had arrived in Lincoln in 1875, almost penniless but vowing to make the village his El Dorado. Allying himself with Tunstall and Chisum, he set about making this vow come true.

Tunstall was born in London in 1853. His father, in addition to his business interests in England, was connected with Turner, Beeton, and Tunstall, Ltd., of Victoria, British Columbia, and in 1872, young Tunstall sailed for Canada. He found his father's partner difficult, the small provincial town dull, and prospects of becoming rich unpromising.

Early in 1876, he set out for California, intent on going into sheep raising there. However, prominent residents of that state advised him to go to New Mexico. He appears to have met McSween and to have been influenced by him to settle in Lincoln County. On McSween's advice, he took up a 4,000-acre ranch along the Rio Feliz.

As an alien, he was ineligible to homestead public lands; it appears that McSween actually filed on the land and then sold it to his friend. In part, the ranch was stocked by animals bought at a sheriff's sale; in part, it was stocked by cattle purchased at rather less than half of their market value, but with the understanding that no questions would be asked about the title to them, provided only that they did not come from Chisum's herds.

Simultaneously, steps were taken to open a store in direct competition with L.G. Murphy and Company, and a bank, the Lincoln County Bank, of which Chisum was to be president and McSween, vice-president.

It has been the custom to present Tunstall as a saintly English lamb fallen among American wolves. But, actually, this young immigrant was very much "on the make." His goal was money—lots of money. His attitude was best revealed by a letter which he wrote to his father April 27, 1877:

> As regards chances of making money here that you can't guess at, I will tell you of one that I am busy on just now. Any work that is done in this county for the county...is paid for in paper called "county scrip," which I can buy at $1.00 and sell for $1.50 without moving from my seat...I have not yet ascertained exactly how much scrip is issued every year, but I intend to control it all if I can....*Everything* in New Mexico that pays *at all*...is worked by a "ring"....I am at work at present making a ring & I have succeeded admirably so far. You see an adventurer like myself does not present a very formidable aspect, if *in the ring*, but any one as well posted as myself can nearly break up an incipient ring single-handed by skirmishing on the outskirts a little....
>
> My ring is forming itself as fast & faster than I had ever hoped & in a cash way that I will get the finest plum of the lot, always providing that I can make my points, which up to now I have done quite successfully. I propose to confine my operations to Lincoln County, but I intend to handle it in such a way as to get the half of every dollar that is made in the county by anyone....

Apparently, all went well with his operations, since on May 27, 1877, he wrote his father:

> I have made arrangements to corner all the corn in the county and will make a large profit upon it. I am going to work to corner the wheat....I have found a lot of ranches that I can buy for a trifle that are worth in many instances 4 and 5 times what they would cost me, and in fact I can make more out of in one year than they will cost me to buy. I have worked into a strong young and independent ring....I shall also make quite a neat thing out of hay this year...when I see that you made only 10 per cent net profit on your capital last year...you can understand how I feel....In addition a chance is looming...of acquiring a very profitable business, viz. the Post Tradership at Fort Stanton....And if I could but get that position, I could make a *great deal* of money every year as I should so entirely control the county that I could make the prices of everything just to suit myself.

It is unlikely that he had sufficient funds to support all of these activities and it seems probable that much of the resources of the Lincoln County Bank must have come from Chisum. Following his initial delivery of cattle to Fort Sumner, Chisum had continued to trail herds from Texas to New Mexico. He established his headquarters on South Spring River, about five miles south of Roswell, and set out to pre-empt all the land in sight.

This brought him into conflict with the small farmers living in the vicinity of Seven Rivers, a community which had been settled by a caravan of thirty Texans and their families in 1870. Their cattle became mixed with those of Chisum, and the farmers soon became accustomed to picking up a few of Chisum's animals when they cut their own out of his herds. As "Billie" later informed Governor Lew Wallace, "The Beckwith family made their boasts that they came to Seven Rivers a little over four years ago with one milch cow borrowed from John Chisum. They had when I was there a year ago one thousand, six hundred head of cattle."

On April 20, 1877, Chisum and about thirty of his men surrounded the Beckwith house, cut off its water supply, and demanded that its inhabitants surrender. Instead, they fought Chisum to a standstill. His men began to rebel, saying that they had been hired to herd cattle, not to fight, and that they did not propose to get killed for $30.00 a month.

Chisum thereupon withdrew, but at the June term of court, the grand jury issued indictments charging him with unlawful assembly, riot, and larceny. By waging the Pecos War, Chisum had accomplished only one thing: he had made bitter enemies of a group of dangerous men. In time, these men would destroy McSween because of their fear of Chisum.

This, then, was the situation in the county at the time McSween was trying to settle the Fritz estate. Arriving in St. Louis, he decided that he required legal aid, and employed a firm there to assist him, promising them $2,800 for their services. Levi Spiegelberg of New York, who had been working on the case, was paid $700 for his services and dismissed. In his stead, Donnell, Lawson, and Company were retained.

Charles Fritz watched McSween's machinations with mounting alarm, and in July, 1877, Probate Judge Florencio Gonzales, who had succeeded Murphy, instructed the New Yorkers to place the money to the credit of Fritz in the First National Bank at Santa Fe, subject to the order of the probate court.

Unfortunately, they had just paid $7,148.94 to McSween. Legally, McSween was obligated to turn these funds over to Fritz and Mrs. Scholand immediately; instead, he deposited them in his personal account in an East St. Louis, Illinois, bank and presented the heirs with a bill for $4,095.15 for his fees and expenses.

After considerable maneuvering by both sides, McSween agreed to appear in court on the first Monday in January, 1878, and pay over the money due Mrs. Scholand. In December, however, he suddenly announced that he was going back to the States. Mrs. Scholand promptly swore out a warrant charging him with embezzlement and had him arrested and jailed at Las Vegas.

Simultaneously, Chisum, who was traveling with the McSweens, was arrested at the request of Thomas B. Catron, head of the Santa Fe Ring, who alleged that he had failed to pay the amount due on a judgment obtained against him by Alexander Grzelachowski. Chisum refused to pay and was promptly clapped in jail, where three other lawsuits were filed against him.

Tunstall struck back by writing a letter to the Mesilla *Independent* in which he alleged that Sheriff William Brady had mishandled tax money and that these funds had been diverted to the use of Dolan and Company, as the firm was now known. Dolan retorted that the money was on deposit with them and that Sheriff Brady had been unable to go to Santa Fe to settle his accounts due to illness in the family.

Territorial Treasurer Antonio Ortiz y Salazar stated a few days later that Brady had paid every cent for which he was accountable. Nevertheless, the damage had been done. Tunstall's failure to appreciate that he was dealing with men who would reply to legal chicanery by gunplay was about to cost him his life.

McSween was taken to the home of Judge Warren Bristol at Mesilla for a hearing. Tunstall allegedly testified under oath that he and McSween were partners in J.H. Tunstall and Company. McSween afterward admitted that this was false, although he said there was an agreement that they were to enter a partnership in May, 1878. Bail was fixed at $8,000 and the case remanded to the April term of court.

On the night of February 6, the McSween party camped at Shedd's ranch. The next morning, Dolan and Evans came to them. Dolan berated Tunstall about his letter to the *Independent* and challenged him to settle the matter by shooting it out then and there. When Tunstall replied that he was not a fighting man, Dolan departed, warning as he did so, "You won't fight this morning, you damned coward, but I'll get you soon."

That same day, Fritz and his sister obtained a writ of attachment on McSween's real and personal property. Acting on Tunstall's testimony before Judge Bristol, Sheriff Brady levied the attachment upon the interest which McSween assertedly possessed in the store and its stock. A week later Brady sent a posse to the Los [Rio] Feliz to attach whatever interest McSween had in Tunstall's ranch and stock. They were accompanied by "The Boys," who alleged that one of Tunstall's men, Billy the Kid, had some horses which they had lent him and which they wanted to recover before the attachment was served.

Upon the posse's arrival at the ranch, it was informed by Robert Widenmann, manager of the Tunstall store, that McSween had no interest in the horses and cattle there and that they would not be released without an order from Tunstall. Since Widenmann was backed by Tunstall's cowboys, the posse decided to return to Lincoln for further instructions.

Tunstall sought help from the Chisum family, but it was refused. He decided not to fight and sent word to the posse that it could have the animals. On the morning of February 18, Tunstall, Widenmann, Billy the Kid, Richard Brewer, and John Middleton started for Lincoln, driving nine horses before them. The posse, which had received reinforcements, including Dolan, arrived at the ranch and learned from the cook, Godfrey Gauss, that a few horses had been started for Lincoln.

Dolan immediately sent a number of possemen under the command of William Morton to recover the animals. As they rode up, Tunstall's men fled. Tunstall himself turned and rode toward them. As nearly as can be concluded from the evidence, Morton shot him in the breast and as he fell to the ground, Tom Hill, another of "The Boys," shot him through the back of the head. At the April term of court, the grand jury commented, "The murder of John H. Tunstall for brutality and malice is without a parallel and without a shadow of justification. By this inhuman act our county has lost one of our best and most useful men."

Tunstall's friends, however, had already taken the law into their own hands. The outcome was the Lincoln County War, which resulted in the death of McSween, the defeat of his party, and the total loss of the $25,000 which the elder Tunstall had invested in his son's ranch and store. As for the Fritz insurance money, the heirs received a total of $200. Years later, Mrs. McSween told the Dolan family that the balance had gone to buy stock for the Tunstall store and to pay for the house which the McSweens had built in Lincoln.

5.

Prelude to War: The Murder of John Henry Tunstall

The English Westerners' Brand Book, January 1970

Although the Pecos War presented grave difficulties for New Mexico cattle baron John Simpson Chisum, it did not absorb all of his energies. Even before his neighbours' guns frustrated his attempts to extend his range in Doña Ana County, he had leagued with John Henry Tunstall and Alexander A. McSween in an attempt to wrest control of Lincoln County from its political and economic dictators—Lawrence G. Murphy, James J. Dolan, and John H. Riley, known as "The House."

About the middle of March 1877, it was announced that Murphy had retired as head of the firm of L.G. Murphy & Co. and that the business would be carried on by Dolan and Riley under the firm name of James J. Dolan & Co. Designedly or otherwise, the announcement came just as his opponents were starting a vigorous campaign to unseat him. Almost simultaneously with his retirement, the Lincoln County Bank was opened, with Chisum as president, McSween as vice-president, and Tunstall as cashier, and J.H. Tunstall & Co., a mercantile concern in direct competition with Dolan & Co., was established, with Deputy U.S. Marshal Robert A. Widenmann in charge. In August, the two new businesses moved into their own building. This structure also housed the law office of McSween & Shield, a partnership composed of McSween and his brother-in-law, David P. Shield.

Little is known of McSween's early life. He is believed to have been the adopted son of Murdock McSween, of Prince Edward Island. On 23 August 1873, he had married Sue Ellen Homer at

Atchison, Kansas. On that occasion, the young lawyer gave his age as 29 and his residence as Eureka, Kansas. Miss Homer had been born at Gettysburg, Pennsylvania, on 30 December 1854. The couple soon emigrated to New Mexico, arriving in Lincoln on 3 March 1875, where McSween became the legal representative of Otero, Sellar & Co., of El Moro, six miles north of Trinidad, Colorado, and of L.G. Murphy & Co.

Tunstall had been born in London on 6 March 1853. On 20 August 1872, he had emigrated to the New World to seek his fortune. He had worked for Turner, Beeton & Tunstall, a Victoria, Vancouver Island, firm of wholesale and retail merchants in which his father had an interest, but differences with the resident partner, J.H. Turner, led him into leaving that city. The young Englishman arrived in San Francisco in February 1876, intent on going into the sheep business in California. However, Colonel John Hays advised him to go to Arizona or New Mexico. Rolando Guy McClellan, to whom Mrs. Ann Clark, a saleslady at the Victoria store, had given Tunstall a letter of introduction, and Colonel William Wells Hollister wholeheartedly agreed with Hays.[1] McClellan presented the young Englishman with a letter of introduction to his friend Samuel Beach Axtell,[2] governor of the territory of New Mexico. In their efforts to be of assistance, these people unwittingly set in motion the chain of events which was to result in the violent death of their protégé. How this came about is the theme of this paper.

Tunstall arrived in Lincoln County in November 1876. He had bought a large quantity of goods from Otero, Sellar & Co. and Sellar had given him a letter of introduction to McSween.[3] A strong friendship sprang up between these two ambitious young men. Murphy allegedly offered McSween $5,000 to use his influence to induce Tunstall to purchase the Murphy ranch at Fairview, some 35 miles from Lincoln. This the lawyer refused to do, contending that Murphy had no good title to the property.[4] Instead, the Englishman took up 4,000 acres of public land on the Rio Feliz under the Desert Land Act. Since he was not a citizen, it was necessary for McSween to file on the land and then sell it to his friend. The range was initially stocked by the purchase of 400 head of cattle which had been seized and auctioned off by the sheriff at $1.98 a head to satisfy a judgment Dolan had obtained against the Casey family. Richard M. Brewer, a local rancher who had formerly worked for Murphy, was hired as foreman and was sent on a trip through Lincoln County to purchase stock. Allegedly, he offered less than half of their market value, but made it clear that he would not inquire as to their title, provided that none of the animals came from Chisum's ranch.[5]

It has been the custom to present Tunstall as a saintly English lamb fallen among Lincoln County wolves. The fact of the matter is that he was simply a fortune hunter, determined to get everything on which he could lay his hands. His attitude was well depicted in a letter which he wrote home on 27 April 1877.[6] [See Chapter 4, p. 47, ed.]

Perhaps fortunately for himself, Tunstall was in St. Louis on a buying trip when Frank Freeman and Charles M. Bowdre made an attack on Chisum on 12 August. On the return trip, he fell ill of smallpox. While he was incapacitated at Las Vegas, "The Boys," a gang of rustlers led by Jessie J. Evans, stole a number of horses and mules belonging to Tunstall, McSween, Brewer, and Widenmann. Brewer, Josiah G. "Doc" Scurlock, and Bowdre trailed the rustlers to W.F. Shedd's San Agustin Ranch, but were unable to effect the return of the animals. During their absence, the Caseys rounded up the cattle Tunstall had purchased at the sheriff's sale and started for Texas. Brewer sent a party led by John Middleton[7] in pursuit and was successful in repossessing the animals in the vicinity of the Beckwith ranch.

On the 17th of October, Sheriff William Brady, acting under heavy pressure from McSween and Tunstall, arrested Evans, Frank Baker, whose real name was Hart, Tom Hill, also known as Tom Childron [Chelson], and George Davis, alias Tom Jones, said to be Evans' brother, at the Beckwith ranch and placed them in jail at Lincoln. Tunstall fatuously visited the jail, laughing and joking with the prisoners. Later, he sent them a bottle of liquor. About the first week in November, Catarino Romero, confined for the murder of Prudencia Garcia, made his escape. When safely away, he wrote jailer Juan B. Patrón that tools were in the possession of The Boys, with which they had filed their shackles and cut through the logs composing the wall of their cell. Brady investigated and found affairs as described, but took no action in the matter. Patrón thereupon resigned. The sheriff appointed Lucilla Archuletta [Diego Archuleta] to the post, but failed to swear him in or turn the keys over to him.

On the night of 16 November, there was no guard at the jail and the doors were left unlocked. The prisoners simply walked out. Horses furnished by Andrew Boyle and other friends waiting in the nearby hills took them to Brewer's ranch, where they equipped themselves with horses, saddles, and arms belonging to Tunstall and Brewer. McSween claimed that the tools had been furnished by Panteleon [Pantaleon] Gallegos, a Dolan & Co. employee; Brady accused Tunstall of having arranged the escape in exchange for the return of his horses and those of his friends, and refused to rearrest The Boys. The truth may never be known, but both Boyle[8] and Evans[9] signed affidavits implicating McSween in the jail break. Tunstall[10] wrote a letter in which he boasted of the esteem in which the outlaws held him and commented that all but one of his horses had been returned. As a result of this episode, feeling between Brady and Tunstall became so bitter that the sheriff hinted that the Englishman had not long to live.

These troubles, however, were but minor compared with those which were about to burst around the unfortunate Tunstall. His affiliation with McSween had involved him in the latter's bitter feud with Murphy-Dolan-Riley. In 1874, Emil Fritz,[11] a partner in Murphy & Co., had died of dropsy in Stuttgart, Germany. Among the assets in his estate was an insurance policy for $10,000. This the insurance company refused to pay, alleging that Fritz had actually died of tuberculosis, which voided the policy. A brother, Charles Fritz, and a sister, Emilie Scholand, were eventually appointed administrators of the estate. In the fall of 1876, they sent McSween east to investigate the situation. Arriving in St. Louis, McSween employed a firm there to assist him, promising them $2,800 for their aid. On their recommendation, he placed the case in the hands of Donnell, Lawson & Co., of New York City. The policy was finally paid in July 1877 and Donnell, Lawson & Co. credited McSween's account with $7,148.94 just before receving instructions from Probate Judge Florencio Gonzales to place the money to the credit of Charles Fritz in the First National Bank at Santa Fe, subject to the order of the probate court. Legally, McSween was obligated to turn these funds over to the administrators immediately; instead, he deposited them to his personal account in an East St. Louis, Illinois, bank. He then returned to Lincoln, where he presented the heirs with $100 each and the administrators with a bill for $4,095.15 for his fee and expenses. He then filed an application for release as surety on administrator's bond, contending that if the money was paid to Fritz and his sister, it would be misappropriated by them, leaving the sureties to make good their defalcations.

Dolan & Co., as successors to Murphy & Co., demanded that the money be paid over to them, alleging that Fritz's estate owed the partnership $76,000. In November 1877, Judge Gonzales appointed a commission consisting of Juan B. Patron, T.G. [Follett] Christie, and McSween to examine the books of Dolan & Co. They reported back that Murphy was indebted to the Fritz estate for something over $20,000, while Charles Fritz owed it about $2,000. Fritz promptly paid The House $1,000 on account and demanded that suit be brought against Murphy for the amount he owed. Mrs. Scholand's attorney, John B. Bail, then prepared to institute proceedings against Murphy at the next term of court and allegedly arranged for McSween to appear in court on the first Monday in January 1878 to pay over the money due her.

In December, however, McSween suddenly announced that he was going to St. Louis. He left Lincoln on the 18th, but Mrs. Scholand sued out a warrant[12] charging him with embezzlement and had him arrested and jailed at Las Vegas. There he remained until the end of January, when Deputy Sheriff Adolph P. Barrier was ordered to take him to Mesilla for a hearing before Warren Bristol, associate justice of the Supreme Court of the Territory of New Mexico and judge of the Third Judicial District Court. It may be stated here that the heirs received a total of $200 from the Fritz insurance. According to their descendants, Mrs. McSween once remarked that the balance went to build her house and to stock the Tunstall store. It is a fact, at least, that in 1877, George W. Peppin supervised the building of a large home for McSween, located just west of the Tunstall store.

A second blow was dealt the new ring on 28 December, when Chisum, who had accompanied the McSweens, was placed in the Las Vegas jail in connection with a suit over a debt which he owed U.S. District Attorney Thomas B. Catron, head of the Santa Fe Ring and president of the First National Bank at Santa Fe, financial backers of Dolan & Co. It was not until late in March that he posted bond and was freed. No fighting man, Chisum was careful to avoid any personal participation in the conflict which his actions had assisted in precipitating.

Competition from the Tunstall store had seriously undermined Dolan & Co. Already indebted to the Lincoln County Bank for a $1,000 loan, obtained about 29 September 1877, they were now forced to seek additional financial assistance from the First National Bank. On 19 January 1878, Dolan & Riley gave Catron a mortgage on forty acres of land adjoining Lincoln on the west, their store, its stock, and 1,500 cattle on Black River (near present-day Carlsbad) to secure him for endorsing their note.

Tunstall relentlessly closed in to eliminate his opponents. In a letter published in the 26 January 1878 issue of the Mesilla *Independent*, he intimated that Brady had mishandled tax monies and that these funds had been diverted to the use of Dolan & Co. This was equivalent to signing his own death warrant. In the following issue (2 February), Dolan retorted that Brady

> deposited with our house Territorial funds amounting to nearly $2000, subject to his order and payable on demand. Owing to sickness in the family of Sheriff Brady he was unable to be at Santa Fe in time to settle his account with the Territory....If Mr. J.H.T. was recognized as a gentleman, and could be admitted into respectable circles in our community, he might be better posted in public affairs.

Hon. Antonio Ortiz y Salazar, territorial treasurer, confirmed that Brady had paid into the treasury every cent for which he was accountable.[13]

During the hearing at Judge Bristol's home on 2 and 4 February, the administrators contended that McSween had gone to New York on private business and pleasure and now demanded that the estate pay all of his expenses; that he had paid Mr. Spiegelberg, of New York, $700 for the insurance policy, although he had neither reason nor authority to do so; that the payment to Donnell, Lawson was evidence of fraud on its very face; that McSween had been long since notified that his services were no longer required, but that they had been unable to bring him to a settlement.[14] McSween protested that he had left behind him in Lincoln sufficient assets to pay all of his debts. Tunstall allegedly testified under oath that he and McSween were partners in J.H. Tunstall & Co., and that McSween's interest in the business was worth at least $5,000.[15] McSween, however, later admitted that he was not actually Tunstall's partner at the time, although there was an agreement that he was to become so in May.[16]

Bail was fixed at $8,000, which, commented the *Grant County Herald*, "would seem to indicate that the prosecution had made out a strong case,"[17] and the case was remanded to the April term of court in Lincoln County. Bristol directed Barrier to take McSween to Lincoln and to deliver him to the sheriff of that county. On the night of 6 February, Barrier, McSween, Shield, Tunstall, and John B. Wilson camped at Shedd's ranch. Baker, Evans, and Jack Long, alias Frank Rivers, arrived shortly afterwards, followed later in the night by Dolan, Fritz, and James J. Longwell. The next morning, Dolan and Evans came over to the McSween-Tunstall camp. Dolan berated Tunstall about his letter to the newspaper and tried to provoke him to fight. When Tunstall inquired whether Dolan was asking him to fight a duel, the latter replied, "You damned coward, I want you to fight and settle our difficulties." Tunstall replied that he was not a fighting man and did not make his living that way. At this point, Barrier intervened. Dolan left the camp, throwing back as he did so the threat, "You won't fight this morning, you damned coward, but I'll get you soon!"[18] Barrier took McSween on to Lincoln, but, when Brady grimly remarked that McSween and Tunstall had reported that he was a defaulter on county funds but would find that he would not default in jailing McSween and taking the spirit out of him, became alarmed for his prisoner's safety and decided to retain him in his own custody. For this he was later arrested and charged with contempt of court. On 7 February, Fritz and his sister obtained a writ of attachment from Judge Bristol in the sum of $8,000 on McSween's real and personal property.[19] Two days later, Brady, accompanied by Deputy Sheriff George W. Peppin, Deputy Sheriff Jacob B. Mathews (a Dolan & Co. partner),[20] William Morton, Long, Longwell, John Clark, and T.G. [Follett G.] Christie, proceeded to the Tunstall store and levied the attachment on the interest which McSween was believed to have in the stock and premises. Tunstall's testimony thus had consequences which he had certainly not anticipated. Widenmann refused to deliver the keys, on the grounds that McSween had no interest in the store. He was thereupon placed under arrest and they were taken from him by force. In a towering rage, Tunstall wrote to Chisum that "the Sheriff has attached my store and threatens to attach my stock; but G-D d—n him he'll find I can't stand everything."[21]

Once home in Lincoln, McSween wasted no time in striking

back at his tormentor. One of his first moves was to circulate a petition requesting the removal of Dolan as postmaster. The records of the Post Office Department for this period have been destroyed, and all that is known of the situation is contained in a published excerpt from a report made to that department by Special Agent Charles Adams and published in the Santa Fe *Weekly New Mexican* of 3 August 1878:

> The charges contained in the petition are not true in the main, and were gotten up by a man (McSween) to injure Mr. Dolan, the petition being signed by one person in his employ. Since this petition was sent to you, and even before I could in person visit the office, a gang of robbers and murderers, led by this man McSween, had virtually accomplished the purpose of driving Dolan out of the country, and, under the protection of the military authority at Fort Stanton, N.M., he had tried to discharge his duties. At least a dozen men have been murdered by this gang, all being friends of Dolan, and it was for some time extremely hazardous to travel in that part of New Mexico for any person in sympathy with Dolan or his friends, unless protected by soldiers. The law of Congress has taken this protection from parties needing it, under the posse comitatus clause of the army bill, and in consequence the whole county of Lincoln has virtually been turned over to a gang of cut throats. The civil authorities are powerless, the sheriff himself having been killed by the gang, and Dolan has sold his business and left the country. It is a long story of murder and retaliation, and if it was not that the person recommended (Mr. Walz) is a stranger and may satisfy both parties, I would recommend the discontinuance of the office. Under no circumstances could I recommend this petition of McSween be considered.

McSween moved also to secure the lucrative Mescalero Apache contracts for Tunstall & Co. In a letter to Secretary of the Interior Carl Schurz, he charged that Dolan & Co. provided the Indians at the Mescalero Reservation with bad wheat and beef and obtained and sold supplies issued by the government for the use of the Indians. Because of these conditions, he alleged (falsely), the Indians were forced to depredate upon the local residents. Dolan & Co., he stated, employed the agency clerk, Morris J. Bernstein, to keep their books. He recommended that the agent, Frederick C. Godfroy, be removed and that Widenmann be appointed in his stead.[22]

To the secretary of the Presbyterian Board of Missions, who had recommended Godfroy's appointment, McSween complained that Godfroy "keeps nobody, outside of his family about him but Roman Catholics, tho' others could be had,"[23] and requested that a Presbyterian missionary be sent to Lincoln. Godfroy was the sole Protestant member of a Catholic family. Dolan and Riley had been raised as Catholics and they reared their own children in that faith. However, finding that preferment in the Santa Fe Ring, which practically controlled the economic and political life of New Mexico, was restricted almost exclusively to Masons, both had left the church and become members of that fraternal organisation. Whatever material benefits thereby accrued to them were achieved at the cost of an uneasy conscience. In later years, Dolan died so suddenly that there was no time for his family to summon a priest. Perhaps to forestall a similar fate, Riley left the Masons and became a devout Catholic. Their religious background probably gave Dolan, Riley, and Godfroy certain advantages in dealing with the citizens of a predominantly Catholic community.

It has been alleged that McSween felt that "the ennobling and refining influence of a Christian church would raise the standards of the whole community."[24] Yet the lawyer must have had some degree of education[25] and any educated man would realise that the introduction of a Protestant church into a largely Catholic community could not but put one more strain on a social fabric already stretched to dangerously near the breaking point. Superficially, McSween's actions might be interpreted as those of a bigot raising the banner of religious intolerance against Godfroy or as those of a man desiring his own brand of religious edification. Viewed within the frame of reference of the place, the time, and the situation, it appears likely that they were actually a carefully calculated attempt to secure certain financial advantages and to weld the Anglos of the area into a block which he could manipulate to his own advantage.[26]

Simultaneously, McSween counterattacked Fritz and Mrs. Scholand by filing a petition in probate court arguing that they were wasting the estate by bringing suit against him and contending that this was done at the instigation of Dolan. Dolan and Riley wrote to District Attorney William L. Rynerson,[27] a leader in the Santa Fe Ring, advising him of what was occurring. Rynerson's reply boded ill for McSween and Tunstall:

> I have received letters from you, mailed the 10th inst. Glad to know you (Dolan) got home O.K. and that business was going on O.K. If Mr. Wiederman [sic] interefered with or resisted the sheriff in the discharge of his duty, Brady did right in arresting him and any one else who does so must receive the same attention. Brady goes into the store in McS's place and takes his interest. Turnstall [sic] will have the same right then he had before, but he neither must not obstruct the sheriff, nor resist the discharge of his duties. If he tries to make trouble, the sheriff must meet the occasion firmly and legally. I believe Turnstall is in with the swindles of that rogue McSween. They have the money belonging to the Fritz estate, and they know it. It must be made hot for them all, the hotter the better. Especially is this necessary now that it has been discovered that there is no hell.
>
> It may be that the villian [sic] Green—"Jusif Baptista" Wilson—will play into their hands as alcalde. If so he should be moved around a little. Shake that McSween outfit up till it shells out and squares up, and then shake it out of Lincoln. I will aid to punish the scoundrels all I can. Get the people with you. Control Juan Patron if possible. You know how to do it. Have good men about to aid Brady, and be assured I shall help you all I can, for I believe there was never found a more scoundrelly set than that outfit.[28]

The day after Dolan mailed his letter McSween had attempted to post an appearance bond. True to his promise to help, Rynerson refused to accept it, alleging that McSween was a fugitive from justice. Dolan's henchmen then threatened and cajoled the bondsmen into withdrawing their support.

Brady's threat to attach Tunstall's stock was no empty one. On 13 February, he sent Deputy Sheriff Mathews, accompanied by John Hurley, Manuel Segovia, Andrew L. "Shotgun" Roberts (also known as Bill Williams), and George W. Hindman to attach the Englishman's horses and cattle. On the way to the ranch, the posse was joined by Evans, Baker, Hill, and Long. According to Evans, it was at Mathews' invitation; according to Mathews, it was on the pretext that they had loaned horses to "Kid" Antrim (an alias for Henry McCarty[29]) and wished to recover them before the attachment was levied.

The presence of these escaped criminals was to prove a serious source of embarrassment to Sheriff Brady. He tried to disclaim responsibility for their being in his deputy's posse by publishing a letter which he had given to Mathews:

> You must not by any means call on or allow to travel with your posse any person or persons who are known to be outlaws, let your Mexican round up the cattle and protect them with the balance, be *firm* and do your duty according to *law* and I will be responsible for your acts.[30]

Mathews protested that, "None of these men were part of the posse, but on the contrary were ordered away by me,"[31] a statement which cannot be given any degree of creditability. Why it should have been necessary for a sheriff to warn a deputy not to select "persons who are known to be outlaws" as part of a posse or why a deputy would not arrest such individuals on sight was never explained. The implications so far as Tunstall was concerned seem clear.

On the posse's arrival at the ranch, it was met by Widenmann, who informed it that McSween had no interest in the horses and cattle there and that they would not be released without an order from Tunstall. Since he was backed up by Brewer and several cowboys, Mathews felt it best to return to Lincoln for instructions and reinforcements. Widenmann urged his companions to assist him in arresting The Boys, but they refused on the grounds that if they did so, they would surely be murdered later on. The outlaws then rode off to Paul's ranch. Widenmann, Fred T. Waite, and Antrim accompanied the posse to Lincoln, but returned to the ranch the next morning.

Mathews sent Telesforo López to the Murphy-Dolan cow camp on the Pecos with instructions for foreman William S. Morton, who was said to have killed four men, to raise as large a force as he could to assist the posse. The resulting group included Mathews, Morton, Hurley, Segovia, Hindman, Roberts, Dolan, Gallegos, A.H. Mills, John Wallace Olinger, Thomas Moore, Robert W. Beckwith, Ramon Montoya, Juan Andrew Silva, Felipe Mes, E.H. Wakefield, Pablo Piño y Piño, Thomas Green, Charles Woltz, Thomas Cochran [Cochrane], "Dutch Charley" Kruling, George B. Kitt, Charles Marshall, Samuel R. Perry, and perhaps others. The Boys joined them at Paul's ranch and the party arrived on the Rio Feliz on the 18th.

Tunstall rode to South Spring, but Jim Chisum, John's brother, refused his pleas for assistance. The Englishman then followed his employees back to his ranch. He decided that saving the stock was not worth risking the lives of his men and sent William McCloskey, who was on friendly terms with several of the possemen, to inform Mathews that they could have the animals. McCloskey was also instructed to arrange for a neighbour, "Dutch Martin" Mertz, to stay at the ranch until matters could be arranged through the courts.

On the morning of the 18th, Tunstall, Brewer, Widenmann, Antrim, and Middleton started along the old Ham Mills trail to Lincoln, driving nine horses before them; Waite followed on the road in a wagon. With them for the first mile or so rode Henry Brown,[32] a former Murphy employee who had left The House after a dispute over wages. Only one man was left at the ranch, Godfrey Gauss, a cook who had had his own bitter experience in dealing with Murphy. About 30 miles from the ranch, Brewer and Widenmann rode off the trail to shoot some turkeys. Middleton and Antrim being towards the rear, Tunstall was left alone. At that moment, a detachment of the posse swept down upon him. Middleton put spurs to his horse, frantically calling to his employer, "For God's sake, follow me," but Tunstall seemed confused and only answered, "What, John? What, John?"[33] It seems likely that in view of his belief that he had the regard and friendship of The Boys, Tunstall did not consider that he was in any personal danger from the possemen. If so, his error was the kind a man makes but once.

On arriving at the ranch, the posse had learned from Gauss that a few horses had been started for Lincoln. Mathews and Dolan immediately despatched Morton to recover the animals. To assist him, they assigned Hurley, Segovia, Hindman, Gallegos, Olinger, Beckwith, Montoya, Green, Cochran, Kruling, Kitt, Marshall, and Perry. With them went The Boys. Morton urged haste: "Hurry up, boys, my knife is sharp and I feel like scalping someone."[34] According to the story he told later, he called on Tunstall to halt and waved the attachment at him. Tunstall wheeled his horses around and rode towards the posse, with his hand on his revolver. The men called to him to throw up his hands, promising that he would not be hurt. Instead, the Englishman pulled his gun and fired twice, whereupon Morton, Evans, and Hill returned the fire.

"As no one else was present at the time," remarked the Santa Fe *New Mexican* (23 March 1878), "...the statements of the parties are uncontradicted and will have to be taken for what they are worth."

There was good reason for the editor's scepticism. Accounts related by other members of the posse suggest that actually as Tunstall approached, Morton shot him through the breast. As he fell to the ground, Hill shot him through the back of the head. The murderers then killed Tunstall's horse and fired two shots from his revolver. It is significant that Tunstall's body was found about 100 yards off the trail, an area to which the possemen need not have penetrated if their only object was to recover the horses.

The murder took place about 5:30 p.m. About midnight, Riley appeared at the McSween house much the worse for drink. He emptied his pockets to show that he had no weapons on his person and then reeled out into the night. Left on the table was a notebook which was said to have contained a detailed account of the dealings of The House with The Boys. When Riley sobered up, he went out to Catron's cattle ranch near Seven Rivers, remaining on the range during the troubles which followed.

During the night, John Newcomb, with the assistance of Patnen Lonjillo [Patricio Trujillo], Florencio Gonzales, Lázaro Gallegos, and Roman Barogan [Ramón Baragón], brought Tunstall's body into Lincoln. An autopsy was conducted by Assistant Surgeon Daniel M. Appel, U.S.A. He reported that he found two wounds:

> one in the the shoulder passing through and fracturing the right clavicle near its center coming out immediately over the superior border of the right scapula passing through in its course the right sub clavicle artery. This would have caused his death in a few minutes and would have been likely to have thrown him from his horse....The other wound entered the head about one inch to the right of the median line almost on a line with the occipital protuberance and passed out immediately above the border of the left orbit. A wound of this kind would cause instantaneous death....
>
> It is my opinion that both of the wounds could be made at one and the same time and if made at the same time were made by different persons from different directions and were both most likely made while Tunstall was on horseback in as much as the direction of the wounds were slightly upwards.
>
> There being no powder marks on the body to indicate that the wounds were made at a short distance and the further fact that the edges of the wounds of the exit were not very ragged, I am of the opinion that they were both made by rifles....[35]

A jury consisting of Justice of the Peace John B. Wilson, George B. Barber, R.W. [Robert M.] Gilbert, Benjamin Ellis, John Newcomb, Samuel Smith, and Frank B. Coe rendered the following report:

> We the undersigned Justice of the Peace and Jury who sat upon the inquest held this the 19th day of February A.D. 1878 on the body of John H. Tunstall here found in Precinct No. (1) number one of the county of Lincoln and Territory of N.M. find that the deceased came to his death on the 18th of February A.D. 1878 by means of divers bullets shot and sent forth out of and from deadly weapons there and then held by one or more of the men whose names are here witnessed, Jessie Evans, Frank Baker, Thos. Hill, G. Hindman, J.J. Dolan, William Morton and others not identified by witnesses, that testified before the coroners Jury, we are undersigned to the best of our knowledge and belief from the evidence at the coroners inquest believe the above statement to be a true and impartial verdict.[36]

Tunstall was buried in back of his store on the morning of the 21st. His body is said to have since been taken up and reinterred with those of McSween, Harvey Morris, and Huston I. Chapman, behind the Penfield residence.

The day of Tunstall's murder, Brady authorised his deputies at the store to give some hay to a U.S. Army detachment. The next morning, McSween sued out a warrant from Justice Wilson, charging the sheriff with misappropriation of Tunstall's property. On the 20th, Brewer, Constable Antonacio [Atanacio] Martinez, Scurlock, Middleton, Antrim, Sam Smith, Samuel R. Corbet, the two Coe cousins, George Washington, George Robinson, Ignacio Gonzales, Jesus Rodriguez, Esiquio Sanches, Barogan [Baragón], Frank MacNab, Waite, and one Edwards forcibly took possession of the Tunstall building. The men in charge of the store were arrested and Widenmann again took control. Brady was examined before Wilson and remanded to the April meeting of the grand jury.

At the April term of court, the grand jury indicted Evans, Rivers, Davis, and Segovia for the Tunstall murder, and commented on the Lincoln County troubles in the following words:

> The murder of John H. Tunstall for brutality and malice is without a parallel and without a shadow of justification. By this inhuman

act our County has Lost one of our best and most useful men. One who brought intelligence, industry and capital to the development of Lincoln County....

Your honor charged us to investigate the case of Alex. A. McSween, Esq., charged with the embezzlement of ten thousand dollars, belonging to the estate of Emil Fritz, deceased; this we did but are unable to find any evidence that would justify that accusation. We fully exonerate him of the charge, and, regret that a spirit of persecution has been shown in this matter.[37]

Coming on the heels of Judge Bristol's decidedly pro-Murphy charge to the jury, these findings must have been a bitter blow to The House's hopes of using the courts to crush its opponents.

Tunstall had invested over $25,000 of his father's money in the ranch and the store. Only a few months after his son's death, the senior Tunstall suffered the additional blow of learning that his entire investment had vanished. The ill news came in a letter from Lincoln written by Corbet, who had been left in charge of the store when Widenmann had to go to Mesilla to attend court as defendant in three charges of resisting an officer[38] and as a witness in other cases. After describing the death of McSween[39]at the hands of the Murphy adherents on the 19th of July, Corbet wrote:

The same night, after McSween was killed the Sheriff's posse broke open the store of J.H. Tunstall, deceased, and taken out everything they wanted. The following morning I went to Sheriff Peppin (he was then in the store), and beg him for protection of life and property. He told me he was not responsible for nothing. I told him, if him or any of his posse wanted anything, I would let them have it; but, for God's sake, not to destroy everything. He told me again he was not responsible for nothing his posse done. They were then carrying out things; by the assistance of a few citizens I got them out and nailed up the store, but that night they broke it open again, and hauled out loads with wagons. After they got everything they wanted, they invited their friends to come and help themselves while they guarded the store, and it was not long until nothing was left....When they destroyed everything, I left town to save my life. I expect every day to hear of them stealing the cattle on the Felix [sic]. I am satisfied they will take them before they leave the country.[40]

Corbet's fears regarding the cattle were well founded. John Kinney's gang rounded up the herd and by the end of August, the last of the animals had been swept off the ranch. Even Mertz's wagon and team were stolen. Eventually, Mrs. McSween, as administrix, recovered 166 head of cattle, worth $976.50, at a cost of $842.45. She also collected $574.33 rent on the Tunstall building, while spending $572.00 for repairs. Another $146.00 was paid to Huston I. Chapman for legal services.[41] The ranch itself finally came into the possession of Dolan.

At the suggestion of both McClellan and McSween, John Partridge Tunstall, John Henry's father, authorised a reward of $5,000 for the apprehension and conviction of the murderers of his son. Widenmann had immediately appraised the British minister of Tunstall's murder, and on 9 March, Sir Edward Thornton requested Secretary of State William M. Evarts to take such measures as might be necessary to investigate Brady's conduct and to bring the murderers to justice. This was to prove only the opening communication in what was to develop into a protracted argument between the United States and Great Britain.[42]

On 12 November, Tunstall wrote to the Marquis of Salisbury complaining that the affair had left him almost penniless, and suggested that $150,000 should be the minimum amount which the United States should offer him in the way of pecuniary compensation. That same month, the British minister asked the secretary of state what results had been achieved, and sent him a pamphlet which had been published by the Tunstalls containing copies of newspaper articles and letters from John's associates. In response to the request of the secretary of state for information with which to reply to the British minister, the attorney general answered that he had "directed the United States Attorney for New Mexico to institute thorough inquiry and report to me," but as that officer had not "at once undertaken such investigation," it had been necessary to send an agent to the territory to investigate the situation.[43] The reason for the United States district attorney's apparent dereliction of duty was simple; he was Murphy-Dolan-Riley's backer, Catron.

Since both Morton and Hill had been killed, the British minister pressed for the arrest of Evans, in the hope that he might have valuable evidence to present. Catron resigned and was replaced by Sidney M. Barnes as U.S. attorney. The attorney general directed Barnes to use his influence to have the appropriate authorities in New Mexico investigate the affair and secure the punishment of those implicated. Two years later, the attorney general was forced to admit that he had received no response to his instructions to Barnes. Evans had meanwhile been arrested in Texas and was in the state prison at Huntsville, a fact of which the Department of Justice seemed blissfuly unaware. It is hard to understand why the attorney general would tolerate such neglect of specific instructions other than on the assumption that the influence of the Santa Fe Ring reached into Washington itself.

On 23 June 1880, Sir Edward submitted a request for the payment of compensation to J.P. Tunstall for the murder of his son and destruction of his property. He argued that since all territorial officers derived their authority from statutes enacted by the Congress, Sheriff Brady was actually an agent of the United States and they were responsible for his acts. To this, Secretary of State Evarts replied that the laws of the various states and territories were administered entirely free from federal control. Sir Edwards retorted that inasmuch as foreign governments had no diplomatic relations with individual states, they were obliged to look to the central power for redress. Secretary of State Frederick T. Frelinghuysen eventually proposed that if Congress approved, the matter should be submitted to the Court of Claims or some other judicial body for decision. The British representative, now L.S. Sackville-West, agreed to this proposal, provided that the United States would admit liability in the case. When this condition was rejected, negotiations came to something of a standstill.

About 1885, the Tunstall family published an "Address to Lord Granville." Subtitled "Resumé of the Facts Connected with the Murder of J.H. Tunstall and the Plunder of His Property in Lincoln County, New Mexico in 1878," it laid the blame for Tunstall's death squarely on the shoulders of the Santa Fe Ring, specifically Brady, Catron, Rynerson, Riley, and Dolan. However, repeated British requests for some sort of action in the case were met by the noncommittal answer that the matter was still receiving the consideration of the Department of State. Finally, on 1 June 1885, a lengthy letter from Secretary of State T.F. Bayard informed Sackville-West that the United States government could not admit any liability in the case. Bayard pointed out that it was an established principle of national and international law that the United States were not liable for the debts or torts of officers of a state or territory. Further, in countries subject to English common law, damages must be redressed through the courts and not through diplomatic intervention by the sovereign of the interested party. In similar instances affecting citizens of the United States, particularly in the case of Henry George, and those of other countries suffering injury in Great Britain, no claim had been made by the states of the individuals involved for pecuniary compensation. To admit such a claim would utterly confuse the boundaries between judicial, executive, and legislative branches of the government, nor did the executive department possess machinery for investigation of such suits. In any case, there was ample precedent for the fact that a citizen could not ask the state to intervene until he had "exhausted the means of legal redress afforded by tribunals of the country in which he had been injured." In this particular case, Mr. Tunstall was domiciled in New Mexico and hence had no title to the intervention of a foreign sovereign.

With this, the correspondence on the subject between the two countries came to a close. A resumé of the case has been cited in some detail in Moore's *A Digest of International Law*.[44] The murder of John Henry Tunstall is probably the only instance on record in which a killing by western desperadoes resulted in the establishment of principles of law between nations.

ACKNOWLEDGMENTS

The writer takes pleasure in acknowledging the assistance received from R.N. Mullin, Frederick W. Nolan, Mrs. Bessie Dolan Chester, Mrs. Carrie Dolan Vorwark; James de T. Abajian and Miss Riva Castleman, California Historical Society; Miss Frances Coleman, Kentucky Historical Society; Miss Gertrude Hill, Miss Ruth E. Rambo, and Mrs. Edith O. McManmon, Library of the Museum of New Mexico; Mr. and Mrs. John Boylan, Old Lincoln County Memorial Commission; and Thad Page, National Archives.

NOTES

[1] For the life of Hays, "the founder of the city of Oakland," see James Kimmins Greer, *Colonel Jack Hays* (New York: E.P. Dutton Co., Inc., 1952). McClellan was born on Prince Edward Island on 25 March 1831. He

arrived in San Francisco in 1855 and worked as a miner before becoming a lawyer and author. He died on 15 June 1896. A brief account of Hollister appears in Frank Sands' *A Pastoral Prince* (Santa Barbara, 1863), pp. 176–79.

[2] Axtell was born near Columbus, Ohio, 14 October 1819. He attended Western Reserve College and was admitted to the bar. In 1851, he went to California. Upon organisation of Amador County, he was elected district attorney, holding office for three terms. Moving to San Francisco, he served two terms in the House of Representatives as a Union-Democrat. He then changed his political allegiance and was appointed governor of Utah in 1875. That same year, he was transferred to New Mexico, where he was reunited with many of his old friends who had served in the California Column and had chosen to remain in New Mexico after their discharge.

[3] Miguel Antonio Otero, *The Real Billy the Kid* (New York: Rufus Rockwell Wilson, Inc., 1936), pp. 28–29.

It should be noted that Frederick W. Nolan, *The Life & Death of John Henry Tunstall* (Albuquerque: University of New Mexico Press, 1965), p. 180, refers to a letter written by Tunstall on 28 October 1876, mentioning that he had met McSween.

[4] Alexander McSween, Unpublished Affidavit, with Frank W. Angel, "Report to the Department of Justice in the Matter of the Cause and Circumstances of the Death of John H. Tunstall, a British Subject." In National Archives.

[5] Andrew Boyle, Unpublished Affidavit, 17 June 1878. In Record Group 75, Records of the Bureau of Indian Affairs, National Archives.

[6] John to My Much Beloved Father, 27 May 1877.

[7] "Middleton is about the most desperate looking man I ever set eyes on (& that is not saying a *little*) I could fancy him doing anything ruffianly that I ever heard of..." John H. Tunstall to My Much Beloved Parents, 29 November 1877.

[8] Andrew Boyle, Unpublished Affidavit, 17 June 1878, op. cit.

[9] Jessie J. Evans, Unpublished Affidavit, 14 June 1878. In Record Group 75, National Archives.

[10] John H. Tunstall to My Much Beloved Parents, 29 November 1877.

[11] Fritz was born in Ludwigsburg, Germany, on 3 March 1832. After serving in the 1st Regiment of Dragoons, he was appointed a captain and organised Company B, 1st Regiment California Cavalry, at Camp Merchant, California, on 16 August 1861.

[12] Civil Docket Case No. 141, Lincoln County.

[13] Santa Fe *Weekly New Mexican*, 9 February 1878.

[14] Silver City *Grant County Herald*, 9 February 1878.

[15] Mesilla *Independent*, Supplement 20 April 1878.

[16] Alexander A. McSween, op. cit.

[17] 9 February 1878.

[18] Adolph P. Barrier, Unpublished Affidavit, with Frank W. Angel, op. cit.

[19] Civil Docket Case No. 141, Lincoln County.

[20] Brady was born in Covan, Ireland, in 1825. During the Civil War, he served in the 1st New Mexico Cavalry. Before becoming sheriff, he worked for Murphy. Mathews was born in Woodbury, Tennessee, on 5 May 1847, and served in the 5th Tennessee Cavalry. He died on 3 June 1903. Peppin was born about 1849. He enlisted in Company A, 5th Infantry, California Volunteers, at Allegheny, California, on 2 October 1861, and was stationed at Fort Stanton from March 1863 to May 1864. He died on 18 September 1904. There is some evidence that Mathews was actually a silent partner in Dolan & Co.

[21] Santa Fe *Weekly New Mexican*, 10 August 1878.

[22] Alex. A. McSween to Carl Schurz, 11 February 1878. In Record Group 75, National Archives.

[23] A.A. McSween to Lowry [John C. Lowrie], 25 February 1878. In Record Group 75, National Archives.

[24] Ruth R. Ealy, "Medical Missionary," *New Mexico Magazine*, 32, 14 March 1954.

[25] Frazier Hunt's *The Tragic Days of Billy the Kid* (New York: Hastings House, 1956) states that McSween graduated from St. Louis University. This Catholic university has no record of his ever attending there. James V. Jones to P.J. Rasch, 29 June 1956.

[26] Lincoln was nominally under the spiritual care of Padre John Ralliere. Ralliere was in residence at Tomé, 25 miles south of Albuquerque, and travelled to the Lincoln area only once a year or so. See Florence Hawley Ellis, "Tomé and Father J.B.R.," *New Mexico Historical Review*, XXX:89–114, April 1955.

[27] Rynerson was born in Mercer County, Kentucky, probably on 22 February 1828. he went to California in the '50s, where he ran a butcher shop and studied law. He enlisted in the 1st Infantry Regiment of California Volunteers in Amador County and was discharged in 1866 with the rank of captain. He had received considerable notoriety as the result of killing Chief Justice John P. Slough in La Fonda at Santa Fe on 15 December 1867. Catron, Rynerson, and Riley were partners in the Tularosa Ranch and Rynerson and Dolan were two of the partners in the Feliz Cattle Co. He died on 26 September 1893.

[28] William L. Rynerson to Friends Riley and Dolan, 14 February 1878.

[29] The background of this individual has been studied in Rasch and Mullin, "New Light on the Legend of Billy the Kid," op. cit.; Rasch and

Mullin, "Dim Trails—The Pursuit of the McCarty Family," op. cit.; Rasch, "The Twenty-One Men He Put Bullets Through," op. cit.; Rasch, "A Man Named Antrim," op. cit.; Rasch, "More on the McCartys," op. cit.; Rasch, "Clues to the Puzzle of Billy the Kid," English Westerners' *Brand Book* (old series), 4:n.p., December 1957–January 1958; Rasch, "And One Word More," Chicago Westerners' *Brand Book*, XVIII:41–42, August 1961; Rasch, "Old Problems—New Answers," *New Mexico Historical Review*, XL:65–67, January 1965. [All appear in *Trailing Billy the Kid.*] See also W.E. Koop, *Billy the Kid, The Trail of a Kansas Legend* (privately printed, 1965).

[30] Mesilla *Independent*, 30 March 1878.

[31] John Middleton, Unpublished Affidavit, with Frank W. Angel, op. cit.

[32] The story of the life of this individual has been told in P.J. Rasch, "A Note on Henry Newton Brown," Los Angeles Westerners' *Brand Book*, 5:58–67, 1953.

[33] John Middleton, Unpublished Affidavit, with Frank W. Angel, op. cit.

[34] Godfrey Gauss, Unpublished Affidavit, with Frank W. Angel, op. cit.

[35] Daniel M. Appel, Unpublished Affidavit, 1 July 1878, with Frank W. Angel, op. cit.

[36] Mesilla *Independent*, 9 March 1878.

[37] Mesilla *Independent*, 4 May 1878.

[38] See Cases No. 251, 252, 261, Lincoln County. Following the session of court, Widenmann went to England to visit the Tunstall family, so took no part in the following troubles in Lincoln County.

[39] For a detailed account of this, see Philip J. Rasch, "Five Days of Battle," Denver Westerners' *Brand Book*, 11:294–323, 1956. [See Chapter 9.]

[40] Samuel R. Corbet to Dear Sir [John Partridge Tunstall], 24 July 1878.

[41] "Statement of Sue E. Barner Administrix of the Estate of John H. Tunstall deceased, as to the receipts and disposition made of effects of said estate up to date October 30th, 1880." In Probate Files, Lincoln County, New Mexico.

[42] For a discussion of this correspondence from the British point of view, see Frederick W. Nolan, "A Sidelight on the Tunstall Murder," *New Mexico Historical Review*, XXXI:206–222, July 1956. The correspondence between the United States and Great Britain may be found in the General Records of the Department of State, Record Group 59, in the National Archives.

[43] Chas. Devens to Wm. M. Evarts, 10 January 1879.

[44] John Bassett Moore, *A Digest of International Law* (Washington, D.C.: Government Printing Office, 1906), VI:662–66.

6.
Chaos in Lincoln County

Brand Book of the Denver Westerners, 1963

In the years following the Civil War, Lawrence G. Murphy, James J. Dolan, and John H. Riley became the political and economic dictators of Lincoln County, New Mexico.[1] In 1877, their domination was challenged by a combine composed of Alexander A. McSween, John H. Tunstall, and John S. Chisum. On February 18, 1878, Tunstall was murdered by a posse composed of Murphy-Dolan-Riley adherents. Open warfare broke out between the two parties.[2] Having fought a war with Chisum themselves,[3] the small ranchers of the Pecos Valley feared that if he were victorious in this clash, he would become powerful enough to drive them from their homes. Reinforced by a band of cattle rustlers led by Jessie J. Evans, who had their own interest in keeping Chisum from becoming too strong, they rallied around Murphy-Dolan-Riley. In July, 1878, a five-day pitched battle was fought for the control of Lincoln, the county seat. The result was a decisive defeat for the McSween-Chisum force. McSween was killed, his home was burned, and his Regulators were driven from the village.[4]

Flushed with their victory, Sheriff George W. Peppin and a twenty-three-man posse pursued the beaten partisans to the Pecos, but by the middle of August, it became impossible to maintain any sort of a force in being. When the sheriff complained that the Board of County Commissioners refused even to issue warrants to purchase rations for his posse, Chairman Juan B. Patrón and the other officials retorted tartly that the county had no funds, due to the failure of the sheriff to collect the taxes. The warriors from Seven Rivers and the Pecos country dispersed to their homes, and the county was overrun by bands of thieves attracted by the rich opportunties for looting. When the sheriff appealed to Lieutenant Colonel N.A.M. Dudley, Ninth Cavalry, commanding Fort Stanton, for help, he learned that the colonel had been forced to issue orders that "under no circumstances" would his men "aid or in any way assist the sheriff or other parties in making arrests for any purpose." Neither would they "furnished any aid in guarding property for which the Sheriff, Deputy U.S. Marshal, or baliff, may be responsible."[5]

No longer held together by their fear of a mutual enemy, the expossemen were soon fighting each other as enthusiastically as they had fought the Regulators. On the 2nd of August, Jim Reese rode into Tularosa, where he fell into a dispute with the Sanches brothers, who claimed that he was riding one of their horses. In the ensuing quarrel, Reese was shot in the head. George A. ["Roxy"] Rose sent for Dr. Joseph H. Blazer, but the wounded man died before his arrival. Next of the party to fall was William H. Johnson, killed by his father-in-law, Hugh [Henry] M. Beckwith, on August 17. Tradition offers two explanations for the murder: one is that Beckwith, an ardent Confederate, resented the fact Johnson had served in the Federal Army; the other is that Johnson and the younger Beckwiths were trying to make Hugh's life so miserable that he would move out and leave the ranch to them. Seriously wounded himself, Beckwith was arrested by County Sheriff A. McCabe and placed in the hospital at Fort Stanton. Since the county had neither jail nor jailer, there was no recourse but to free him when he had regained his health. Andrew Boyle began breathing mysterious threats that he was going back to Lincoln "to wind things up."[6] Whatever this may have meant, Riley published a letter warning that Boyle was trafficking in stolen cattle and that his concern had no business connections with him.[7]

The vanquished Regulators also went through a period of regrouping. Both Chisum and the Ellis family withdrew their support, while Evans became their ally. In the end, the McSween partisans became almost more dangerous than before. Their threats against Captain Saturnino Baca became so strong that Dudley stationed a corporal and two privates in his home for his protection. Their first concern, however, was to obtain mounts to replace those which they had lost at Lincoln. On the 5th of August, Josiah G.

"Doc" Scurlock, William Bonney, alias The Kid, Charles Bowdre, John Scroggins, Henry Brown, John Middleton, George and Frank Coe, Joe Bowers, "Dirty Steve" Stevens [Stephens], Fernando Herrera, Ignacio Gonzales, Isacio Sanchez, Jim French, and others to the number of about nineteen raided the horse herds on the Mescalero Apache Reservation. Hearing shooting, Chief Clerk Morris J. Bernstein rode to the scene and fired at the rustlers. He was promptly killed and robbed. Contemporary opinion inclined to Martinez as the murderer, but years later, Mrs. McSween named Sanchez as having fired the fatal shot.[8]

Dudley sent Captain Thomas Blair, 15th Infantry, to investigate. He reported he was convinced that the affair was a premeditated attempt "by the band of outlaws known as the McSween party" to murder Indian agent Frederick C. Godfroy and Bernstein, and that the shots were only a ruse to draw them into the open. Blair called attention to the fact that Bernstein had had a severe quarrel with Dr. Blazer, who had beaten on a table with his fist, warned that he could have sixty Mexicans there in ten hours and that no one could call him a liar and live, and demanded (unavailingly) that Godfroy discharge the clerk. "I invite special attention to the Statement of Dr. Blazer," wrote Blair, "to a person wholly disinterested in the affair, they are remarkable."[9] Godfroy himself alleged that the whole incident had been instigated by Mrs. McSween in an attempt to murder him in accordance with the plans of her husband.[10]

A guard under Second Lieutenant George W. Smith, Ninth Cavalry, was stationed at the agency, and Second Lieutenant Millard F. Goodwin, Ninth Cavalry, was sent in pursuit of the murderers, but failed to come up with them. Corporal Thomas S. Baker, 15th Infantry, later reported that a Mr. Stracie, employed by Dr. Blazer, had overheard the Coes say that they had not wanted to kill Bernstein, but the whole party had returned his fire when he had ridden up and shot at a Mexican.[11] George Coe's own version was that the party was en route to Blazer's Mill to learn what disposition had been made of the body of their former leader, Dick Brewer, who had been killed in an earlier fight. Coe, Billy the Kid, and Brown stopped at a spring to get a drink. Some Mexicans in their party rode on ahead and were suddenly attacked by five men, one of whom they killed.[12]

In forwarding Blair's report, Dudley had complained of the failure of his superior, Colonel Edward Hatch, Ninth Cavalry, commanding the District of New Mexico, to provide directives to guide his actions during these trying times. Perhaps stung by the justice of this criticism, Hatch sharply retorted that Dudley's action in leaving troops in Lincoln to protect the lives and property of Baca and other citizens was "entirely illegal and must be stopped immediately."[13] Dudley immediately withdrew the soldiers, and again asked for instructions to guide his actions. As soon as the troops left, French, who made his headquarters with Mrs. McSween, Scurlock, Bowdre, Scroggins, Billy the Kid, Tom O'Folliard, Fred Waite, Middleton, and Brown practically took over the village, openly threatening the lives of Dudley, Goodwin, and others who had assisted the sheriff in making arrests of their friends.

On August 15, Sheriff Peppin executed a long affidavit before Captain Blair, setting forth his inability to execute the duties of his office without help from the military. He did not, he stated, even dare to go to the county seat without the protection of fifteen or twenty men. Dudley forwarded the original to Governor Samuel B. Axtell and a copy to the attorney general of the United States. In his accompanying letter, he estimated that there were not less than 200 outlaws and desperadoes in the county. He commented, "The Sheriff is powerless, and the military has its hands fairly tied."[14] Dudley went on to predict that an Indian war would break out unless some steps were taken to protect the Apaches from the thieves. Probate Judge Florencio Gonzales, County Commissioner Saturnino Baca, who had sought refuge at Fort Stanton, Justice of the Peace George Kimbrell, and County Treasurer Ta Montana [Jose Montaño] presented a petition to the governor setting forth that the probate judge was unable to hold court, the commissioners could not hold their regular sessions, the sheriff lacked the power to execute the laws, the county was bankrupt, and the United States was not furnishing the protection guaranteed the citizens under the terms of the Treaty of Guadalupe Hidalgo. The governor promptly forwarded the two documents to President Rutherford B. Hayes, with a request "for protection for this Territory from domestic violence." In part, he wrote,

> The S.E. portion of the Territory is over run by bands of armed men numbering in all about two hundred, who almost daily commit the

> most atrocious crimes, such as murder, rape, arson and robbery. Some of these bands come from Texas and some from Old Mexico. One band when asked who they were and where they came from; replied, "We are Devils just come from Hell" and when ordered by the Sheriff of the County to disband and return to their houses and ordinary avocations; they replied: "We have no houses; we are at our ordinary avocations"
>
> These men are not only living upon the good people of the Territory but are constantly committing acts of wanton cruelty and violence; many men have been murdered and several women and young girls, mere children have been ravished and large quantities of property stolen and destroyed.[15]

Both Mrs. McSween and Godfrey Gauss, formerly cook at the Tunstall ranch, wrote to John Partridge Tunstall, father of the murdered John H., begging for financial assistance, as the war had left them destitute. Gauss informed him,

> The war is raging now as fiercely as ever, and the country is over-run by horse and cattle thieves, and there is no law in force. The thieves took, last Sunday, the herd of cows, about 200 in number, worth perhaps $2,500, the last of the property belonging to your son's estate which could have been at present turned into ready money.[16]

Instead of two big gangs, each possessing some claim, however tenuous, to acting under legal authority, many small ones now roamed the countryside, most of them bent only on loot and rapine. The whereabouts of some of those intimately concerned in the Murphy-McSween troubles can be documented. The Coes, and some fifteen other men, were camped in the mountains near Tularosa. Juan Patrón headed a gang of about twenty-five Mexicans wandering around the Pecos. Robert Widenmann, formerly manager of the Tunstall store, was at Mesilla, charged with three counts of resisting the sheriff and his deputies. Samuel R. Corbet, a clerk in the store, and Antanacio Martinez were under similar charges, but the former, at least, had stayed in the vicinity of Lincoln, trying to salvage for the estate what little he could recover from the wreck of Tunstall's dream of an empire. A party of about nine under one McDonald, formerly of John Kinney's rustlers, operated between Fort Sumner and Puerto de Luna. About the 1st of September, Billy the Kid and his friends assisted Scurlock and Bowdre to remove their families to Fort Sumner. The whole party, with the exception of Scurlock, who went to work for Pete Maxwell, then started out on a raid through the county. On the afternoon of September 6, Bowers and Sam Smith appeared at the home of Charles Fritz, eight miles east of Lincoln, ordered his two sons off their horses, and drove off the seventeen horses and 180 cattle in the lads' custody. Others of the gang took in the ranch of Alexander Grzelachowski at the Alamogordo and those located in the vicinity of Juan de Dios and Puerto de Luna. Bowdre is said to have sold his interest in the stolen stock to his companions and to have joined Scurlock.[17]

The rustlers drove thirty-five or forty head of horses north to Tascosa, in the panhandle of Texas. Here Waite, Brown, and Middleton decided to leave the territory for good. There is a story that Waite changed his name and became a substantial citizen of Oklahoma. Middleton opened a grocery store in Kansas. After living in one or another of several small towns in the state, he eventually disappeared. Brown became a highly respected marshal in Caldwell, Kansas. In 1884, however, he was involved in an attempt to rob the bank at Medicine Lodge. The robbers were captured and Brown was shot on April 30 when a mob burst into the jail and he attempted to escape.[18] On September 11, 1878, French was indicted for stealing two mules from Jose Maria Aguallo, and apparently left the county shortly afterwards. Whether he was the man killed by Colonel Irwin during the attempted robbery of Reynolds & Company's store at Catoosa, Oklahoma, in 1895 has not been determined.

Bad as things were, they were to get worse before they got better. In September, a marauding band led by John Selman, and alleged to include Thomas Selman, Charles Snow, alias Johnson, Reese Gobly [Gobles], V.S. Whittaker, John Nelson, Robert Speakes, Gus Gildea, James [John W.] Irvin, William Dwyer, John Collins, and others appeared on the scene. After stealing everything of value from the Coe ranchhouse at Tinnie, they burned it to the ground. They wrecked Hoggins' Saloon (the old Murphy brewery) near Lincoln, abused his wife and sister, and severely pistol whipped a man named Sheppard when he remonstrated against their treatment of the women. On the Hondo, they wantonly murdered two boys, Clato and Desiderio Chavez [Chaves], and a crazy boy named

Lorenzo Lucero. Stealing what horses they could find, they proceeded to the Martin Sanchez [Sanches] ranch, where they killed Gregorio, his fourteen-year-old son. A few nights later, they raped the wives of two employees of a man named Bartlett, who operated a small grist mill on the Rio Bonito eleven miles below Fort Stanton.[19]

Dudley sent a report to Colonel Hatch which left no doubt of his feelings:

> I respectfully and earnestly ask in the Name of God and humanity, that I may be allowed to use the forces at my command to drive these murderers, horse-thieves, and escaped convicts out of the Country.[20]

After the rape of the two women, he sent Captain Henry Carroll, Ninth Cavalry, with twenty men to afford protection to the citizens. This brought an immediate reaction from his superiors:

> The Department Commander directs that you be notified that your action in sending out Capt. Carroll with twenty men to afford protection to Citizens, is entirely in violation of orders and opposition to law, and is disapproved.
>
> The party must be at once withdrawn.
>
> Hereafter you will see that the orders given on this subject are explicitly complied with.[21]

Brigadier General John Pope, commanding the Department of the Missouri, must have taken no more pleasure in issuing these orders than Dudley did in receiving them. In his annual report, he concisely and accurately summarized the situation:

> The county of Lincoln, New Mexico, has for twelve months past been in a state of anarchy. Lawlessness and murder have run riot in it, and there has not been, and is not now, any civil or other power in New Mexico able to restore order, except the United States military authorities. I have sent from time to time reports of the commanding officers of Fort Stanton giving a very complete history of a reign of lawlessness and outrage unparalleled in our history. I believe that Governor Axtell, of New Mexico, has done everything in his power to restore order and to enforce the laws, but neither he nor any other civil governor in that Territory is able, in my opinion, to do so with

> any means in his power to command. The United States military authorities are prohibited by law from assisting to keep the peace in any manner whatever, and have been compelled to stand by and see houses, containing women and children, attacked, and many people, and some of them undoubtedly persons innocent of any part or lot in these quarrels, killed or driven to seek refuge on the military reservation of Fort Stanton. The state of things existing in that county is disgraceful to civilization, and demands the exercise of stronger power than is lodged in the civil authorities of New Mexico.
>
> I simply report these facts for the information of the government. Having no power to defend any one—men, women, or children—against these outrages, I deem it at least within my province to inform those who have the power of a condition of affairs for which changes of civil functionaries are no remedy.[22]

The secretary of war appears to have been in full agreement with these remarks. In his own annual report for 1878, he stated that

> The inability of the officer in command of the troops in that vicinity to aid the officers of the law in making arrests was one of the principal causes which led to the most disgraceful scenes of riot and murder, amounting, in fact, to anarchy.[23]

Their protestations were without avail insofar as any change in the law was concerned. Seventy-nine years later, it was still in effect, and it was to be charged that the use of troops to maintain order in Little Rock, Arkansas, during desegregation troubles was a direct violation of the Posse Comitatus Act of 1878 which so effectually hamstrung the Army in Lincoln County.[24] And even before they wrote, Secretary of the Interior Carl Schurz and President Hayes had taken action which they hoped would remedy the situation.

In mid-May, 1878, Frank Warner Angel, acting under an appointment as a special agent of the departments of Justice and of the Interior, had commenced a thorough investigation of conditions in the county.[25] Arriving at his home in New York City on August 24, he settled down to write his final reports, but three days later was ordered to Washington to give a verbal account of his findings. After hearing his account, Schurz recommended that Axtell be immediately removed as governor of the territory and that General

Lew Wallace be appointed in his stead. Hayes promptly concurred.[26] For better or for worse, a change in civil functionaries was to be tried as a means of settling the problems which had proved too much for Axtell.

NOTES

[1] Philip J. Rasch, "The Rise of the House of Murphy." Denver Westerners *Brand Book*, XII:55–84, 1957. [See Chapter 1.]

[2] Philip J. Rasch, "Prelude to the Lincoln County War: The Murder of John Henry Tunstall." Los Angeles Westerners *Brand Book*, 7:78–96, 1957. [See Chapter 5.]

[3] Rasch, "The Pecos War," op. cit.

[4] Rasch, "Five Days of Battle," op. cit. [See Chapter 9.]

[5] M.F. Goodwin to Thomas Blair, July 23, 1878. Records of the War Department. Office of the Adjutant General. 1405 AGO 1878. Consolidated File Relating to the Lincoln County War, New Mexico. In National Archives.

[6] Mesilla *Independent*, August 3, 1878.

[7] Ibid., August 31, 1878.

[8] Otero, *The Real Billy the Kid*, op. cit., p. 118.

[9] Thos. Blair to Post Adjutant, Fort Stanton, August 9, 1878. 1405 AGO 1878.

[10] F.C. Godfroy to E.A. Haugh [Hayt] and Carl Schurz, November 21, 1878. Record Group 75. Records of the Bureau of Indian Affairs. Letters Received: New Mexico, 1879, G-6.

[11] Thomas S. Baker to Post Adjutant, Fort Stanton, 5 September 1878. 1405 AGO 1878.

[12] Coe, *Frontier Fighter*, op. cit., pp. 77–78.

[13] John S. Loud to Commanding Officer, Fort Stanton, August 15, 1878. 1405 AGO 1878.

[14] N.A.M. Dudley to Charles Devens, August 15, 1878. Records of the Department of Justice, Classified File No. 44-4-6-3, Correspondence and newspapers relating to the Lincoln County, New Mexico, trouble (1878–1879). Record Group 60. In National Archives.

[15] S.B. Axtell to His Excellency, The President of the United States, August 20, 1878. 1405 AGO 1878.

[16] G. Gauss to J.P. Tunstall, August 22, 1878.

[17] Garrett, Pat F., *The Authentic Life of Billy, the Kid*. Norman: University of Oklahoma Press, 1954, p. 80–81.

[18] Rasch, "A Note on Henry Newton Brown," op. cit.

[19] Rasch, "Exit Axtell: Enter Wallace." *New Mexico Historical Review*, XXXII:231–245, July, 1957. [See Chapter 15.]

[20] N.A.M. Dudley to Asst. Adjt. General, District of New Mexico, September 29, 1878. 1405 AGO 1878.

[21] Loud to Comdg. Officer, Fort Stanton, October 8, 1878. 1405 AGO 1878.

[22] Report of Brigadier-General John Pope, October 4, 1878. In *Report of the Secretary of War*. Washington: Government Printing Office, 1878, pp. 39–44.

[23] Ibid., p. VI.

[24] David Lawrence, syndicated column, October 5, 1957.

[25] Philip J. Rasch, "The Federal Government Intervenes." *The Denver Westerners Monthly Roundup*, XVI:13–21, September 1960. [See Chapter 10.]

[26] Rasch, "Exit Axtell: Enter Wallace," op. cit.

7.
WAR IN LINCOLN COUNTY

THE ENGLISH WESTERNERS' BRANDBOOK, JULY 1964

In the years following the Civil War, Lincoln County, New Mexico, fell under the political and economic domination of L.G. Murphy & Co. In 1874, one of the partners, Emil Fritz, died in Germany. Eventually, James J. Dolan and John H. Riley were taken into the company and the name changed to Dolan & Co. Fritz had left a $10,000 life insurance policy, with his brother, Charles Fritz, and his sister, Emilie Scholand, as beneficiaries. The insurance company objected to paying the claim and the heirs finally authorised a Lincoln lawyer, Alexander A. McSween, to make collection. McSween employed a firm of St. Louis attorneys to assist him, promising them $2,800 for their services. Eventually, their efforts were successful and they credited McSween with $7,148.94. Legally, he was obligated to turn these funds over to the heirs immediately; instead, he deposited them to his personal account in an East St. Louis, Illinois, bank. He then returned to Lincoln, where he presented the heirs with $100 each and a bill for $4,095.15 for his fees and expenses.

McSween allied himself with John H. Tunstall, an Englishman whose avowed goal was to get half of every dollar made by anyone in the county, and John S. Chisum, a cattle baron who desired the whole southeastern quarter of the territory for his range. The trio opened a store and bank in Lincoln and promptly challenged Dolan & Company's political and economic control of the county. The caustic comment of Lieutenant General Philip H. Sheridan, commanding the Military Division of the Missouri, suggests that in his opinion there was little to choose between the two groups. "One of these parties," he wrote, "is made up of cattle and horse-thieves, and the other party of persons who have retired from that business."[1] Years later, Mrs. McSween told her friends that the bulk of the Fritz insurance money went to build the McSween house and to stock the Tunstall store.

In December, 1877, McSween and Chisum started back to the States. At Las Vegas, the former was arrested on a warrant charging embezzlement, sued out by Mrs. Scholand, and the latter was jailed in connection with a debt owed to U.S. District Attorney Thomas B. Catron, president of the First National Bank of Santa Fe and financial backer of Dolan & Co. McSween appeared before Judge Warren Bristol at Mesilla on 2 and 4 February 1878. He affirmed that he had left behind him in Lincoln sufficient assets to pay all of his debts, and Tunstall testified under oath that they were partners in J.H. Tunstall & Co. A few days later, Fritz and his sister moved to attach McSween's interest in Tunstall's store and ranch. On the 18th of February, a sheriff's posse appeared at the ranch and Tunstall was shot, apparently by William S. Morton, foreman of the Murphy-Dolan cattle camp on the Pecos, and Tom Hill (Chelson), a rustler.[2, 3]

Among Tunstall's cowboys were a number of desperate men. These promptly set out to avenge their employer. McSween was ill-equipped to ride the whirlwind which his actions had helped to raise. He had displayed his complete lack of understanding of the realities of the situation by asking the Santa Fe Presbytery to send a medical missionary to Lincoln, in the fatuous hope "that the enobling and refining influence of the Christian church would raise the standards of all those who came in contact with it."[4] The ingenuous volunteer who answered this call was Dr. Taylor F. Ealy, of Schellsburg, Pennsylvania, a nephew of Congressman Rush Clark. Accompanied by his wife, his two small daughters, and Miss Susan Gates, a teacher, he arrived at Fort Stanton, nine miles from Lincoln, on the day of Tunstall's murder. The officers there warned him of the disturbed conditions existing in the county and urged that he not go on; Ealy, however, replied that inasmuch as he had no connection with either faction, it should be quite safe for them to proceed.

The following morning, his party reached Lincoln and were invited to stay in the house shared by McSween, his brother-in-law,

David P. Shield, and their families. Ealy found his host apprehensive over his own safety, but determined to do everything possible to bring the murderers to justice. The next day, the attorney sued out warrants for the alleged killers from John B. Wilson,[5] justice of the peace in Precinct No. 1. The following morning, they were placed in the hands of Constable Atanacio Martinez for execution. Calling upon William "Billy the Kid" Bonney[6] and Frederick Waite to assist him, Martinez proceeded to the Dolan store, where some of the men named in the warrants had assembled. On its arrival, the posse was charged with disturbing the peace and placed under arrest by Sheriff William Brady. Martinez was freed late that afternoon, but Bonney and Waite remained in custody.

Ealy's first official acts in Lincoln were to embalm Tunstall's body and to conduct funeral services over it. Following the burial on the 22nd, the citizens of Lincoln held a mass meeting. Probate Judge Florencio Gonzales, Isaac Ellis, Jose Montaño, and John Newcomb were delegated to call on Brady to learn why he had interfered with the constable. His answer was brusque: He had arrested the posse because he had the power to do so. Nevertheless, the two men were released that evening.

Tunstall had sent a letter to the newspapers implying that Sheriff Brady had embezzled county funds. Although the territorial treasurer, Antonio Ortiz y Salazar, had publicly refuted the charge,[7] the sheriff had neither forgiven nor forgotten. He made it clear that he held McSween responsible, and the lawyer prudently started construction of a wall twelve feet high around his house.

When it appeared that open warfare was about to break out, Captain George A. Purington, 9th Cavalry, commanding Fort Stanton, sent troops to the Lincoln plaza to preserve order. He suggested to both sides that they retire to the mountains and fight it out there, a suggestion which went unheeded. To Colonel Edward Hatch, 9th Cavalry, commanding the District of New Mexico, the captain wrote:

> I have the honour to report that the usual Lincoln County war has broken out and a terrible state of affairs exist....The sheriff is utterly powerless and to prevent the destruction of property and the loss of life I sent a detachment of troops to Lincoln. Last night the mob fired on the soldiers and wounded a horse....Mr. Riley is at this post

> demanding protection from the military....I am fully satisfied that the lives of Sheriff Brady, Dolan, Riley and others would not be worth a farthing if turned over to the McSween party....8

Hatch promptly warned his subordinate that the military could not interfere in civil affairs except by order of the president of the United States. Brady thereupon wired Catron, requesting him to arrange for U.S. troops to assist in serving legal papers and in enforcing the law. Governor Samuel Beach Axtell immediately forwarded the request to Washington and started for Lincoln himself, pausing only long enough to persuade U.S. Marshal John Sherman, Jr., to revoke the appointment of Robert A. Widenmann, manager of the Tunstall store, as a deputy marshal.

Following the Martinez fiasco, Wilson appointed Richard M. Brewer a special constable and gave him warrants for Tunstall's murderers. Unfortunately, Brewer was anything but a disinterested party. In addition to being manager of the Tunstall ranch, he had formerly worked for Dolan-Riley and was indebted to them in the sum of $2,000. On leaving their employ, they charged, he had leased from them two of the former Horrell ranches[9] and, advised by McSween, had tried to defraud them of the property by entering it under the Desert Land Act.[10]

About a week later, Bonney and three companions rode to the Tunstall ranch, where they found the sheriff's posse had left Thomas Moore in charge. Moore succeeded in convincing them that he had had nothing to do with Tunstall's murder, and the four men returned to the plaza. Brewer then raised a posse which included Bonney, Waite, Josiah G. "Doc" Scurlock, Sam Smith, Jim French, John Middleton, Charles Bowdre, Henry Brown, Frank McNab [MacNab], and William McCloskey. Styling themselves "The Regulators," they set out for Seven Rivers. At the ranch of "Cap" Amazon Howell, near that point, they captured William Morton and Frank Baker (two members of the posse that had killed Tunstall) after a chase of more than six miles. Thomas Cochrane, a third member of that posse, hid out in a corn crib and was not discovered.[11]

Brewer's party started for Lincoln with their prisoners, stopping at Roswell on 9 March so that Morton could mail the following letter to H.H. Marshall, of Richmond, Virginia:

Some time since I was called upon to assist in serving a writ of attachment on some property, wherein resistance had been made against the law. The parties had started off with some horses which should be attached, and I, as Deputy Sheriff with a *posse* of twelve men was sent in pursuit of same, overtook them, and while attempting to serve the writ our party was fired on by one J.H. Tunstall, the balance of his party having ran off. The fire was returned and Tunstall was killed. This happened on the 18th of February. The 6th March I was arrested by a constables party, accused of the murder of Tunstall. Nearly all of the Sheriff's *posse* fired at him and it is impossible for any one to say who killed him. When the *posse* which came to arrest me and one man who was with me, first saw us about one hundred yards distant, we started in another direction when they (eleven in number) fired nearly one hundred shots at us. We ran about five miles when both of our horses fell and we made a stand, when they came up they told us if we gave up they would not harm us; after talking a while we gave up our arms and were taken prisoners. There was one man in the party who wanted to kill me after I had surrendered, and was restrained with the greatest difficulty by others of the party. The constable himself said he was sorry we gave up as he had not wished to take us alive. We arrived here last night en-route to Lincoln. I have heard that we were not to be taken alive to that place, I am not at all afraid of their killing me, but if they should do so I wish that the matter be investigated and the parties dealt with according to law if you do not hear from me in four days after receipt of this, I would like you to make inquiries about the affair.

The names of the parties who have me arrested are, R.M. Bruer [Brewer], J.C. Skurlock, Chas. Bowdre, Wm. Bonney (Goodrich!) Henry Brown, Frank McNab [MacNab], "Wayt" [Waite] Sam Smith, Jim French Middleton (and another named McCloskey and who is a friend.) There are two parties in arms and violence expected, the military are at the scene of disorder and trying to keep peace. I will arrive at Lincoln the night of the 10th and will write you immediately if I get through safe. Have been in the employ of Jas. J. Dolan & Co. of Lincoln for 18 months, since 9th of March 1877 and have been getting $60 per month, have about six hundred dollars due me from them, and some horses &c. at their cattle camps.

I hope, if it becomes necessary, that you will look into this affair, if anything should happen I refer you to T.B. Catron U.S. Attorney Santa Fe N.M. and Col. Rynerson District Attorney La Mesilla N.M. they both know all about the affairs as the writ of attachment was issued by Judge Warren Bristol La Mesilla N.M. and everything was legal. If I am taken safely to Lincoln I will have no trouble but let you know.

If it should be as I suspect. Please communicate with my brother Quin Morton Lewisburg W.V. Hoping that you will attend to this affair if it becomes necessary and excuse me for troubling you if it does not.[12]

The next evening, McNab returned to Roswell, explaining to Postmaster Ash Upson:

When we had ridden some 20 miles, and had reached a point some 5 or 6 miles from Black Water, Morton was riding side by side with one of the *posse*, McCloskey, when he suddenly snatched McClosky's [sic] pistol from the scabbard and shot him dead.

Although mounted upon a poor slow horse, he put him to his best speed, closely followed by Frank Baker, they were speedily overtaken and killed.[13]

When the bodies were found, it was observed that both Morton and Baker had been shot in the breast eleven times. Since there were eleven men in the posse, this suggests that he too had been executed rather than shot in an attempt to escape.

Morton is said to have come from a good Virginia family, although it was alleged that he had killed four men, but Upson's remarks regarding Baker are illuminating:

This fellow, Frank Baker, has shot innocent men when they were on their knees, pleading for life. With a brutal laugh has held a pistol to their heads, and after blowing their brains out, kicking the inanimate body and face to a jelly. His countenance was the strongest argument that could be produced in favour of the Darwinian theory. Brutish in feature and expression, he looked a veritable gorrilla. He boasts that his father killed 18 men before he was hung in Texas, and that his three brothers had killed a deputy sheriff in Texas. That he was twenty-two years of age, the last of the family and had killed 13 men and wanted twenty before he was 25 years old.

I have often heard of the family. Their names are Hart, not Baker. They had no friends and no companions even among the vilest outlaws, except companions compelled by fear. They were a fearful curse to whatever section they went....[14]

It would be interesting to know whether his father was the Hart who had participated in the atrocious murder of Deputy Sheriff Joseph Haskins in Lincoln County during the Horrell War,[15] but this has not been established.

Oddly enough, the other man suspected of the murder of Tunstall was killed almost simultaneously. On 9 March 1878, Tom Hill and Jessie J. Evans attempted to rob the wagon of John Wagner, a sheep drover camped at Alamo Spring, near present-day Alamogordo. When the driver, a half-breed Cherokee, objected, they fired at him, wounding him in the leg. As the thieves were rummaging the wagon, the herder crawled back and shot Hill. Evans was wounded in the wrist, and was later forced to surrender at Fort Stanton to secure medical attention.

Meanwhile, events were taking a turn decidedly unfavourable to the McSween partisans. On Axtell's arrival at Fort Stanton, he learned that the secretary of war had instructed the Army to support the civil authorities in maintaining order and in enforcing legal process, in spite of General Sheridan's grumpy complaints about the expense involved. There was, however, doubt in Purington's mind as to who were the rightful officials, and he was uncertain whether he should aid Deputy United States Marshal Widenmann or Sheriff Brady. Hatch settled the question by directing the captain to render assistance to the sheriff,[16] thereby doing much to determine the eventual outcome of the Lincoln County War.

After consulting with Dolan, Riley, and Brady, Axtell called on McSween, Widenmann, and Ealy, informing them that he was issuing the following "Proclamation to the Citizens of Lincoln County":

> The disturbed condition of affairs at the County Seat brings me to Lincoln County at this time. My only object is to assist good citizens to uphold the laws and keep the Peace. To enable all to act intelligently it is important that the following facts should be clearly understood.
>
> 1st. John B. Wilson's appointment by the County Commissioners as a Justice of the Peace was illegal and void, and all processes issued by him were void, and said Wilson has no authority whatever to act as Justice of the Peace.
>
> 2nd. The appointment of Robt. Widenmann as U.S. Marshall [sic] has been revoked, and said Widenmann is not now a peace officer,

> nor has he any power or authority whatever to act as such.
>
> 3rd. The President of the United States upon an application made by me as Governor of New Mexico has directed the Post Commander Col. Geo. A. Purington to assist Territorial Civil officers in maintaining order and enforcing legal processes. It follows from the above statement of facts that there is no legal process in this case to be enforced, except the writs and processes issued out of the Third Judicial District Court by Judge Bristol, and there are no Territorial Civil officers here to enforce these, except Sheriff Brady and his deputies.
>
> Now therefore in consideration of the premises I do hereby command all persons to immediately disarm and return to their homes and usual occupations, under penalty of being arrested and confined in Jail as disturbers of the Public Peace.

When his listeners requested that he first call a mass meeting of the citizens to ascertain the facts, the governor exclaimed, "God deliver me from such citizens as you have in Lincoln," to which Widenmann tartly retorted, "The citizens are right, but God deliver me from such executive officers."[17]

Axtell spent something less than three hours in Lincoln. His justification for the removal of Wilson was that the latter had been appointed by the county commissioners upon the resignation of James H. Farmer, whereas the law called for justices of the peace to be elected. There is something unsatisfactory about this. The governor himself had signed the Commissioners Act of 1876, which provided that in the case of any vacancy being created in an office in a county or a subdivision thereof, the county commissioners should have the power to fill such vacancy by appointment until an election could be called. If he now challenged the provisions of that act, it is evident that this should have been settled by a decision of the courts, not by executive action, but one will search in vain for any protest by Judge Warren Bristol over this usurpation of his authority. Neither is it at all clear on what grounds Axtell held that warrants which might be issued by other justices of the peace in Lincoln County were also void.

One thing was all too plain to McSween's henchmen: if Wilson had no authority to appoint Brewer a constable, the actions of his posse were without legal sanction, and in effect its members were outlawed as murderers. The Regulators promptly fled to the mountains, the immemorial refuge of outlaws in Lincoln County.

Ealy was also to learn that not all elements of the community looked upon his coming as an unmixed blessing. Stopping him on the street one day, Jack Long bluntly informed him that he had helped to hang a preacher in Arizona, and would as soon see a whore come to Lincoln as Ealy. However, Long graciously added, he would not help to hang the missionary—at least not as long as the latter treated him properly.[18]

On 28 and 30 March, the Regulators sortied from their mountain retreat, entered the village, were met with gunfire, and withdrew. McSween was not present on either occasion. Fearing for his life, he had hidden out near the Bottomless Lakes, while his wife had gone to stay with the Chisums. Brady was eager to arrest him, but was unable to raise a posse among the townsfolk. On 29 March, Second Lieutenant George W. Smith, 9th Cavalry, informed Mrs. McSween that if her husband would come to Fort Stanton, he would be guaranteed protection. McSween accepted this offer and set out for the fort, arriving at Lincoln on 1 April. He found the plaza in a fever of excitement.

During the night of 31 March, Bonney, Brown, Waite, McNab, Widenmann,[19] Middleton, French, and perhaps others had stolen into the town and hidden behind the walls of a corral which extended east from the rear of the Tunstall store. About 9 o'clock the next morning, Brady and his deputies, Jacob B. Mathews, George Hindman, George W. Peppin, and Jack Long, started down the street to the courthouse. Through a clerk's error, notice had been given that court would open the first Monday in April; Brady's mission was to inform the citizens that it would actually convene on the second Monday. The group stopped for a moment to speak with three members of the grand jury, Timeoto Analla [Timoteo Anaya], Ignacio Torres, and Navor Chaves, and then strolled on.

A volley rang out as the sheriff and Hindman passed the corral. Brady was killed instantaneously, sixteen shots afterwards being found in his body. Hindman was mortally wounded by a single bullet, traditionally said to have been fired by McNab. Across the street, Justice Wilson, hoeing in his garden, was painfully injured by a wild shot that passed through the back of both thighs. Long, Peppin, and Mathews dashed into Lupe Cisneros' [Lola Sisneros'] house. Peering out of a window, they saw Bonney run out and seize

Brady's new Winchester. Mathews fired just as he straightened up again, the bullet passing through the inside of his left thigh.

The murderers retired to the McSween home, where the Kid's wound was treated by Ealy, but where McSween furiously upbraided them. As the crestfallen gunmen rode off to Brewer's camp on the Peñasco, Sam Corbet sawed a hole in the floor under his bed in the rear storage room which was part of the main Tunstall building. There he hid the Kid, and Brady's friends, following the trail of blood down the street, searched in vain for his hiding place.

These cold-blooded murders were one of the turning points of the Lincoln County War. Whatever McSween's regrets, they constituted a major strategical blunder. In eliminating two of their enemies, the Regulators irreparably damaged their cause in the eyes of the community. This cowardly ambush of public officials on the main street of the county seat while in pursuit of their official business alienated public opinion and gave the McSween cause a blow from which it never recovered. Even the welcome appearance of John Chisum, who had finally negotiated his release from the Las Vegas jail, could not alter the situation, nor did it add anything to their fighting strength.

At Deputy Sheriff Peppin's request, Purington immediately led his troops to the plaza. McSween, Widenmann, Shield, and two of McSween's coloured servants, George Washington and George Robinson, were arrested. At their own request, they were taken to Fort Stanton for safe-keeping. Purington and Lieutenant Smith had a sharp verbal clash with Montague R. Leverson, a pompous Englishman who was staying with Juan B. Patrón, chairman of the county commissioners, while in search of a locality in which to establish an English colony. The officers finally damned Leverson as an ass and bluntly told him to shut up. Deeply wounded in his self-esteem, Leverson began a barrage of letters to President Rutherford B. Hayes, Secretary of the Interior Carl Schurz, and other federal officials, demanding an investigation of the state of affairs in New Mexico and eventually proposing himself for governor of the territory.

On 5 April, Lieutenant Colonel Nathan Augustus Monroe Dudley, 9th Cavalry, relieved Captain Purington as commanding officer of the post. He ordered the prisoners released, as he could find no authority for their detention. Widenmann thereupon promptly placed Evans under arrest. The erstwhile captives demanded that they be allowed to stay on the post for protection from the Dolan-Riley forces. This request was granted and they remained there at liberty until Judge Warren Bristol arrived on 8 April and ordered McSween arrested for embezzlement and the others held on a charge of alleged murder.

The Regulators had assembled at the home of George Coe, who had his own troubles with Brady.[20] Reinforced by his cousin, Frank Coe, they set out to seize George Kitt and Bill Williams, known in Lincoln County as Andrew L. "Buckshot" Roberts, two members of the posse who had killed Tunstall. About 11 a.m. on the 4th of April, fourteen Regulators rode up to the home of the U.S. Indian Agent, Frederick C. Godfroy, at South Fork, on the Mescalero Apache Reservation, and asked for lunch. While they were eating, Roberts himself rode up. Dismounting, he asked Frank Coe to step to one side to talk, and the two men seated themselves on a porch. Brewer entered the building, while Bonney lounged in front of it, engaged in casual conversation with David M. Easton, manager of a store owned by Dr. Joseph H. Blazer and justice of the peace in Precinct No. 3. Bowdre, Middleton, Brown, McNab, and George Coe quietly slipped around the corner and suddenly demanded Roberts' surrender.

"Not much, Mary Ann," snapped the Texan, drawing his revolver. His first shot glanced off Bowdre's cartridge belt, his second took off George Coe's trigger finger, his third tore through Middleton's chest, inflicting a serious wound. As he stepped back into Blazer's room, Bowdre shot him in the right side, just above the hip joint, the bullet ranging upward through the abdomen and inflicting a mortal wound. Once in the room, Roberts found Blazer's Springfield and a cartridge belt hanging on a wall. Dragging a mattress off a couch, he placed it before the open door and lay down behind it.

Brewer demanded that Easton put Roberts out of the house, which the justice refused to do. Ignoring Mrs. Godfroy's pleadings, Brewer swore that he would have Roberts if he had to pull the house down. He then proceeded to Blazer's saw mill, about 125 yards from the house. He was heard to fire a shot; a minute or two later, there was a reply from the house. Then all was still. Blazer finally investigated and found Brewer's body, the top of its head blown off. Easton informed the Regulators of their leader's death and they agreed to leave. John Ryan, a clerk in the Dolan store at the agency, then called to Roberts that his enemies had left and offered his help. Assistant Surgeon Daniel M. Appel was summoned from Fort Stanton, but Roberts lapsed into unconsciousness and died the next day.[21] On his way to Blazer's Mill, Appel encountered the McSween gang and gave George Coe's hand first aid treatment. Ealy later amputated the thumb and a finger. In due course, a coroner's inquest found that the deceased came to his death from gunshot wounds at the hands of Brewer, Bowdre, Scurlock, Waite, Middleton, McNab, John Scroggins, Stephen Stevens [Steve Stephens], the Coes, and Antrim, although Easton testified that Jim French and Ignacio Gonzales were also present.

On 9 April, the county commissioners appointed John N. Copeland, a man friendly to the McSween faction, to the shievalty. His term of office was destined to be a short one.

The April session of district court in Lincoln presented a curiously martial appearance. Copeland went about guarded and assisted by a squad of soldiers. Bristol stayed at Fort Stanton, riding to Lincoln and back daily under the protection of a military escort. His sympathies must be presumed to have been with the Murphy-Dolan-Riley party. In 1875, the citizens of Grant County had petitioned for Bristol's removal from office and Murphy had circulated a counterpetition for his retention. There is no reason to believe the jurist unappreciative. In a long charge to the grand jury, he reviewed the causes of the Lincoln County troubles, laid the blame squarely on the shoulders of McSween, denied that the courts were controlled by the Santa Fe Ring, and urged the citizens to do their duty without fear or favour.[22]

The jurors got fairly to work on 15 April. In two reports submitted by Foreman Blazer, they complained of the difficulty of securing witnesses, the presentation of prejudiced testimony, expressed their thanks to the officers at Fort Stanton for their help, condemned the actions of Governor Axtell, and reported that the charge of embezzlement made against McSween was unjust and proposed in a spirit of persecution.[23] Over twenty indictments were found, including ones against Jessie Evans, Frank Rivers, George Davis, and James J. Dolan for the murder of Tunstall.[24] For reasons which are not altogether clear, the jury refused to return indictments against the alleged murderers of Roberts, but at the June term of the United States district court held in Mesilla, the grand jury voted indictments against Henry Brown, Bonney, Middleton, Scroggins, Waite, and George Coe on this charge.[25]

Finding a friendly jury in the box, McSween pressed his campaign to have Godfroy replaced by a man from the Regulators by persuading a former Dolan-Riley teamster, Stephen Stanley, to testify that his employers and Godfroy were systematically defrauding the government on its Mescalero Apache Indian contracts. His story was supported by Farmer; immediately after testifying, both men disappeared. The majority report of the grand jury commented that the Indians were marauding and stealing because they were being regularly robbed of their supplies—a finding which appears to have been completely inaccurate—but noted that federal offences were not indictable in the district court.

Dudley gloomily reported Bristol's chagrin and mortification at the "*total failure* of the District Court to accomplish *anything* which would in any possible way lead to restore harmony and peace in the County...."[26] Foreseeing the on-coming storm, Shield departed for Las Vegas to seek a safer residence for his family.

After court adjourned on 24 April, the citizens held a mass meeting. Probate Judge Florencio Gonzales was elected president, Saturnino Baca and County Treasurer Jose Montaño vice-presidents, McSween and Benjamin H. Ellis secretaries. Speeches were made by Patrón, Montaño, and others. Resolutions presented by a committee composed of Patrón, Chisum, and Avery M. Clenny were unanimously adopted. Included among them were statements that it was the sense of the meeting that the old feuds would cease, a vote of thanks to Dudley for non-partisan conduct, a vote of censure to Axtell for his partisan actions, and a vote of thanks to Copeland for accepting the office of sheriff and for his impartial and efficient discharge of duty. A copy of these proceedings was sent to President Hayes.[27] Murphy, however, had not waited for the adoption of these pious expressions. On 22 April, he had sought sanctuary at Fort Stanton until such time as he could safely go to Santa Fe. He was wise; affairs had passed beyond the point where they could be settled by the adoption of resolutions.

Frank McNab, who had succeeded Brewer as leader of McSween's fighting men, had made yet another of the fatal blunders which culminated in the downfall of his party. Exultant over the murders which seemed to be restoring the Regulators to dominance, he had sent word to Seven Rivers that they would soon clean up the cattle thieves in that area. Dolan wrote to the newspapers that McSween and Chisum had surrounded themselves with armed men and sought to crush Murphy-Dolan-Riley so that they might control the county, and that Isaac Ellis had joined them because he saw a chance to rid himself of a business competitor.[28] Peppin hastened to Seven Rivers to warn the settlers that this was Chisum's fight and that they would lose their ranges and cattle if he won it. With events of the Pecos War[29] still fresh in their memories and with McNab's threat cast into their very teeth, these formidable warriors were not slow to react. Even as the citizens in Lincoln were holding their futile meeting, the cowboys on the Pecos were assembling to ride to the county seat to offer their assistance to the sheriff in arresting the Regulators. The posse was led by William H. Johnson, who had been a deputy under Brady and who seems to have been unaware of the fact that the sheriff's death had terminated his appointment. Under his command rode Peppin, Mathews, Long, Robert W. Beckwith, Milo L. Pierce, William [Thomas B.] "Buck" Powell, Samuel R. Perry, Thomas Gaffney, J.G. [Follett G.] Christie, James J. Longwell, Lewis [Louis] Paxton, John C.H. Galvin, John M. Beckwith, Robert Olinger, Richard Lloyd, Joseph H. Nash, H.D. Leets, John Hurley, Frank Catlin, Charles Guastin, Thomas Cochrane, J.W. Gauce, Wallace Olinger, Tom Green, J. Colvin, "Dutch Charlie" Kruling, J. Packerson [Jim Patterson], Ruben Kelly, and Charles Martin.

On the evening of the 29th, McNab, Frank Coe, and James A. Saunders, Coe's brother-in-law, rode up to Charles Fritz's Spring Ranch. As they dismounted to drink at the spring, the Seven Rivers men fired from ambush. McNab was killed, Saunders seriously wounded, and Coe captured. Assistant Surgeon Appel accompanied an ambulance to the ranch and removed Saunders to the McSween home. McNab is believed to have been implicated in the murder of the Casner brothers in the Panhandle of Texas in 1877. Dudley reported to Hatch:

> His reputation was as bad as it could be; he was looked upon as an outlaw and a murderer. While we may regret the means by which he came to his death, we cannot complain of the riddance.[30]

Resuming their journey to Lincoln, the posse met James Chisum, John's brother, and chased him for 12 miles before giving up the pursuit.

When Johnson's force reached the placita the following day, it was greeted by fire from McSween riflemen concealed in the buildings and on the roofs. The Seven Rivers men split into two squads, one of which was posted along a line of trees bordering the Rio Bonito and the other of which took up positions on the bluffs on the opposite bank. Wallace Olinger was left in charge of Coe, but becoming anxious to get into the fighting, he tossed the prisoner a gun and told him to look out for himself. Firing became general, but the only casualty seems to have been Kruling, who had his leg broken by a magnificent shot by George Coe at a range of over a quarter of a mile.

McSween wrote out a warrant for the arrest of eighteen of the Seven Rivers men and had it signed by Gorgonio [Gregorio] Trujillo, justice of the peace in Precinct No. 2. Copeland then sent to the fort for assistance in serving it. Troops under the command of Lieutenant Smith arrived on the scene about 3:30 p.m. Johnson's men refused to give up their arms to Copeland, explaining that they feared they would be murdered if they did so, but offered to surrender to Smith and to accompany him to Fort Stanton. At the sheriff's request, the officer arrested twenty-two men, including Dolan and Edgar A. Walz, Catron's brother-in-law and personal representative.

On arriving at Fort Stanton, Peppin, Long, and Mathews swore out affidavits accusing members of the Regulators of assault and attempt to murder. Dudley sent the affidavits to Justice Easton, who issued the necessary warrants. These too were placed in the hands of Copeland. Assisted by a squad of soldiers under Second Lieutenant Millard F. Goodwin, 9th Cavalry, he promptly arrested Widenmann, Isaac Ellis, William R. Ellis, Gonzales, Corbet, Scroggins, Washington, and Scurlock. The Seven Rivers men meanwhile petitioned Dudley for a hearing before Justice Easton, alleging that Justice Trujillo was under the influence of McSween and Chisum, and that they were being held for no other reason than to give Chisum time to seize their property. Within thirty-six hours, all of the prisoners were released, since under the law they could not be held longer without a hearing. Copeland thereupon antagonised Dudley by giving him a worthless cheque in payment for the rations furnished his prisoners.

At Dolan's request, Kruling had been brought to the post hospital. Similar treatment was accorded Saunders, but Dudley irritated the McSween party by refusing to permit Frank Coe to stay on the post to nurse him. He reported to Hatch:

> I shall continue to adhere most sacredly to my first resolve, namely, in no way to become myself a partisan to either side, or permit the few troops under my command to be used to improperly carry out the edicts of the chiefs representing either faction....
>
> I think I am safe in making the statement that I fully believe from the official conduct of the newly appointed Sheriff in his relations with myself, he would not hesitate to call upon me for a posse to disarm the Dolan and Riley party if it were not for the fact he knows I would not consent to any such proposal, for it would be making myself and command a sole cause of murdering them all.[31]

Ealy wrote to his uncle, Representative Rush Clark, that nineteen men had been killed or wounded in the different battles, and urged him to beg the president to declare martial law. Rush forwarded the letter to the secretary of war, with the comment that, "there seems to be ample evidence of a reign of terror demanding some action on the part of the Government...."[32] It has not been possible to identify all of the men to whom Ealy referred. At some stage of the fighting, a man named Meeten had been killed and French had been wounded. Another was added to the list on 24 May, when Dan Huff was unpleasantly surprised to find a dead man—so far unidentified—buried in his yard.

Other letters poured in upon the government, one of the more influential being from the highly respected Brooke Herford, pastor of the Church of the Messiah, in Chicago, whose son was in Lincoln attending to Tunstall's estate.

Bankrupt by the disorders, the Dolan-Riley concern was dissolved by mutual consent on 1 May. Catron then foreclosed the mortgage which he held on its buildings and its stock, placing Walz in charge of the store.

Meanwhile, the county officials were in a heated disagreement.

Copeland alleged that he held no warrants for the arrest of the murderers of Brady and Roberts; District Attorney William L. Rynerson protested that he had placed the warrants in the hands of the sheriff and was surprised at his failure to execute them. Dudley commented:

> Some body has jumped the truth here. If Officers of high standing cannot be relied on, the District Commander can readily see how difficult it is for the officer in command here to arrive at facts.[33]

On 19 May, Scurlock, posing as a deputy sheriff, Bonney, Bowdre, Brown, Scroggins, one of the Coe boys, and a number of others, drove off Catron's horse herd at Seven Rivers, apparently in an attempt to make it impossible for him to round up and brand his calves. A herder named Wair, referred to by Dudley as "a bad man,"[34] was killed and some 1,500 head of Catron's cattle were thrown into Chisum's herd. As a result, Riley, who had the government beef contracts, was unable to drive the animals required to supply Fort Stanton and the Mescalero Apache Agency.

Again, the Regulators had blundered. Dudley's view was that since Riley had Johnson's company available, he should recover his cattle by force. With his personal interests violated, Catron requested Axtell to take steps to protect lives and property in Lincoln County. The governor's first action was to remove Copeland from office, the following proclamation being issued on 1 June:

> For the information of all the citizens of Lincoln County I do hereby make this Public Proclamation:
>
> First—John N. Copeland, Esq., appointed Sheriff by the County Commissioners, having failed for more than thirty days to file his bond as Collector of Taxes, is hereby removed from the office of Sheriff, and I have appointed GEORGE W. PEPPIN, Esq. Sheriff of Lincoln County. This has been done in compliance with the laws, passed at the twenty second session of the Legislative Assembly, relating to Sheriffs.
>
> Second—I command all men and bodies of men, now under arms and traveling about the country, to disarm and return to their homes and their usual pursuits, and so long as the present Sheriff has authority to call upon U.S. troops for assistance, not to act as a sheriff's posse.
>
> And, in conclusion, I urge upon all good citizens to submit to the

> law, remembering that violence begets violence, and that they who take the sword shall perish by the sword.

In issuing this proclamation, Axtell conveniently ignored the fact that the amount of the bond to be filed by the sheriff had to be set by the county commissioners after they had ascertained the amount of taxes to be collected. Owing to the unsettled state of affairs, the commissioners had been unable to calculate this figure and consequently Copeland had been powerless to take the required action.

That the Regulators were completely undaunted by the governor's action is evident in a defiant letter which John Middleton wrote to Buck Powell two days later:

> Dear Friend Buck, Dear Sir: I want to ask you a few questions, will you please answer them.
>
> Where do you live at?
>
> Are you a citizen of Lincoln co.
>
> Did you ever live in Lincoln co.
>
> Do you and your posse think we are a set of damned fools, that we would recognise you as a deputy sheriff, if you do you are badly fooled.
>
> Look at the Governor's proclamation and see what he says, dont he [sic] all citizens to go home and lay down his arms, and not allow themselves to be summoned as a sheriff's posse. Look at Peppin the first thing he did was to go into the Plaza with a band of masked men and a posse do you call this wrong or right, if right where is the wrong?
>
> Buck if you had staid on your own range and took no hand in this thing you would never Been Molested...the same with many others, do you think that a half a dozen of us would run from the posse you have—we would like to see them too well. Come and you can find us. I want to life [sic] the Belt John B. [Beckwith] has on. We have run them too often to try and get out of the way. Please answer this and tell me all the news, and what you think of these lines.[35]

At the governor's request, Colonel Hatch instructed Dudley to assist the territorial civil officers in maintaining order and in enforcing legal process; directed him to send Purington and his company to Roswell for the purpose of disarming and disbanding the gangs in that neighbourhood; and transferred Captain Henry Carroll, 9th Cavalry, and his company from Fort Union to Fort Stanton to beef up Dudley's command. However, somewhat uncertain of the legality of his actions, he immediately forwarded copies of these instructions to General John Pope, commanding the Department of the Missouri, requesting that he be advised by telegraph in case Pope felt he had exceeded his authority. Pope considered Hatch's actions virtually constituted an unauthorised establishment of martial law, and ordered his subordinate to suspend all operations under these instructions until directions could be obtained from the War Department. Secretary of War George W. McCrary in turn asked his judge advocate general, W.M. Dunn, for an opinion as to the legality of Hatch's course. The JAG's reply was uncompromising:

> I can but arrive therefore at the conclusion that the furnishing of troops to aid the territorial sheriff to serve warrants, guard prisoners, &c, in this case, was without authority of law, as was also the furnishing of the same, for any purpose, at the demand of the District Judge.[36]

Troops, ruled Dunn, could legally be used only to assist a U.S. marshal or his deputy.

Axtell had appointed Peppin, against whom McSween had obtained three warrants for murder, on the recommendation of District Attorney William L. Rynerson, a member of the Santa Fe Ring. Dunn's decision presented no serious problem for the Ring; it simply arranged for Marshal Sherman to appoint Peppin an acting deputy U.S. marshal and to furnish him with warrants for the arrest of Bowdre, Middleton, Brown, the Coes, Stevens [Stephens], Bonney, Scurlock, Scroggins, and Waite. There is a Lincoln tradition that Rynerson promised Dolan that he would send men to help him. That he kept this promise is suggested by information which Texas Ranger J.A. Tays passed on to his superiors: "The mob of desperadoes that was round El Paso Texas have all left for Lincoln County."[37]

The "mob of desperadoes" to which he referred was a gang of rustlers led by John Kinney. They preyed principally on Chisum's herds and had their own reasons for not desiring to see him control the county.

They headed north at a time when McSween's own force was seriously reduced in fighting strength, as many of his partisans had been summoned to attend district court at Mesilla. At their request,

Dudley had furnished an escort to protect Patrón, Widenmann, Copeland, Washington, Robinson, Martinez, Gauss, and Jose Chaves y Chaves while en route to that city. With them went Evans. Judge Bristol set Evans' bail at $5,000 on the charge of murdering Tunstall and at $1,000 on a charge of rustling and stealing from Widenmann and Brewer. Sheriff Barela appointed E.H. Wakefield a special deputy to deliver Evans to Sheriff Peppin. Lacking a jail, Peppin was forced to turn him loose.

Blustering Bob Widenmann, Tunstall's closest friend, never returned to Lincoln. Perhaps this distressed McSween not at all, since his distrust of the man is evident in a letter which he wrote to Tunstall's father:

> I have given you in a former letter, my views of the propriety of letting Widenmann wind up the estate; there are many reasons why I cannot approve it....No one here would act jointly with Mr. Widenmann. I would rather not say this much, but I must give you an honest opinion. Aside from his incompetency, I think it inadvisable to entrust a young man who has not one dollar with the management of your means. We know not from whence he came nor whither he will go. I advise you to revoke the power of attorney sent by you and make to Mr. Hereford....[38]

It is not likely that his defection made the slightest difference in the final outcome. The Regulators proposed to "whoop 'em up liverly," observed the Mesilla *News*, but might find "The tables may sometime be turned."[39] The editor may have known whereof he spoke.

A few nights after Patrón returned to his home, Jim Reese forced his way into his room with the evident intention of killing him. However, he left when he found a Mr. Cronin with him. The following day, Patrón took refuge at Fort Stanton.

The sheriff now struck hard at the Regulators. On 18 June, Peppin appeared at Fort Stanton with the warrants he had obtained from Marshal Sherman and demanded a detachment to assist him in serving them. Dudley ordered out 27 men under the command of Second Lieutenant Millard F. Goodwin, 9th Cavalry. On the way to Lincoln, his force was joined by Kinney and eleven of his men, whereupon Goodwin refused to permit his troops to enter the plaza. However, he surrounded the village while the sheriff searched it.

None of the individuals for whom he had warrants were found.

On the night of the 27th, Deputy Sheriff Long and 25 men invested the village of San Patricio, where the Regulators had established their headquarters. After Kinney captured Washington, Long and six men proceeded up the river to Newcomb's ranch. Failing to find any of the Regulators there, they headed back to San Patricio. Two miles out of the placita, they encountered McSween, Copeland, Waite, Bowdre, Bonney, French, Scroggins, Stevens [Stephens], Jesus Rodriguez, Martinez, and Eusebio Sanchez. Shots were exchanged and Copeland killed the horses ridden by Long and George A. ["Roxy"] Rose. Kinney's men hastened to their fellows' aid and the McSween party withdrew into the mountains.

Twenty-seven women living in or near the village signed a petition imploring Dudley to send soldiers to protect their lives and those of their children. The widowed Mrs. Brady complained that Scurlock had threatened to kill her oldest son, John. Sheriff Peppin again requested the aid of troops. The colonel despatched Captain Carroll and 35 men to the scene, with Juan Patrón to act as interpreter. The troops pursued the Regulators to Coe's ranch and thence to Agua Azul, but there couriers hastily despatched by Dudley caught up with them with orders for their immediate return to the fort. Word had just been received from the adjutant general of the Army that Congress had inserted a clause in the Army Appropriation Bill which forbade the use of the Army as a *posse comitatus* to assist civil authorities except in such cases and under such circumstances as might be especially authorised by the Constitution or by Act of Congress. No money appropriated by Congress was to be expended to meet the expenses of troops used as such posses, and a fine of $10,000 or two years imprisonment, or both, was provided for violations of the act. The effect of this clause, General Pope later commented, was to force the troops

> to stand by and see houses containing women and children attacked, and many people, and some of them undoubtedly persons innocent of any part or lot in these quarrels killed or driven to seek refuge on the military reservation of Fort Stanton.[40]

Even such a rugged individual as ex-Sheriff Ham Mills, who had led the fight against the Horrells, fled to Texas to save his life.

About 1 July, Copeland was captured by a posse led by Long. On the morning of 3 July, a posse under Deputy Sheriff Jose Chaves y Baca attempted to arrest the McSween partisans. One of his men, Julian López, was badly wounded, but the Regulators again executed a successful withdrawal. Reinforcements sent by Peppin overtook them in the mountains about four miles from San Patricio, and the opposing parties clashed in an hour-long fight. Two of the posse's horses were killed and two of those belonging to the Regulators, including McSween's own mount, were captured. Peppin once more requested aid from the Army, but Dudley pointed out that he was prohibited from furnishing it.

Under Dolan's direction, John Hurley, Chaves y Baca, Juan José Porado, Panteleon [Pantaleon] Gallegos, George Davis, Kinney, and others forcibly searched San Patricio, breaking down doors and insulting the inhabitants, all without any pretence of having search warrants or other legal authority. Captain Thomas Blair, 15th Infantry, with Patrón as interpreter, was despatched to investigate the situation. "The present status of affairs in the county," wrote Dudley,

> is simply shameful and disgraceful.
>
> The action of leading men on both sides, some of whom are holding prominent relations to the Government is infamous and instead of matters improving, they are growing more and more lawless daily....
>
> I would respectfully suggest that these statements be laid before His Excellency the Governor of the Territory, trusting that some measures may be taken to end the present condition of affairs in this section.[41]

He had, he added, been informed that McSween paid his men $3.00 per day.

Following the clash with the sheriff's posse, McSween, Copeland, Waite, Bonney, Bowdre, French, Scroggins, Stevens [Stephens], Rodriguez, Martinez, Sanchez, the Coes, and others of the McSween party proceeded to John Chisum's South Spring River Ranch, where they were surrounded on the 4th of July by a posse led by Deputy Sheriff Powell. Some shots were exchanged at long range, but no damage was inflicted on either side and the deputy's force withdrew during the night. McSween's henchmen then returned to San Patricio, followed at a distance by Powell, who had been reinforced by Deputy Sheriff Marion Turner and twelve or fourteen Seven Rivers warriors.

On 11 July, Bob Beckwith, then at Lincoln, wrote his sister Josie a letter which is one of the most poignant documents to come out of the Lincoln County War:

> We arrived here yesterday in persuit of McSween's mob but did not overtake them. We were under the impression that they were coming to recapture the town but they had not been near it. Today we will start to look after them.
>
> we do not know where about in the country they are but suppose they are at Ruidozo or the Feliz. they have recruted to twenty-five McSween with them in person our party or Sheriff posee numbers about 35 men. the mob are too cowardly to come to us and fight.
>
> we will have to look for them like indians, the mob was Routed from this part of the country on the 3d and had the sheriff persuid them down to the pecos we would have captured them.
>
> but they returned to the plaza and twelve of us only had to contend against them at South Spring River ranch we held them there the [fourth] all day and they did not dare come out and fight us they shot a few shots at us from the houses but did not tuch any one of us.
>
> had the men from here come to our assistance we would have provable got some of them but they did not come untill we sent for them, and when they come McSween's mob had escapted.
>
> Now Dear Sister do not fret yourself about us it does no good. And tell Mother and Camilia & Ellen not to either. God will be with us and those murderers will not tuch a hair on our heads. Dear Sister we are having a Ruff time of it but hope era long we will be about to go home again.
>
> I wrote Father by the men who went down after cattle. I also wrote to Miss Howell requesting her to let you see the letter to let you know how we were. Give my regards to the Howell family. I sent my love to mother Camilia Ellez Lizzie Nick Laura the baby and yourself the love and hart of your Brother's that hope this will find you all well and enjoy yourselfs and try not to worry about us as I said before, it does no good.
>
> Of course you cant help but feel some anxiety about us but I will try and let you know about us at every opportunity.
>
> There will be some soldiers and Navajo Indians go down to Seven Rivers provable to stope about that vicinity.
>
> Charley Woltz was here a few days' ago but did not stay long. he

> was not aware there was anyone here but his kind. Jim Ruce [Reece?] talked very ruff to him but he did not resent it. he said he had nothing against anyone but Dolan Riley & one Seven Rivers man did not say who that was.
>
> tell Father to try and make the flour go as far as possible no chance to get any here at present. New wheat is now coming in. I have not seen any of the Fritzs family nor heard how they were but beleive they are all well.

Events were shaping up for the climax of the troubles. Within a few days, Beckwith, McSween, and several of their fellows would be dead, the McSween home burned, and the Regulators driven from the village in total defeat.[42]

ACKNOWLEDGMENTS

The writer is indebted to Lieutenant Colonel Robert M. Patterson, U.S.A. (Ret.) for a copy of the Beckwith letter. He takes pleasure in acknowledging assistance received from Miss Gertrude Hill, Miss Ruth E. Rambo, and Mrs. Edith McManmon, of the Library of the Museum of New Mexico; William S. Wallace, archivist, New Mexico Highlands University; Mr. John Boylan, curator-custodian, Old Lincoln County Memorial Commission; Mrs. William Wilson, and the staff of the Huntington Library.

NOTES

[1] P.H. Sheridan to Adjutant-General of the Army, 2 May 1878. In Records of the War Department, 1405 AGO 1878. Consolidated File Relating to the Lincoln County War, New Mexico. In National Archives.

[2] Rasch, "The Rise of the House of Murphy," op. cit. [See Chapter 1.]

[3] Rasch, "Prelude to War," op. cit. [See Chapter 5.]

[4] Ruth R. Ealy, *Water in a Thirsty Land*, (Privately printed, 1955), p. 25.

[5] A John B. Wilson had been commissioned a justice of the peace in Hamilton County, Illinois, in 1826, 1829, and 1831. He was commissioned quartermaster of the 13th Odd Battalion on 2 January 1847, but this unit apparently saw no action in the Mexican War. There is some indication that this man was the Justice Wilson of Lincoln County.

[6] For detailed studies of the background of this individual, see Rasch and Mullin, "New Light on the Legend of Billy the Kid," op. cit.; Rasch and Mullin, "Dim Trails—The Pursuit of the McCarty Family," op. cit.; Rasch, "The Twenty-One Men He Put Bullets Through," op. cit.; Rasch, "A Man Named Antrim," op. cit.; Rasch, "More on the McCartys," op. cit.; Rasch, "Clues to the Puzzle of Billy the Kid," op. cit.; Rasch, "And One Word More," op. cit.; [All appear in *Trailing Billy the Kid.*]; Rasch, "Killed by the Kid," *New Mexico Historical Review*, XXXVI:347–348, October, 1961.

[7] Santa Fe *Weekly New Mexican*, 9 February 1878; Mesilla *Independent*, 23 February 1878.

[8] Geo. A. Purington to Act. Asst. Adjt. General District of N.M., 21 February 1878. In 1405 AGO 1878.

[9] Located at the present Glencoe Post Office, on Highway 70.

[10] Santa Fe *Weekly New Mexican*, 25 May 1878.

[11] Al Erwin, Personal Communication, 12 June 1957.

[12] *Mesilla Valley Independent*, 13 April 1878.

[13] Ibid., 16 March 1878.

[14] Ash Upson, 15 March 1878. Quoted in Fulton, "Roswell in Its Early Years," op. cit.

[15] Rasch, "The Horrell War," op. cit. [See Chapter 2.]

[16] John S. Loud to Commanding Officer, Fort Stanton, N.M., 24 March 1878. In 1405 AGO 1878.

[17] D.P. Shield, Unpublished Affidavit, 11 June 1878. In Records of the Office of the Secretary of the Interior, Appointment Division, Letters Received Territorial Governors, New Mexico, 1849–78. Record Group 48, National Archives.

[18] Taylor F. Ealy, Unpublished Affidavit, 18 June 1878. In Selected Documents Concerning the Investigation of Charges Against F.C. Godfroy, Indian Agent at the Mescalero Apache Agency, New Mexico. Record Groups 75 and 48, National Archives. Also Ruth R. Ealy, op. cit., pp. 44–47.

[19] Obscure allusions to "the dog feeder" in contemporary New Mexican papers refer to Widenmann, who admitted being in the corral at the time Brady was shot, but insisted he had gone there only to feed his dog. When asked why he had a rifle and two pistols, he replied that the dog was vicious and he was afraid it might bite him! Widenmann was born in Georgia 24 January 1849 and died in Haverstraw, New York, on 15 April 1930.

[20] Coe, *Frontier Fighter*, op. cit., pp. 49–56.

[21] Testimony of D.M. Easton, 7 June 1879, (Proceedings of a Court of Inquiry in the case of Lt. Col. N.A.M. Dudley. QQ1284. Records of the War Department. Records of the Judge Advocate General. In National Archives); Mesilla *Independent*, 13 April 1878; A.N. Blazer, "Fight at the Blazer Mill," Alamogordo *News*, 16 August 1928; Roberts' murder is Cause 411, Lincoln County. Easton's report of his administration of the estate is still on record. Roberts' horse, pack animal, rifle, clothes, and personal possessions brought $99.50 at public auction, in additon to which he had a cheque from James J. Dolan & Co. for $47.20. Bills, including $30.00 to Dr. Appel for medical services, came to $89.94.

[22] Mesilla *Independent*, Supplement, 20 April 1878.

[23] Ibid., 4 May 1878.

[24] Cause No. 259, Lincoln County.

[25] Indictment found in 3rd Judicial District Court, Territory of New Mexico, 21 June 1878. Cause No. 411, Doña Ana County.

[26] N.A.M. Dudley to John S. Loud, 4 May 1878. In 1405 AGO 1878.

[27] A.A. McSween and B.H. Ellis to Rutherford B. Hayes, 26 April 1878. In Record Group 48, Records of the Secretary of the Interior. In National Archives.

[28] Santa Fe *Weekly New Mexican*, 25 May 1878; Prescott *The Weekly Arizona Miner*, 7 June 1878.

[29] Rasch, "The Pecos War," op. cit. [See Chapter 3.]

[30] N.A.M. Dudley to Act. Asst. Adjutant General, District of N.M., 18 May 1878. In 1405 AGO 1878.

[31] Ibid.

[32] Rush Clark to the Honble The Sec. of War, 28 May 1878. In 1405 AGO 1878.

[33] N.A.M. Dudley to Act. Asst. Adjutant General, District N.M., 18 May 1878. In 1405 AGO 1878.

[34] N.A.M. Dudley to Act. Asst. Adjutant General, District of N.M., 31 May 1878. In 1405 AGO 1878.

[35] Mesilla *News*, 10 August 1878, quoting John Middleton to Buck Powell, 3 June 1878. The misspellings and other faults in the original letter, and in others quoted subsequently, have been closely followed.

[36] W.M. Dunn to George W. McCrary, 8 June 1878. Quoted in *Federal Aid in Domestic Disturbances, 1903–1922*. Supplement to Senate Document 209, 57th Congress, 2nd Session. (Washington, D.C.: Government Printing Office, 1922), pp. 290–291.

[37] J.A. Tays to J.B. Jones, 31 May 1878. Typescript in Webb Collection,

University of Texas.

[38] A.A. McSween to John P. Tunstall, 17 April 1878.

[39] Mesilla *News*, 8 June 1878.

[40] Quoted in *Federal Aid in Domestic Disturbances, 1903–1922*, p. 177.

[41] N.A.M. Dudley to Act. Asst. Adjutant General, District of N.M., 13 July 1878. In 1405 AGO 1878.

[42] Rasch, "Five Days of Battle," op. cit. [See Chapter 9.]

8.
A Second Look at the Blazer's Mill Affair

Frontier Times, December 1963–January 1964

The Battle at Blazer's Mill, New Mexico, between Andrew L. "Buckshot" Roberts and a gang led by Richard M. Brewer has gone down in history as one of the classic gunfights of the Old West. It has been described by numerous authors, most of whom have based their accounts on George Coe's *Frontier Fighter* or Walter Noble Burns' *Saga of Billy the Kid.*

This is natural enough. Coe was one of the participants and his book is easy to obtain. Burns is believed to have secured his material principally from Frank Coe, George's cousin and another of the participants. Unfortunately, both of these men were members of Brewer's crowd. Not only are the Coe-Burns versions suspect, they are demonstrably in error in many respects. Luckily, other—and presumably impartial—eye-witnesses have also left a record of what they saw. They were David M. Easton, manager of Blazer's store and justice of the peace in Precinct No. 3, Lincoln County, and Almer N. Blazer, Dr. Blazer's son, who was then thirteen years of age. Paul A. Blazer, Almer's son, has also written an account of the event as handed down by his father and grandfather.

My purpose is to reconstruct the fight on the basis of the evidence of all the witnesses, rather than on that of just two of the Regulators. There are unresolved discrepancies, of course; for example, some of the eye-witnesses say Roberts was shot in the right side, others that he was shot in the left. In such cases, we can only follow those who seem to have been in the best position to make valid observations.

The background of the trouble has been related on many occasions and is probably familiar to most readers.... [See Chapters 4–7, ed.]

Little is known of Roberts' background. Henry Brown had met him in Texas, where he was using the name Bill Williams. It has been stated that he had been a soldier in the Union Army during the Civil War, a Texas Ranger, and a railroad meat hunter under Buffalo Bill Cody. He is generally depicted as a small man, given to riding a mule. It is said that a crippled arm incurred from a load of buckshot gave him his nickname and made it impossible for him to raise a rifle to his shoulder; hence, he fired from the hip. How much of this description is fact and how much fiction is yet to be proven. Some accounts say that he owned a small ranch on the Ruidoso. So far, no legal record attesting to this has been uncovered, and various old-timers were convinced that he was simply a reward hunter. His role in Lincoln County affairs had been inconspicuous and it would seem doubtful that any of those who knew him suspected that he was the stuff from which heroic legends are made. We now pick up the accounts of those who were there when he proved that he was.

It is said that Roberts had sold his ranch to a man from Santa Fe, who was to mail a check to him at the South Fork Post Office which was operated by Dr. Joseph H. Blazer. In Blazer's employ at the time was a man named Sam Miller, whose friendship with Roberts dated back to the days when they had worked together under Buffalo Bill. Roberts decided to go to Blazer's Mill and to stay with Miller until the check arrived.

On Thursday morning, April 4, some Mescalero Apaches came in to the agency to report that a gang of men had killed a beef in Rinconada the night before. Recognizing the men from the description the Indians gave, Blazer foresaw the possibility of trouble and asked Roberts to leave. The latter replied that he planned to depart the country anyhow and would go to Las Cruces, to which point Dr. Blazer could forward the check when it arrived.

When Buckshot had ridden about eight miles from the mill, he saw the mail carrier coming in on another trail. Thinking his check might be in the mail, he tied his packhorse and rode back to Blazer's establishment, arriving a little after 11 a.m. It was Dr. Blazer's custom to ask his visitors to leave their guns outside. Accordingly, Roberts left his six-shooter belt hanging from the saddle horn and his Winchester in its scabbard when he dismounted.

Seeing Frank Coe in the yard, Roberts asked him to step to one side to talk. The two men seated themselves on the porch. Billy the Kid was in front of the house chatting with Easton. Apparently, Roberts did not even suspect that most of the rest of the gang were in the house eating dinner. Coe told Roberts that they had a warrant for his arrest and were determined to take him, and urged that he surrender quietly. Buckshot refused to do this, reminding Coe of what had happened to Morton and Baker after they had accepted a similar offer of protection after surrender.

Suddenly someone cried, "Here's Roberts!"

Buckshot sprang to his horse, drew his carbine and ran toward the southwest corner of the building. As he did so, Charles Bowdre, John Middleton, Francis MacNab, and Henry Newton Brown ran around the corner toward him. They called upon him to surrender, to which he snapped, "Not much, Mary Ann!" Firing broke out immediately.

A bullet from Bowdre's gun struck Roberts in the left side, ranged through the body, and came out just above his right hip, inflicting a fatal wound. One shot from Roberts' carbine hit Bowdre's belt buckle and put him out of the fight, bounced off the buckle, and struck George Coe's right hand, tearing off his trigger finger. A second went through Middleton's lung and knocked him down. By now, Roberts' rifle was empty. As he backed down the side of the house into Dr. Blazer's office, Billy the Kid closed in for the kill. In his eagerness, he approached so closely that his quarry was able to jab him hard in the belly with the empty weapon just as the Kid fired. The bullet went wild, passing through a corner of the door facing.

In the room, the hunted man found Dr. Blazer's single shot Springfield .45-60 and a belt of cartridges. He pulled the mattress off a cot, threw it behind the partially open door, and lay down on it. Brewer entered the house and ordered Easton to go into the room and put Roberts out—an order which the justice sensibly refused to obey. Mrs. Godfroy, wife of the Indian agent, pled with the constable to leave, but Brewer, greatly enraged, swore that he would have Buckshot if he had to pull the house down to get him.

Brewer and Bowdre went down to the sawmill, about 125 yards away, and crawled through the logs until they could see the door to

Blazer's room. Two or three shots fired into it drew no reply. Bowdre then left and rejoined the rest of the party. The Regulators had two men in serious need of medical attention and it seemed probable that Roberts would die soon anyhow, so they reached a decision to leave as soon as Brewer came back.

The constable, however, was determined to make one last attempt to kill Roberts. As he raised his head above a log for a final sight, a slug from the Springfield took him in the left eye, tearing off the top of his head. His body lay in the hot sun until it was safe to recover it. By then, it was in such a state that it was necessary for the mill carpenter, a man named Beam, to make a coffin and bury him promptly.

Badly demoralized by the loss of their leader, the gunmen decided to leave. Indian Agent Frederick C. Godfroy supplied a government hack and team to take the wounded men to Fort Stanton for medical treatment. A messenger had already been dispatched to the fort to request aid. En route, the party met Assistant Surgeon Daniel M. Appel, U.S.A., post surgeon at Fort Stanton and acting physician at the Mescalero Agency, on his way to the scene of the fighting. Appel rendered what aid he could and sent the party on. (For his thanks years afterwards, he was recalled by George Coe as "Dr. Gordon.") Later that month, Dr. Taylor F. Ealy, a Presbyterian medical missionary in Lincoln, amputated Coe's thumb and finger.

The question at the mill was how to contact Roberts without getting shot in the process. Finally, John Ryan, a clerk in Dolan's store at the Indian agency, waving a white cloth in one hand, slipped up close enough to call to Roberts and explain the situation. Ryan and Easton then entered the room and gave what care they could to the wounded man. Late that night, Appel arrived at the house. He told them there was nothing that could be done other than make the sufferer as comfortable as possible. Roberts died about noon the next day, having been unconscious the last six or seven hours of his life. Beam made a second coffin and Roberts was buried in a grave adjacent to that of Brewer. A coroner's jury found that he had come to his death from gunshot wounds suffered at the hands of Richard Brewer, Charles Bowdre, "Doc" Scurlock, Fred Waite, John Middleton, Frank MacNab, John Scroggins, Stephen Stephens, George Coe, Frank Coe, and W.H. Antrim, alias "Kid."

Easton was appointed administrator of Roberts' estate. This consisted principally of his weapons, clothes, livestock, and a check from Dolan & Co. for $47.20. No heirs could be located. His possessions—other than the check—were sold at public auction in Lincoln. They brought a total of $99.50. When various charges were deducted, including $30.00 to Dr. Appel for professional services and $20.00 to Dr. Blazer for the cost of the burial, the balance of the estate amounted to less than $10.00—surely little enough to show for one's lifetime.

Of those involved in the killing of Roberts, only the Kid was eventually brought to trial for his part in the affair. On March 30, 1881, Billy was arraigned in Mesilla before Judge Warren Bristol, presiding justice, United States Third Judicial District, on a charge of murdering Roberts. Ira E. Leonard, Billy's attorney, immediately objected that since Blazer's Mill was private property, the United States had no jurisdiction in the matter. U.S. Attorney Sidney M. Barnes promptly demurred on the grounds that the reservation was "Indian Country" and the United States had exclusive control over Indian Country. Bristol took the matter under advisement.

In due course, he issued a seven-page opinion in which he held that no part of New Mexico was included in the definition of Indian Country as set forth in the law. He therefore overruled the demurrer and quashed the indictment. Barnes thereupon asked leave for discontinuance as to the seven others implicated in the case.

Billy was next tried before Bristol, sitting as a justice of the territorial district court, for the murder of Sheriff William Brady. For some reason, Leonard did not appear as defense counsel. In his stead, the court appointed Albert J. Fountain, Simon B. Newcomb, and John D. Bail. Their efforts were in vain. The Kid was found guilty and sentenced to be hanged on May 13. James W. Southwick, sheriff of Doña Ana County, appointed Bob Olinger his deputy to take the prisoner to Lincoln. With them went Tom Williams, Billy Mathews, John Kinney, D.M. Reade, and W.A. Lockhard [Lockhart]. The party left Mesilla about 10 p.m. on Saturday, April 16.

En route to Lincoln, the men stopped at Blazer's Mill. The Kid gave them a graphic account of the fight with Roberts, pointing out the hole in the door where his shot had gone through the wood and—according to him—inflicted the fatal wound. Almer Blazer accepted his story as factual, and apparently it was on his authority that a number of writers have credited Billy with the killing. However, on his death bed, Roberts told Easton, Appel, and others that the shot which struck him had been fired by Bowdre. Bowdre is also named by both George and Frank Coe. Under the circumstances, there is little reason to give credence to the vainglorious claims of New Mexico's most famous psychopathic personality.

9.
FIVE DAYS OF BATTLE

BRAND BOOK OF THE DENVER WESTERNERS, 1955

FOREWORD: During the years following the War Between the States, Lawrence G. Murphy and Emil Fritz, doing business as L.G. Murphy & Co., became virtual economic and political dictators of Lincoln County, New Mexico. After the death of Fritz, James J. Dolan and John H. Riley became the active partners in the concern. In 1877, Alexander A. McSween, a Lincoln lawyer, and John H. Tunstall, a wealthy young Englishman, backed by cattle baron John S. Chisum, opened a store and bank in Lincoln, directly challenging Dolan-Riley for the control of the county.

Chisum had already earned the enmity of the small ranch owners who now rallied around Dolan-Riley. On February 18, 1878, Tunstall was murdered by a sheriff's posse composed of Dolan-Riley sympathizers. Open warfare resulted. In quick succession, Sheriff William Brady, George Hindman, William Morton, Frank Baker, William McCloskey, Richard Brewer, Bill Williams, alias Andrew L. Roberts, Frank McNab, James A. Saunders, and Tom Childron, alias Tom Hill, were shot down. Murphy fled to Santa Fe; Riley took refuge on the range. Dolan and the newly-appointed sheriff, George W. Peppin, continued to press the fight against McSween.

Affairs came to a climax in July, 1878, when a pitched battle between the two sides raged for five days in the plaza of Lincoln, the county seat. The fight resulted in a defeat for the McSween partisans, but financially ruined Dolan-Riley. Lincoln County was plunged into anarchy. Murder, rape, arson, and theft became the order of the day, leaving behind a legacy of bitterness which persists to some extent to this day.

The actions of Lieutenant Colonel N.A.M. Dudley were investigated by a Court of Inquiry, which finally exonerated him. The following account of the battle at Lincoln is based primarily on two sources: the weekly reports made by Dudley to his superior, Colonel Edward Hatch, commanding the District of New Mexico, and the sworn testimony given by participants in the affair at the Court of Inquiry. Many of the details are admittedly controversial. The sworn testimony contains statements so directly contradictory that they can be accounted for only on the supposition that at times the truth was deliberately disregarded. Nevertheless, the writer believes that the story as here presented is correct in all essential points.

By the middle of July, 1878, it had become evident that Alexander McSween's Regulators were in desperate straits. Harried on every side by the Dolan-Riley faction, they assembled at San Patricio for a council of war. Their decision was born of their desperation: they decided to stake everything on one throw of the dice and to attempt to seize Lincoln by force. An alliance was effected with Martin Chaves, of Picacho, and his Mexican followers, and on the night of Sunday, July 14, the Regulators took up positions in the plaza. Chaves, Fernando Herrera, and seven other Mexicans manned the Montaño house. McSween, Henry McCarty (alias William Antrim, alias Bill Bonney, alias Billy the Kid), Harvey Morris,[1] Jose Chaves y Chaves, Yginio Salazar, Florencio Chaves, Ignacio Gonzales, Vincente Romero, Francisco Zamora, Jim French, Tom O'Folliard, Jose Maria Sanchez, Joseph J. Smith, Thomas Cullins (alias Joe Rivers), and George Bowers defended the McSween house. Henry Brown, George Coe, and Sam Smith were barricaded in the warehouse behind the Tunstall building, in the back rooms of which were living Dr. and Mrs. Taylor F. Ealy, their two small daughters, and Miss Susan Gates. Charles Bowdre, Josiah G. "Dock" Scurlock, John Middleton, "Dirty Steve" Stevens [Stephens], and others to the number of about a dozen garrisoned the Isaac Ellis home. A group of perhaps five men occupied the Patrón house.

Sheriff George W. Peppin, taken completely by surprise, had only a small force under his immediate command. Deputy Sheriff

Jack Long held the Torreón, a round tower which had originally been erected for defense against Indian raids, with Jacob Mathews, James B. Reese, Sam Perry, Jim McDaniels, George A. ["Roxy"] Rose, and a man known as "The Dummy." Peppin, Panteleon [Pantaleon] Gallegos, Lucien [Lucio] Montoya, Andrew Boyle, and one other man occupied the Wortley Hotel. With them was James J. Dolan, who was recuperating from a broken leg suffered in a fall from his horse. A Mexican was hastily dispatched for Deputy Sheriff William [Thomas] B. "Buck" Powell, who was in the vicinity of San Patricio, ordering him to bring his men to Lincoln at once. As they entered the plaza about six o'clock in the evening, they were fired on from the McSween house and a horse was killed. With reinforcements received the next day, the sheriff's force was brought up to twenty-six or twenty-eight men, including Joseph H. Nash, Robert W. Beckwith, John M. Beckwith, Robert Olinger, Wallace Olinger, John Thornton, Jim Hurley, John Hurley, —— Prince, Benjamin "Buck" Waters, Deputy Sheriff Marion Turner, John Chambers, Charles Crawford (alias Lalacooler or Lally Cooler[2]), John Kinney, John Jones, Tom Jones, Jim Jones, Jessie J. Evans, —— Hart, —— Collins, John W. Irving [Irvin], Jake Owens, Jose Chaves y Baca, M.L. Pierce, William Johnson, K.L. Bryan, Thomas Cochran [Cochrane], and John Galvin, in addition to those previously named.

The sheriff held two warrants each for Antrim, Brown, Scurlock, and Bowdre on charges of murder, one for Jose Chavez for horse stealing, one for Coe for murder, and one for McSween, charged with assault to kill. The next morning, Long made the gesture of attempting to serve the warrants, was greeted with gunfire, as he no doubt anticipated, and beat a hasty retreat.

The presence of Dolan-Riley partisans in the Torreón, which was on property owned by McSween, led to trouble between Saturnino Baca and the McSweens. Mrs. McSween had already accused Baca of having sent men to San Patricio to kill her husband and had warned that if he was harmed, she would retaliate, come what might. Baca, although a Dolan-Riley supporter, occupied a house owned by McSween adjacent to the tower. McSween was furious when he learned that Baca had permitted Long and his men to enter the Torreón. He immediately sent his rentor a written notice to vacate within three days because "You have consented to the improper use of the property by murderers for the purpose of taking my life."[3]

When Assistant Surgeon D.M. Appel was sent to the plaza to attend Julian López, a posseman who had been wounded in the fighting at San Patricio, the Bacas told him that they were in fear for their lives and begged for a guard. Appel visited McSween to discuss the situation. Livid with rage, McSween informed the doctor that the Bacas were on his ground and harboring his enemies, and that they would leave if he had to burn them out. He had been hiding in the hills long enough, he snapped; he had now returned to his home and no one would drive him away alive. Quieting down then, he gave the officer his written consent for the soldiers to occupy the Torreón to protect the Baca family. Baca, however, decided to move and wrote Dudley for the loan of wagons, pleading in justification for this aid his five years of service in the Union forces and the recent confinement of his wife.

Scurlock appeared before Justice Wilson and executed an affidavit denying that he had threatened to kill Colonel Dudley and Johnny Brady. Isaac Ellis and his son Benjamin signed affidavits to the effect that Crawford had threatened their lives and stolen their best horse. Appel returned to Fort Stanton with these papers to lay the matter before his commanding officer.

Things remained quiet the rest of the day, but about midnight Dan Huff, a citizen of Lincoln, died in agony, in spite of the ministrations of Dr. Ealy. He had tried to remain neutral, but is supposed to have been poisoned by a relative who objected to the fact that he had been friendly with the McSweens. The next evening, two of McSween's colored servants, George Washington and Sebrian Bates, dug a grave adjacent to that of Tunstall and were in the process of lowering the body into it when they were driven away by shots from the Torreón.

On the 16th, Peppin wrote Dudley, requesting the loan of a howitzer. Until this time, Dudley's weekly reports had been scrupulously fair in their attitude toward the two factions. His answer to Peppin, however, threw off all pretense and allied him firmly with the Dolan-Riley side:

> ...and in reply would state I fully realize your difficult situation. My sympathies and those of all my officers are most earnest and sincere-

> ly with you on the side of law and order....I do not hesitate to state now that...were I not so circumscribed by laws and orders, I would most gladly give you every man and material at my Post to sustain you in your present situation....[4]

To Hatch, he reported that "The...Dolan-Riley faction...I fear will get the worst of it."[5]

Private Berry Robinson was sent to Lincoln with the letter for the sheriff. As he reached the outskirts of the plaza, several shots were fired at him. Peppin immediately capitalized on the incident by writing Dudley that

> The McSween party fired on your Soldier when coming into town. My men on seeing him tried there [sic] best to cover him, but of no use. The soldier will explain the circumstances to you.[6]

The following morning, Dudley appointed Captain G.A. Purington, Captain Thomas Blair, and Appel a board of officers to investigate the shooting. In spite of McSween's denials, they concluded that the shots had come from his house. While in Lincoln, they learned that Peppin had sent Crawford, Montoya, and three other men up in the hills south of the town to drive the McSween riflemen off the roofs of the buildings held by them. Crawford had been shot by Herrera and was lying helpless on the hillside. Blair and Appel went to assist him, whereupon either they or the wounded man were fired upon from the Montaño house. However, Crawford was taken to the post hospital, where he died a week later.

The 17th was relatively quiet, although that night Ben Ellis was shot in the neck while in his corral feeding his mules, but this was the proverbial lull before the storm. Fighting was resumed on the morning of the 18th and continued almost incessantly.

During the day, Thomas Cullins was killed and buried in the cellar of the McSween house. George Bowers was seriously wounded. In spite of these reverses, the high morale of the Regulators is evident in a letter written by Joseph Smith the next morning:

> I thought I would write you a few lines to let you know what the people are doing up here. We have taken the town. One was killed yesterday, and one wounded. Ben Ellis was shot through the neck by one of the guards. Everything is fair in war. Seen Jim Reese the other

> morning walking down the street. I heard Collins sing hunger the other morning. I heard Jim Reese cried because he was on the other side. He says he is in it and can't get out of it. All of them have taken an oath to stand by each other until death, so I guess we will get to kill a lot of them fore they get away. Capper, you must not think hard of a fellow for quitting you; but I wanted to go, so I went. The U.S. troops have stepped aside, and given us full swing. There is 45 of us citizens have turned out. I tell you it makes a fellow's hair stand up when bullets come whistling through the air; then I get cooled down, I don't mind it much. Best respects to Sam. Harvey Morris sends his respects to all. Had a little excitement yesterday evening. The Murphy's told some woman in town that they got a condemned cannon and was going to bombard the town. Tried to scare us out, but we didn't scare worth a darn.
>
> Well, I must quit writing. Good luck to you.
>
> Tell Bill Nagle he can have them gloves.[7]

From the standpoint of the sheriff, the situation was becoming desperate. Johnson and two other men had been wounded in the shooting and removed to the post hospital. Many of the possemen were discouraged and wanted to leave the fight. Dolan, Kinney, Perry, Roxie [Rose], and several others went to Fort Stanton to consult with Dudley. They told him frankly that there was no way of getting the McSween men out of the house without his assistance. The colonel was noncommittal. He answered that he had had numerous appeals for help from non-combatants; that his howitzer was broken but that blacksmith Nelson would work on it all night and on the following day troops would go to Lincoln to protect women and children.

That evening, he called a conference of his officers. At the suggestion of Captain Purington, those present signed their names to the following statement:

> General N.A.M. Dudley Lieut Col 9th Cavalry having asked the undersigned Officers their Opinions and advice as to the advisability of placing Soldiers in the Town of Lincoln for the preservation of the lives of the women and Children, and in response to the numerous petitions received from persons in that town, do hereby place on record their concurrence in the measures adopted by General Dudley believing them to be in the Course of right and humanity.

About ten o'clock on the morning of the 19th, Dudley rode into the plaza, accompanied by five officers, thirty-five men, the howitzer, and a Gatling gun. Drawing rein in front of the Wortley Hotel, Dudley issued a grim warning:

> Mr. Sheriff, I want you to understand that I have not come to Lincoln to assist you in any way. I have come solely to protect the women and children; the men can take care of themselves. I propose to go into camp within half a mile of the town. If my camp is attacked, or an officer or man killed or wounded from a shot fired by either party from any house, I shall demand the parties who did the firing be turned over to me, and in case of failure I shall request the women and children to leave the house, and I shall open fire on it with my howitzer, and arrest the parties in the house. I do not know what houses your party or McSween's occupy; I shall treat both parties exactly alike.[8]

The posse heard him out in silence. Plans had already been made to assault the McSween house. As the troops marched on, the possemen took up their asigned positions. Robert Olinger led a party into the Stanley house. John Hurley was sent to the Wilson jacal. Dolan moved into the Mills house. Peppin took up position in the Torreón. Matthews, Gallegos, Jim Jones, and Perry entered the Schon residence.

Dudley went into camp about 300 yards east of the McSween house and about 30 yards from the Patrón home, on property leased by Washington from Ellis. The men occupying Patrón's house promptly abandoned it. The colonel ordered the howitzer trained on the door of the Montaño building and sent Captain Blair to repeat his ultimatum to Chaves and to advise that the women and children should leave. Chaves soon led his men down to the Ellis home. Mrs. Montaño then sent word to Dudley that she had prepared a room for him and his officers, but he replied that they would stay in the camp. Dr. Appel was instructed to inform Ellis of the purpose of the troops. He soon returned to camp for some bandages for Ben Ellis, bringing Isaac with him so that the colonel could talk with him personally.

Sergeant Andrew Keefe was ordered to tour the village and inform the people that the Army would give them protection if they would come to the camp. He found the plaza almost deserted; not more than a dozen families were still present.

Upon his return, the colonel sent him for Peppin. Dudley told the sheriff that a number of the McSween supporters had congregated at Ellis', and suggested that they be headed off. After some delay, Peppin, Jim Hurley, Robert Beckwith, John Jones, and Thornton ran down to the Ellis place. They found the defenders were riding off into the hills to the north of the town. Shots were exchanged and Jones was slightly wounded. While Peppin searched the house and store, Beckwith obtained a bucket of coal oil. As the men returned up the street, Dudley remarked disgustedly that they could have captured the men in the Montaño house if they had come when he first sent for them.

About ten minutes after the troops went into camp, McSween's seven-year-old niece brought the commanding officer a note:

> Would you have the kindness to let me know why soldiers surround my house. Before blowing up my property I would like to know the reason. The constable is here and has warrants for the arrest of Sheriff Peppin and posse for murder and larceny.[9]

To this, Dudley ordered his adjutant, Lieutenant M.F. Goodwin, to reply that

> I am directed by the Commanding Officer to inform you that no soldiers have surrounded your house, and that he desires to hold no correspondence with you; if you desire to blow up your house, the commanding officer does not object providing it does not injure any U.S. soldiers.[10]

On receipt of this answer, Mrs. McSween decided to go to the camp and talk with Dudley personally.

"Colonel Dudley," she asked, "what is your object in bringing your troops to Lincoln?"[11]

"Mrs. McSween, I am not aware that I have to report my movements to you. However, I am here simply to offer protection to women, children, and non-combatants, and to prevent the wanton destruction of property."

"Then why do you not protect myself, my sister, and her children?"

"I cannot protect them while they are in that house. Your sister or your husband or anyone else who comes to my camp will be given protection."

"Colonel Dudley, my husband and I hold you in high regard."

"I thank you, Madam, for the compliment," replied the officer, lifting his hat.

"Will you not have the firing stopped so that I can remove my things from my house?"

"I am sorry, but I cannot interefere with the civil authorities. I understand that the sheriff has warrants for various parties, including your husband, and he must be the judge of the means to be used in serving them."

"I have been told that you are going to blow my house up."

"You have been misinformed. But that should not worry you much, since I have a letter from your husband stating that he is going to blow your house up himself."

"If you have received any such letter, I do not believe that my husband wrote it."

"I will read it to you." The colonel stepped back into his tent, picked up the letter and read it aloud.

"I do not believe that my husband wrote that. Let me see the handwriting," exclaimed Mrs. McSween, reaching for the note.

"I will not trust you to handle it, because I believe you would tear it up if you had the chance," replied Dudley, stepping backward. "If your husband will surrender, I will give you my word of honor as an officer that he will not be molested or hurt in any way. I will take him to the post and give him all the protection that I can."

"I must say one thing before I leave, Colonel," answered Mrs. McSween. "Your being in town with your troops today looks a little too thin."

Dudley blinked. "Will you repeat that?"

"Your being in town with your troops today looks a little too thin."

"I do not understand such slang phrases, Mrs. McSween. The ladies with whom I am accustomed to associate do not use such language and I do not understand what you mean by 'too thin.'"

Mrs. McSween turned to leave, but paused to ask one more question. "Colonel, why do you have that cannon pointed at my house?"

"Madam, if you will look again, you will see that it is pointed in the opposite direction."

"I believe you know more about guns than I do," Mrs. McSween laughed as she left the camp.

Dudley sent for Justice of the Peace John B. Wilson and demanded that he issue a warrant for the arrest of McSween for the attempted murder of Private Robinson. Purington, Blair, and Appel accompanied the justice back to his office to make the necessary affidavit, but Wilson returned to the camp and demurred that a writ for an offense involving a soldier should legally be issued by a U.S. commissioner. When the colonel became abusive and threatened to put him in irons if he did not issue the paper promptly, Wilson went back to his office and prepared the warrant. It was delivered to Sheriff Peppin, who appointed Bob Beckwith a deputy sheriff and instructed him to serve it.

The sheriff then ordered the McSween's three colored servants, Washington, Bates, and Joseph Dixon, to join the posse and carry lumber to burn the McSween house. However, Washington, who had been captured at San Patricio, was exempted when Dudley objected that he was a parolled prisoner.

The combined Chaves-Ellis party now advanced over a hill opposite the camp and started firing at the posse. The shots were returned by a detachment of the posse led by Peppin, and the soldiers turned the howitzer in their direction. When the attacking party saw this, they ran back over the hill. They did not again appear on the scene, although later on, a group of six or seven men gathered opposite the camp and fired promiscuously into the western end of the town.

As the morning wore on, a group of about thirteen or fourteen men, led by Deputy Sheriff Turner, made a dash to the front of the McSween house, tried to pry the window sills off with their butcher knives, poked their guns through the windows, and demanded that the defenders surrender. Jim French replied that they had warrants in their guns for all of the posse.

About half past one, Long entered the besieged house and poured the coal oil on the floor of the northeast kitchen (a part of the building occupied by the Shield family) and The Dummy started a fire. This burned out in about ten minutes. After leaving the house, Long and The Dummy came under heavy fire from the Tunstall store and were forced to jump into the privy sink. Here, they were shortly joined by Powell, who had come under the defenders' sights while getting water. Boyle was grazed along the neck by a bullet from the Tunstall marksmen, but half an hour later piled a sack of shavings and chips and some kindling thrown to him by Nash against the back door of the northwest kitchen and succeeded in getting a fire started.

Gunfire became so heavy that Dudley and his men were forced to seek refuge inside an unfinished adobe building just west of their camp.[12] Dr. Ealy sent Miss Gates to ask Dudley for an escort of soldiers to remove his personal property from his rooms in the Tunstall building, since he had received word that it too would be burned. That ill-feeling may have existed between the two men is suggested by the fact that she also brought a note to Appel, asking him to use his influence to obtain this favor.[13] Appel, Blair, Goodwin, and three enlisted men went to the Ealy residence and removed a wagonload of goods. However, the soldiers reported to Dudley that Ealy had used "some threatening and impudent language"[14] to them, and he refused to permit them to return. Around 5:30 that evening, Dudley received letters from Mrs. Ealy (written on the advice of Appel) apologizing for her husband's conduct and asking for a guard to remove her family and Miss Gates from their home. A wagon was hitched up and Captain Blair and Dr. Appel, with five enlisted men, went up to the Tunstall building. Mrs. McSween requested the same protection from Blair, and with her sister, Mrs. Shield, and the latter's five children, the Ealy family, and Miss Gates, was assigned quarters in the Patrón house.

Appel then inquired of Washington, "George, can't you take me to some near place where we can see the fun?"[15] Washington guided him to the Wilson jacal. Appel afterwards remarked feelingly, "I don't think I cared to get any nearer to the fight...."[16] Later claims were made that while attempting to escape from the burning house, members of the McSween party were fired upon by soldiers. In evaluating them, it is important to remember that Appel was the only soldier out of the camp at the climax of the fight.

The fire burned down the west side, across the front, and back up the east side of the McSween home. During the afternoon, there was an explosion within the building and the fire began to gain rapidly. The house became a huge torch, lighting up the hills on both sides of the town. The occupants were driven into the sole remaining room, the northeast kitchen. Three choices were open to them: to burn, to make an attempt to escape, or to surrender. Bowers chose the first alternative. Unable to move, he preferred death in the burning building to surrender to the posse.

His fellows chose the second. About half an hour after dusk, the defenders burst from the house in two groups. The first group, including Antrim, Chaves y Chaves, French, O'Folliard, and Morris, dashed from the kitchen through the gate in the plank fence along the east side of the building, apparently bound for the Tunstall store. Morris was killed just as he reached the gate. Three members of the posse suddenly appeared around the corner of the Tunstall building and fired almost point blank at the fleeing men. The fugitives turned toward the Rio Bonito and made their escape into the friendly darkness.

The second group, in which were McSween, Gonzales, Romero, Zamora, and Salazar, attempted to reach safety through the gate in the adobe fence on the north side of the house. Rifle fire from possemen concealed behind the wall was so heavy that they were driven back into the dark corner between the chicken house and the wood pile. About five minutes later, they made a second attempt to reach the gate and were again repulsed. Two of the Mexicans sought shelter in the chicken house. The scene was set for what Boyle[17] later succinctly termed "the big killing."

After a pause of perhaps ten minutes, McSween called out, "Will you take us as prisoners?"

Beckwith answered, "I will. I came for that purpose but it seems necessary to kill you to take you."

"I shall surrender."

"I am a deputy sheriff and I have a warrant for you." As Beckwith stepped forward, followed by Nash, John Jones, and The Dummy, McSween cried despairingly, "I shall never surrender."[18] Immediately, a shot from the chicken house killed Beckwith. Retribution was so swift that McSween's body fell on top of Beckwith's. His men made another desperate attempt to escape, and this time some of them got through the gate and into the covering night. Nash and Boyle got a log, poked a hole into the chicken house, and demanded that the men in there surrender. They replied that they would not and had never intended to do so. Boyle then fired a few shots into the inside of the structure. It is not apparent from the evidence whether these men were Romero and Zamora, both of whom were killed at this stage of the fighting.

Salazar had been shot in two places and had fallen close to the adobe wall. Boyle gave him a couple of kicks and was about to add a finishing shot, but Pierce called to him, "Don't waste another shot on that damn greaser; he is already dead and we may need all our ammunition later on."[19] During the night, Salazar crawled the thousand yards to the home of Jose Otero, where his sister-in-law, Nicolasita Pacheco, was staying.

About eight o'clock, the firing died away. Beckwith's body was then taken up to the former Dolan-Riley store.[20] Dudley seems to have been much moved by his death. He wrote Hatch that Beckwith had been

> a gentleman well known in the country and recognized as one of the most upright, energetic, and industrious men of the community, who I believe lost his life in the conscientious discharge of loyal duty. He belonged to one of the best families in his section of the Country, and his loss will be deplored by every good citizen, who had the good fortune to know him. I personally know that this slight tribute to his memory is equally appreciated by the Officers of my command and the citizens of this county.[21]

With his permission, the body was interred at Fort Stanton with military honors, an action which the judge advocate of the Department of the Missouri later cited as a positive demonstration of partisanship.[22]

The following morning, Justice Wilson convened a coroner's jury. The jury found that McSween, Morris, Zamora, and Romero "came to their deaths by rifle shots from the hands of the Sheriffs posse, while they the above named persons were resisting the Sheriffs posse with force and arms," and that Beckwith "came to his death by two rifle shots from the hands of the above named persons...in the discharge of his duty...."[23] Peppin prepared to bury McSween, but Mrs. McSween hysterically forbade him to touch her husband's body. Dudley himself chased off the fowl who were pecking at the dead man's eyes and ordered the corpse covered with a quilt.

Kinney and three of his men noticed the blood stains Salazar had left on the ground and trailed him to the Otero house. They threatened to kill the wounded man, but left when Dr. Appel, who had answered a plea from Nicolasita, warned that if they harmed his patient, he would personally see to it that all four were hanged. Justice Wilson was called and Salazar[24] executed an affidavit giving a brief account of the fight. This was supplemented by an "On Honor" statement prepared by Appel,[25] which contained additional information given by Salazar, including confirmation of the fact that Beckwith was killed only after McSween's party had agreed to surrender.

David M. Easton, the local business manager for Catron, had some Mexicans carry the bodies of McSween and Morris up to the Tunstall store. They were wrapped in blankets, placed in boxes, and buried near Tunstall and Huff without ceremony of any kind. On his arrival at the store, Easton found that the door had been broken in and the merchandise was being carried off. Jessie Evans and Kinney were trying on new suits. Jake Owens was putting on hats. Boyle and others were looking for items which suited their fancy.

Easton sent for Sam Corbet, who was nominally in charge of the store, and Sheriff Peppin. The sheriff stated that he was almost powerless to stop the looting, but would assign a guard of two men to assist Corbet. Corbet, however, refused to remain at the store. Dudley and Appel came in and looked around. Appel told Corbet that he would have the looters arrested if he would swear out warrants, but Corbet said he was afraid that he would be killed if he did so. Easton and Corbet then nailed up the store and left.

About four o'clock that afternoon, Dudley took his troops, with the exception of a small guard left for the protection of the Bacas and others who might care to avail themselves of it, back to Fort Stanton. With them went the Ealys and the Shield family. Dudley's undisguised contempt for Ealy made it impossible for them to stay at the fort for any length of time, and about a week later, these refugees left for Las Vegas.[26]

The five days of fighting had resulted in a decisive victory for the Dolan-Peppin forces, but Dudley took a somber view of the prospects for the future:

> One thing is sure, both parties are still determined, the fearful sacrafice [sic] of McSween's clique on the 19th inst does not seem to satisfy either side. A deep revenge will be sought by the sheriffs posse for the loss of their pet leader *Beckwith*, and if possible a still stronger spirit exists on the part of the McSween men to retaliate for the death of their headman, McSween.

> ...Men who have the reckless courage to attack a building in bright mid-day, its walls forming a perfect protection, against any modern musketry to its inmates, pierced as this castle of McSween's was, with scores of loop holes for rifles on every side and angle, to say nothing of the flat roof, protected by a perfect wall of defence, and for hours hugging the walls, exposed to the fire of not only from the loop holes, but from the roof and adjacent buildings held by McSween men, charging this position across a space perfectly exposed to the fire of McSween's men for a distance of nearly three hundred yards, are not of a character to be easily induced to abandon a course they believe is only half completed. A similar remark can be made of the party holding this structure, who held the same fortification for the five days, the last nine hours gradually retreating from one room to another, as the heat compelled them to do what no amount of leaden missles from the rifles of the attacking party could do, and for an hour finally, all huddled in one room, nearly surrounded by the flames, some as it is claimed, preferred to being burnt rather than surrender to the Sheriff's posse.
>
> More desperate action than was exhibited on this unfortunate day by both sides is rarely witnessed.[27]

On the morning of the 21st, Easton and Edgar Walz found a mob of Mexicans pillaging the Tunstall store. They claimed that they had been told by Mrs. McSween to take what they wanted. When Easton[27] asked Mrs. McSween about this, she replied, "I would rather have the Mexicans living on the creek have the goods than any of Peppin's gang of murderers."

"You can do as you please," Easton answered. "If you have any interest in having the goods saved, I will aid you, but if the goods are to be allowed to be stolen by anyone, I will go home."

"If you think the store will not be burned down and that the goods can be saved, I would be glad to have you help put the goods back," she replied.

Easton and Walz were able to recover some of the property and once more nailed up the doors and windows. That afternoon, the store was again broken open. Corbet refused to come down, so Easton had Bates and Dixon nail it up again. Apparently, it was not disturbed thereafter.

The question of why the Regulators, possessing the twin advantages of surprise and superiority in numbers, were so decisively defeated is an interesting one. The advantage of surprise was lost when they took up defensive positions instead of mounting an attack against the sheriff's force before it could obtain reinforcements. The advantage of superiority in numbers was dissipated by the placement of the men in houses too widely dispersed to permit communications, cooperation, and mutual support.

That Long, Boyle, and The Dummy were able to enter the McSween house, set a fire and leave without interference, and that Turner and his men were able to reach the very walls of the house and fire through the windows without the loss of a man indicates that the defense was not properly organized. The thirteen men still effective, aided by an enfilading fire from the Tunstall building, should have been able to put up a better defense than they did.

The men at the Ellis house should certainly have been able to hold it against the sheriff and his handful of possemen. Having abandoned this strongpoint, their failure to press home a determined assault to relieve their beleagured companions permitted the moment of decision to pass to the posse. Even at the very climax of the battle, a diversionary attack from across the Rio Bonito could have driven Boyle and his party away from the adobe wall north of the McSween house and provided the defenders with an opportunity for a successful escape.

The arrival of Dudley and his troops tremendously increased the psychological pressure on the Regulators, but can hardly have been the decisive factor. The key to the problem is the fact that the comparatively large number of men originally posted in the homes of Montaño, Patrón, and Ellis took practically no part whatever in the fighting. Seizure of a large part of the village without any sort of a strategic plan for exploiting this move and the complete absence of tactical control over the various units into which the aggressive force was divided spells only one thing: a lack of competent leadership.

In spite of the partisan actions of Dudley, the rout of the McSween force appears to have resulted primarily from the fact that Dolan, Peppin, and his deputies provided more determined and effective leadership than was available to their opponents. McSween, like Tunstall, was ill equipped by nature and training for the role he aspired to play among the desperate men of Lincoln County. Their failure to recognize that the society of Lincoln

County was one that would respond to the symbols of legal chicanery with gunfire[28] resulted in their own destruction and that of many of their followers. The end had been foreshadowed by the previous failure of the Regulators to win even a single victory in their clashes with the sheriff's posse.

NOTES

[1] According to R.N. Mullin, Morris was a tubercular patient who was reading law with McSween.

[2] According to the Tombstone *Prospector*, January 17, 1892, a lally cooler was three diamonds and a pair of clubs. It composed the highest hand in the deck, but could be played only once an evening.

[3] A.A. McSween to Capt. Saturnino Baca, July 15, 1878.

[4] N.A.M. Dudley to G.W. Peppin, July 16, 1878.

[5] N.A.M. Dudley to Acting Assistant Adjutant General, District of New Mexico, July 16, 1878.

[6] George W. Peppin to N.A.M. Dudley, July 16, 1878.

[7] Joseph J. Smith to Howard Capper, July 19, 1878.

[8] N.A.M. Dudley to Acting Assistant Adjutant General, District of New Mexico, July 20, 1878.

[9] A.A. McSween to Gen. Dudley, July 19, 1878.

[10] From testimony of Lieut. M.F. Goodwin at the Dudley Court of Inquiry, June 24, 1879.

[11] This conversation is a composite from the testimony at the Dudley Court of Inquiry and is not to be understood as being verbatim.

[12] R.N. Mullin believes that this building was being erected as a Presbyterian church and school for the Rev. Dr. Ealy.

[13] D.M. Appel "On Honor" statement, July 20, 1878.

[14] Ibid.

[15] Testimony of George Washington at the Dudley Court of Inquiry, May 26, 1879.

[16] Testimony of D.M. Appel at the Dudley Court of Inquiry, June 25, 1879.

[17] Testimony of Andrew Boyle at the Dudley Court of Inquiry, June 17, 1879.

[18] Ibid.; Testimony of Joseph Nash at the Dudley Court of Inquiry, June 18, 1879.

[19] Otero, *The Real Billy the Kid*, op. cit.

[20] On January 19, 1878, U.S. District Attorney Thomas B. Catron, president of the First National Bank at Santa Fe, had accepted a mortgage on the

store, its stock, 40 acres of land adjoining Lincoln on the west, and 1,500 cattle on Black River (near present-day Carlsbad) to secure him for endorsing a Dolan-Riley note. When the partnership was dissolved by mutual consent on May 1, 1878, he sent his brother-in-law, Edgar A. Walz, to take over the store. Riley went out on Catron's cattle range near Seven Rivers and took no part in the fighting in Lincoln. Catron later sold the merchandise to J.C. Delaney [DeLany], who operated the store until the building was sold to Lincoln County in 1880. See Edgar A. Walz, *Retrospection*, Santa Fe: Privately printed, 1931, and J.W. Henron, "The Old Lincoln Courthouse," *El Palacio*, XLVI:1–18, January, 1939. Robert W. Beckwith, son of H.M. Beckwith and Refugia Pino Beckwith, was born October 10, 1850.

[21] N.A.M. Dudley to Acting Assistant Adjutant General, District of New Mexico, July 20, 1878.

[22] D.G. Swain to Assistant Adjutant General, Department of the Missouri, September 23, 1879.

[23] Proceedings of Coroner's Jury, July 20, 1878.

[24] Affidavit of Hinio Salacar [Yginio Salazar], July 20, 1878.

[25] N.A.M. Dudley to Acting Assistant Adjutant General, District of New Mexico, July 23, 1878.

[26] For subsequent events in the life of the Ealy family, see Ruth R. Ealy, "Medical Missionary II," *New Mexico Magazine*, 32:22 *et seq.*, April, 1954. Miss Gates married J.Y. Perea at Zuñi on December 25, 1878.

[27] Testimony of David M. Easton at Dudley Court of Inquiry, May 21, 1879.

[28] S.I. Hayakawa, *Language in Thought and Action*. New York: Harcourt, Brace and Company, 1949, pp. 196–197.

10.
The Federal Government Intervenes

The Denver Westerners Monthly Roundup, September, 1960

In the years following the Civil War, Lincoln County, New Mexico, fell under the domination of L.G. Murphy & Co. On June 26, 1871, Emil Fritz, a partner in the firm, died at his parents' home in Stuttgart, Germany. As part of his estate, he left an insurance policy for $10,000 with his brother, Charles, and his sister, Emilie Scholand, as heirs. The policy was retained by Murphy, who alleged that Fritz owed the firm an amount far in excess of its value. The insurance company, however, raised difficulties about making payment, and a Lincoln lawyer, Alexander A. McSween, was finally retained to go to New York City to investigate the situation. Upon obtaining a settlement, he paid some of the expenses which had been incurred and placed the balance to his personal account in an Illinois bank. He then returned to Lincoln, but on December 18, 1877, again set out for the East, without having made a settlement of his accounts with the heirs.

Allegedly at the instance of James J. Dolan, who had taken over the management of Murphy & Co., Mrs. Emilie Fritz Scholand, sister of Emil Fritz, thereupon had him halted at Las Vegas and placed under arrest. In due course, he was taken to Mesilla for a hearing before Judge Warren Bristol.[1] The attorney protested that he had made his intention to return to the States public well in advance of his departure, had left behind him in Lincoln assets more than sufficient to cover all of his debts, and was ready to settle with the administrators of the estate at any time.[2] The heirs maintained that McSween had actually gone to New York upon private business and pleasure and had then demanded that the estate pay all his expenses; that he had disbursed monies from the estate without authority to do so; that at least one of these disbursements was evidently a fraud; that he had been notified that his services were no longer required, but that he had persistently evaded all attempts to obtain a settlement.[3] Judge Bristol placed the defendant under $8,000 bond and remanded him to the April term of court in Lincoln.

All of this was largely tactical maneuvering in a deadly serious struggle for power. In the winter 1877–78, McSween had allied himself with John H. Tunstall, a local merchant and rancher, in an effort to wrest control of Lincoln County from Murphy, Dolan, and their partner, John H. Riley. The duo were backed by, and appear to have been "front men" for John S. Chisum, a cattle baron who desired the county for his range and who had a happy faculty for being elsewhere when trouble was rampant. Once back in Lincoln, McSween wasted no time in striking back at his tormentor. One of his first moves was to circulate a petition requesting the removal of Dolan as postmaster. The records of the Post Office Department for this period have been destroyed,[4] and all that is known of the situation is contained in a published excerpt from a report made to that Department by Special Agent Charles Adams:

> The charges contained in the petition are not true in the main, and were gotten up by a man (McSween) to injure Mr. Dolan, the petition being signed by one person in his employ. Since this petition was sent to you, and even before I could in person visit the office, a gang of robbers and murderers, led by this man McSween, had virtually accomplished the purpose of driving Dolan out of the country, and, under the protection of the military authority at Fort Stanton, N.M., he had tried to discharge his duties. At least a dozen men have been murdered by this gang, all being friends of Dolan, and it was for some time extremely hazardous to travel in that part of New Mexico for any person in sympathy with Dolan or his friends, unless protected by soldiers. The law of Congress has taken this protection from parties needing it, under the posse comitatus clause of the army bill, and in consequence the whole county of Lincoln has virtually been turned over to a gang of cut throats. The civil authorities are powerless, the sheriff himself having been killed by the gang, and Dolan has sold his business and left the country. It is a long story of murder and retaliation, and if it was not that the person recommended (Mr.

> Walz) is a stranger and may satisfy both parties, I would recommend the discontinuance of the office. Under no circumstances could I recommend this petition of McSween be considered.[5]

Long before the publication of this report, McSween had opened an assault on a second front. This time, his target was Frederick C. Godfroy,[6] who was agent for the Mescalero Apaches and friendly to the Dolan interests. In February, 1878, McSween began a campaign against him. He wrote Secretary of the Interior Carl Schurz, charging that Godfroy sold supplies destined for the Indians to Dolan & Co., with the result that the Apaches were forced to depredate on the citizens. He recommended that Godfroy be removed and that Robert A. Widenmann be appointed in his stead.[7] Widenmann,[8] the manager of the Tunstall store, also wrote Schurz, alleging that supplies provided for the Indians were sold at the Dolan store, that the firm was furnishing stolen cattle on its government beef contracts, and was diluting their flour with bran.[9] To the Presbyterian Board of Missions, McSween complained that Godfroy, a nominee of that Board, hired only Catholics, and was locally known as the "Presbyterian fraud."[10]

Tunstall, a naive young Englishman, injected himself into the fray by writing letters to the newspapers implying that Sheriff William Brady had diverted county tax receipts to the benefit of Dolan & Co. Apparently, his charge was completely mendacious, since Territorial Treasurer Antonio Ortiz y Salazar confirmed that Brady's accounts were in order. If so, Tunstall had little time to regret his cavalier handling of the truth. On February 18, 1878, he was killed by a sheriff's posse, allegedly while resisting service of an attachment on his property.[11]

At the April term of the grand jury, the majority of the members, under Foreman Joseph H. Blazer, signed a report written by Juan B. Patrón alleging that the Indians were being systematically robbed by their agent and were forced to steal from and murder the citizens. Godfroy immediately demanded an investigation. Colonel E.C. Watkins, U.S. Indian inspector, was ordered to report on the situation. The colonel arrived at the reservation on Jue 13, 1878, and carefully examined the records of the agency. In a long letter to his superior, Commissioner E.A. Hayt, he stated that he had found Godfroy was forced to pay exorbitant rent for entirely unsuitable quarters leased from Blazer. He considered the Agency poorly located, but observed that the Indians were quiet, well disposed, and very much attached to their agent. He was especially complimentary regarding the school conducted by Godfroy's daughter, Katherine, and evaluated Godfroy's management of the Indians as "eminently successful."[12]

Watkins submitted 46 affidavits from witnesses he had interrogated. He commented that he had had a bit of difficulty getting in touch with McSween, "the head and moving spirit of a Banditti," because the attorney had assumed that the military escort furnished for Watkins' protection by Lieutenant Colonel N.A.M. Dudley, 9th Cavalry, commanding Fort Stanton, was a sheriff's posse and had fled to the mountains.

Dudley, his adjutant, 2nd Lieutenant Samuel S. Pague, 15th Infantry, and Assistant Surgeon David M. Appel[13] reported that they had personally visited the agency and that the Indians were quiet and perfectly satisfied with their condition. Dudley warned that McSween was a dangerous, unreliable man whose reputation was very bad and who could not be believed under oath where his own interests were concerned.[14] Even those who had signed the majority report of the grand jury admitted that they had no personal knowledge of any depredations by the Indians and had acted largely on the basis of testimony taken from James H. Farmer and Stephen Stanley, both of whom had since left the county. These charges, Watkins concluded, "were manifestly false."

All concerned freely conceded that Godfroy had loaned government supplies to Dolan & Co., Dr. Blazer, and Pat Coughlin [Coghlan], but contended that this sort of cooperation between agents and traders was a common practice on all reservations, and that the supplies had invariably been returned. They flatly denied that Godfroy had made any personal profit from these exchanges, or that the Indians had suffered in any way as a result of them. The weakness in their argument was that no bookkeeping entries were made of any of these loans, which made the transactions both "inexcusable and suspicious."

Chisum had presented a claim against the government for $47,000 for reimbursement for horses and cattle allegedly stolen by the Apaches. This claim was also carefully investigated. Jessie J. Evans, whom Watkins characterized as being "a notorious horse thief" but "having the reputation of telling the truth," Andrew Boyle and others made affidavits that McSween had offered to buy cattle without asking questions about their origin, provided only that they did not belong to Chisum. Evans, Frank Baker, Tom Hill, Frank Rivers, Henry Goodman, Sam Blendon, Jerry Blendon, Charles Wilson, Jim McDaniels,[15] William Young, Dick Swift, Marion Turner, James Reynolds, and one Teaugne or Tagne were specifically mentioned as being among those whom Chisum had hired. Watkins' conclusion minced no words:

> I think the evidence shows conclusively that in the matter of horse stealing Mr. Chism is far ahead of the Indians and that a balance should be struck in their favor....The testimony shows conclusively that John S. Chism, whose agent and advisor McSween was, systematically robbing the Indians of their horses, through the instrumentality of men whom he hired for the purpose.[16]

His investigation was cut short by orders assigning him duties in connection with the removal of the Utes and Arapahoes from Cimarron and Abiquiu. He therefore requested Frank Warner Angel, a special agent of the Department of Justice and of the Department of the Interior, and Lieutenant Colonel Dudley to make an accurate count of the number of Indians on the reservation. Godfroy had been drawing supplies for 1,150 Indians. When Angel and Captain Henry Carroll, 9th Cavalry, reported that they had actually counted only 373, Watkins concluded that issues had been made on a false basis and recommended that Godfroy be dismissed at once.[17]

The investigation was continued by Angel, who took a number of additional affidavits which corroborated the statements made to Watkins but which shed little new light on the situation. Angel was inclined to believe that perjury had been committed on both sides. He expressed the opinion that Godfroy "was the best indian agent that the government had so far as control and care of the Indians are concerned," but regretfully arrived at the conclusion that by reporting a fraudulent number of Indians, he had been able to appropriate and sell vast quantities of government property to his personal benefit. In view of the agent's outstanding record in dealing with the Apaches themselves, he recommended that he be permitted to resign.[18]

Godfroy fought vigorously to retain his post. He maintained that he had been innocent of any wrong doing and that he was actually the victim of A.A. McSween, a "notorious Scoundrel," an "unprincipled petty fogging lawyer," and leader of the "McSween Cutthroats," who had committed murder at the agency and had stolen the government's animals. On a salary of only $1,500, he pleaded, he had not been able to lay up a cent and his situation was difficult in the extreme.[19] His protestations proved to be in vain. His superiors made no recommendation for clemency in their reviews of his case and on August 2, 1878, President Rutherford B. Hayes suspended the unfortunate agent from his position.[20] Early in March, 1879, S.A. Russell arrived at South Fork to take charge of the reservation.

Less than a year later, Commissioner Hayt himself was summarily dismissed from office. "Mr. Hayt," commented the New York *Tribune*, "has made a few friends and many enemies since he has been in office. As he has judged others harshly so have they judged him."[21] Probably, Godfroy felt that he was at least partially vindicated by Hayt's removal.

Vital as this investigation was to Godfroy, it was only an incident in Angel's work. The continued disturbances in Lincoln and Colfax counties had resulted in a deluge of complaints to the federal government. With the murder of Tunstall, these took on an international aspect, as the British ambassador unceasingly pressed for a full investigation of the killing and for compensation for Tunstall's parents for his death and the destruction of his property. Eventually, Angel was sent to examine and report upon the situation.

Little is known of his background and what is does not make it evident why he was selected to carry out this task. Unfortunately, his original instructions cannot be located in the National Archives,[22] but their general tenor is indicated by two of his reports:

> Under your instructions I visited New Mexico for the purpose of ascertaining if there was any truth in the repeated complaints made to the Department as to the fraud incompetency and corruption of United States officials....
>
> I have investigated charges against two Indian Agents, U.S. District Attorney, Surveyor General, the Governor, the Tunstall murder and the cause of the troubles in Lincoln County....[23]

He had also looked into the matter of the Una de Gato Grant and the murder of Pierre Buisson.[24] That his task was no easy one is seen from his statement that

> I was met by every opposition possible by the United States civil officials and every obstacle thrown in my way by them to prevent a full and complete examination—with one exception and that of the surveyor general who not only sought but insisted on a full and thorough examination....[25]

The private notebook in which Angel recorded his uncensored opinions of the individuals he met on his travels through the territory is still preserved in the files of the William Henry Smith Memorial Library of Indiana Historical Society, and provides the present day reader with fascinating insights into his personal impressions of most of the individuals who played leading roles in the troubles in Lincoln.

Angel arrived in Lincoln itself about the middle of May, 1878, and proceeded to collect literally hundreds of pages of testimony. The opening paragraphs of his report on the condition of affairs in that county in effect summarize his findings:

> The history of Lincoln County has been one of blood shed from the day of its organization.
>
> These troubles have existed for years with occasional outbreaks, each one being more severe than the other.
>
> L.G. Murphy & Co., had the monopoly of all business in the County; controlled government contracts, and used their power to oppress and grind out all they could from the farmers, and force those who were opposed to them to leave the county.
>
> This has resulted in the formation of two parties, one led by Murphy & Co. and the other by McSween (now dead). Both have done many things contrary to law, both violated the law. McSween, I firmly believe, acted conscientiously—Murphy & Co. for private gain and revenge.[26]

He went on to recommend that the governor of New Mexico be given assistance in enforcing the law and protecting property, pointing out that the territory had no militia and the outlaws were in such firm control of the county that it was impossible even to hold court within its boundaries.

In the matter of Tunstall's murder, Angel reached three conclusions:

> The cause of Tunstall's death was the enmity of a certain faction in Lincon County.
>
> Tunstall had been shot in cold blood, not while resisting an officer of the law, by two of the following: William Morton, Jessie Evans, Tom Hill.
>
> The death of Tunstall was not brought about by lawless and corrupt conduct of United States officials.[27]

U.S. District Attorney Thomas B. Catron appears to have presented a particularly thorny problem for Angel, as he continually dissembled and repeatedly sought extensions of a time to enable him "to gather evidence." When the investigator finally submitted a written "Interrogatory" to him, Catron retorted that the affidavits on which it was based were simply an electioneering ruse on the part of his Democratic opponents. He averred that he could answer every allegation in them perfectly and convince every candid mind that there is no reasonable foundation for the charges if only he were given sufficient time to prepare his answers.[28, 29] Unfortunately, many of the pertinent records, including the "Interrogatory," the affidavits Catron filed in reply, a number of affidavits executed by McSween supporters, and Angel's first report concerning the charges against Governor Samuel B. Axtell, appear to have disappeared from the files of the National Archives.[30] It is, however, a matter of record that Dudley refused to certify to the attorney general of the United States that certain of the parties who made charges against Catron were unreliable and unprincipled men, on the grounds that the individuals in question were unknown to him. This brought on a furious quarrel between the attorney and the officer he had once defended so successfully, culminating in Catron's threat to volunteer his services to prosecute certain legal charges against Dudley if he were not employed for that purpose.[31] It is also a matter of record that Angel concluded that the Una de Gato Grant was a fraud, and that it had been engineered by Catron.[32]

While Catron temporized, Senator Samuel B. Elkins worked furiously on his behalf in Washington. His efforts proved unavailing. The pressure became too great to be withstood and on October

10, 1878, Catron submitted his resignation to the Department of Justice. His successor, Sidney M. Barnes, took his oath of office on February 4, 1879, with a stern injunction from Attorney General Charles Devens to use his influence to have the murder of Tunstall fully investigated and those implicated punished—an injunction which he signally failed to heed.

Axtell made a very poor impression upon Angel. The latter recorded in his notebook that the governor was "Conceited. Egotisical. Easily flattered. Tool unwittedly of the Ring. Goes off 'half cocked.'" In his report, he made a detailed analysis of twelve allegations [against] that official in connection with the Colfax County and the Lincoln County troubles. He concluded that

> The Governor has taken strictly partisan action in the troubles in Lincoln County.
>
> He had refused to listen to the complaints of the people of that county.
>
> The fact that Dolan's partner, John H. Riley, had loaned him $1800 in 1876 may have influenced his subsequent action.
>
> He had arbitrarily removed Justice of Peace Wilson.
>
> He had artbitrarily removed Sheriff John Copeland and appointed a Dolan-Riley leader, G.W. Peppin, sheriff.
>
> His actions had increased rather than quieted the Lincoln County troubles.
>
> He had appointed officials "who were supported by the worst outlaws and murderers that the territory could produce."
>
> He had knowingly appointed a badman (Peppin) to office.
>
> "He was a tool of designing men, weak and arbitrary in exercising the functions of his office."
>
> There were no substantial facts to show that he was a Mormon.
>
> He had "conspired to murder innocent and law abiding citizens" (Clay Allison and his friends) because "they opposed his wishes and were exerting their influence against him."
>
> "He arbitrarily refused to restore the courts to Colfax County and refused to listen to the petitions of the people of that county for the restoration thereof."[33]

Axtell protested that he had gone to Lincoln in person immediately upon receipt of word of the murder of Tunstall, and insisted that the situation there had worsened only because McSween refused to follow his advice and act according to law. He contended that Wilson had not in fact ever been a justice of the peace, and that Copeland had failed to file the bond required by law, which made it the governor's duty to remove him. Peppin, a respected resident of the county, had been appointed upon the advice of District Attorney William L. Rynerson, and his services had been praiseworthy. His loan from Riley, he averred, had been repaid in 1876.[34] In a later letter, Axtell replied to the charges made against him in regard to affairs in Colfax County. He denied that there was any conspiracy to murder Allison, alleging that it had been planned to use only as much force as was necessary to effect his arrest. So far as the courts were concerned, he had supported their return to the country just as soon as peace and good order had been restored. His defense was summed up in his final paragraph:

> Whatever I have done in Colfax and Lincoln counties I have done with a sincere desire to restore order and preserve the public peace. I have never taken any interest whatever in party politics in this territory. I have gone home to Ohio every year to vote and have considered my relation to the people of this territory simply official. My family are not here nor have I any property here. I repeat again, I am in no way whatever connected with any personal cliques in New Mexico.[35]

The evidence against him was too damning. Angel advised the secretary of the interior that Axtell was "not fit to be entrusted with any power whatever." "It is seldom," he added, "that history states more corruption, fraud, mismanagement, plots and murders, than New Mexico, has been the theatre under the administration of Governor Axtell."[36]

This was not the first time the governor had been under heavy fire. In 1877, he had successfully defended himself against charges filed against him with the secretary of the interior rising out of his actions in affairs in Colfax County.[37, 38, 39] This time, he was not so fortunate. Angel arrived home on August 24 and settled down to write his reports. Almost immediately, however, he was summoned to Washington to give a verbal account of his findings. Upon hearing what he had to say, Secretary Schurz immediately wrote to the president: "I telegraphed you an hour ago about the New Mexico and the St. Louis business. After listening to Mr. Angels verbal report, it became clear to my mind that we ought to make a change in the Governorship of N.M. the sooner the better, and as Gen. Wallace has indicated his willingness to serve, we ought to have him on the spot as speedily as possible."[40] President Hayes concurred in the Secretary's recommendation. On September 4, Schurz sent Wallace an order appointing him governor of the territory of New Mexico and Axtell's political career was at an end.[41]

ACKNOWLEDGMENTS

The writer is indebted to Miss Alice J. Pickup, librarian, The Buffalo Historical Society; Rutherford D. Rogers, chief of the Reference Department, New York Public Library; Mrs. M.K. Comes, reference librarian, Free Public Library of Jersey City, N.J.; Watt P. Marchman, director, The Hayes Memorial Library; and members of the staff of the National Archives for their assistance in preparation of this paper.

NOTES

[1] Rasch, "The Rise of the House of Murphy, op. cit. [See Chapter 1.]

[2] Las Cruces *Eco del Rio Grande*, January 24, 1878.

[3] Silver City *The Grant County Herald*, February 9, 1878.

[4] Meyer H. Fishbein to P.J. Rasch, December 2, 1957.

[5] Santa Fe *Weekly New Mexican*, August 3, 1878.

[6] Godfroy was born in Monroe, Michigan, on May 15, 1828. He died at Plattsburg Barracks, New York, May 15, 1885. The records of the time frequently refer to him as Major Godfroy, but neither the National Archives nor the adjutant general of the state of Michigan have any record of an officer by this name.

[7] Alex A. McSween to Carl Schurz, February 11, 1878. In selected Documents Concerning the Investigation of Charges Against F.C. Godfroy, Indian Agent at the Mescalero Apache Agency, New Mexico. Record Groups 75 and 48, National Archives.

[8] Widenmann was born in Georgia on January 24, 1849. He died in Haverstraw, New York, on April 15, 1930.

[9] Robt. A. Widenmann to C. Schurz, March 11, 1878. Record Groups 75 and 48.

[10] A.A. McSween to Lowry (John C. Lowrie), February 25, 1878.

Record Groups 75 and 48.

[11] Rasch,"Prelude to War," op. cit. [See Chapter 5.]

[12] E.E. Watkins to Sir (E.A. Hayt), June 27, 1878. Record Groups 75 and 48.

[13] Appel and Miss Godfroy were married at the Agency on February 13, 1879.

[14] N.A.M. Dudley to E.C. Watkins, June 20, 1878. Affidavit No. 42 with E.C. Watkins to Sir.

[15] For a brief account of the life of this individual, see Philip J. Rasch, "The Chronicle of Jim McDaniels, *Corral Dust*, IV:28 et seq., December, 1959.

[16] E.C. Watkins to E.A. Hayt, July 14, 1878. Record Groups 75 and 48.

[17] Ibid.

[18] Frank Warner Angel to C. Schurz, October 2, 1878. Records of the Bureau of Indian Affairs. Report to Frank W. Angel, October 2, 1878, Concerning F.C. Godfroy, Indian Agent at the Mescalero Apache Agency, New Mexico. Record Group 75.

[19] F.C. Godfroy to Dear Judge (I.T. Christiancy), September 6, 1878. In Records of the Office of the Secretary of the Interior, Appointment Division, Letter Received. Record Group 48.

[20] R.B. Hayes to Fred C. Godfroy, August 2, 1878. Records of the Bureau of Indian Affairs. Letters Received, New Mexico, 1878, P-678. In National Archives.

[21] New York *Tribune*, January 30, 1880.

[22] Marion Johnson, Reference Service Report, June 27, 1955.

[23] Frank Warner Angel to Chas. Devens, August 9, 1878. Report in the Matter of the Troubles in Lincoln County, New Mexico. General Records of the Department of Justice, Records Relating to Frank W. Angel, Record Group 60.

[24] Philip J. Rasch, "The Gory Case of Pierre Buisson." Los Angeles Westerners *Branding Iron*, June, 1959, n.p.

[25] Frank Warner Angel to C. Schurz, In the Matter of the Investigation of the Charges Against S.B. Axtell, Governor of New Mexico. Records of the Office of the Secretary of the Interior, Appointment Division. Letters Received, Territorial Governors New Mexico, 1849–78. Record Group 48.

[26] Frank Warner Angel to Charles Devens, October 7, 1878. In the Matter of the Lincoln County Troubles. Record Group 60.

[27] Frank Warner Angel to Charles Devens, undated. In the Matter of the Cause and Circumstances of the Death of John H. Tunstall, a British Subject. Record Group 60.

[28] T.B. Catron to Charles Devens, September 13, 1878. Classified File No. 44-4-8-3. Correspondence relating to the Lincoln County, New Mexico, trouble (1878–1879). In National Archives.

[29] T.B. Catron to F.W. Angel, August 10, 1878. Record Group 60.

[30] Bess Glenn to P.J. Rasch, April 24, 1957, and February 5, 1958; Jane F. Smith to P.J. Rasch, February 12, 1958.

[31] N.A.M. Dudley to Charles Devens, September 16, 1879. In National Archives. For a brief account of Dudley's life, see P.J. Rasch, "A Note on N.A.M. Dudley," Los Angeles Westerners *Brand Book*, 1949, pp. 207–214.

[32] Frank Warner Angel to Charles Devens. In the Matter of the Una de Gato Grant. Records of the General Land Office. In National Archives.

[33] Angel to Schurz, In the Matter of the Investigation of the Charges Against S.B. Axtell, Governor of New Mexico, op. cit.

[34] S.B. Axtell, undated, unaddressed letter (to F.W. Angel about August, 1878). Records of the Office of the Secretary of the Interior. In National Archives.

[35] S.B. Axtell to F.W. Angel, September 11, 1878. Records of the Office of the Secretary of the Interior.

[36] Angel to Schurz, In the Matter of the Investigation of the Charges Against S.B. Axtell, Governor of New Mexico, op. cit.

[37] W.B. Matchett and M.E. McPherson to the Secretary of the Interior, March, 1877. Record Group 48. Records of the Office of the Secretary of the Interior, Appointments Division. Letters Received Concerning Samuel B. Axtell. In National Archives.

[38] S.B. Axtell to Carl Schurz, May 30, 1877. Record Group 48.

[39] Samuel B. Axtell to Carl Schurz, June 14, 1877. Record Group 48.

[40] C. Schurz to Mr. President Rutherford B. Hayes, August 31, 1878. In Rutherford B. Hayes Memorial Library.

[41] Rasch, "Exit Axtell: Enter Wallace," op. cit. [See Chapter 15.]

11.
Frank Warner Angel, Special Agent

Corral Dust, Potomac Corral of the Westerners, April 1962

In 1878, complaints of political corruption in the territory of New Mexico became so numerous and so vociferous that the Federal government was forced into long overdue action. One Frank Warner Angel (records exist in which he signed his middle name as Warren) was instructed to investigate the situation. His reports resulted in the prompt removal of the governor of the territory and directly affected the careers of a number of its most prominent citizens. He thus ensured for himself a permanent niche in the history of that state, yet, curiously enough, the earlier events of his life and the reasons which led to his selection for this important mission are all but unknown.

Angel was born somewhere in the state of New York on June 30, 1845, the son of William H. and Harriet Angel. He was admitted to the bar in New York City in 1869, but what law school he attended, if any, is unknown, and he was never a member of the Association of the Bar of the City of New York. The fact that the New Mexican papers referred to him as Judge Angel suggests that he may have had experience on the bench, but at the time of his assignment to this investigation, he was engaged in private practice, with his office at 61 Wall Street. Except for this scanty data, his life up to the year 1878 remains a closed book.

In April of that year, Angel was appointed a special agent of the departments of the Interior and of Justice, and "authorized and directed to make certain investigations in matters in New Mexico in which the United States is concerned."[1] His original instructions cannot be located in the National Archives,[2] but it is evident from his reports that he was to investigate the murder of John H. Tunstall;[3] examine the charges which had been preferred against Frederick C. Godfroy, agent of the Mescalero Apaches,[4] Thomas B. Catron, United States district attorney, Samuel B. Axtell, governor of the territory, and the surveyor general; and to inquire into the conditions surrounding the Una de Gato land grant. Later, he was instructed to report on the murder of Pierre Buisson.[5]

Angel arrived in Santa Fe the end of April or the first week in May, and spent the latter part of May and most of June in Lincoln County. His final report on the charges against Axtell sheds a clear light on the reception which he received.[6] [See Chapter 10, p. 142.]

In spite of this opposition—or perhaps because of it—he collected nearly 2,000 pages of testimony, much of which has since disappeared from the National Archives.[7] On August 17, President Hayes decided the problems involved were so serious that prompt corrective action was mandatory, and Angel was summoned to the capitol to report in person. His findings so shocked Secretary of the Interior Carl Schurz that he recommended to the president that an immediate change be made in the governorship of the territory. As a result, Axtell was replaced by Lew Wallace.[8]

Presumably as a reward for a difficult job well done, Angel was appointed assistant to the attorney of the United States for the eastern district of New York (Brooklyn), a post which he held until his resignation early in 1886. After several changes of address during the next few years, Angel settled down at 320 Whitson St., Jersey City. He took an active interest in Republican politics, which did not go unappreciated by the party chieftains. On January 1, 1902, Angel was appointed a member of the Board of Fire Commissioners of Jersey City. Apparently, he later resigned from this board to accept the post of commissioner of appeals for the regulation of tax assessments, a position which he held until 1905. Angel died of a cerebral hemorrhage on March 15, 1906, after an illness lasting nearly two years. He was survived by his wife, Sadie W. Angel, and a married daughter, a Mrs. Van Dien. Interment was in the Greenwood Cemetery.

There is, of course, nothing in his later career to suggest what background he possessed for the New Mexican assignment or why he was selected for it. Perhaps someday one of the active members of the Potomac Corral will blow the dust off the pertinent documents in the National Archives and uncover the data necessary to clarify this minor mystery.

ACKNOWLEDGMENTS

The writer is particularly indebted to Rutherford D. Rogers, chief of the Reference Department, New York Public Library; Mrs. M.K. Comes, reference librarian, Free Public Library, New Jersey; Miss E. Marie Becker, reference librarian, The New York Historical Society, and Miss Louise W. Turpin, chief, History Division, Brooklyn Public Library, for their assistance in the preparation of the above material.

NOTES

[1] Charles Devens to John E. Sherman, April 16, 1878. Department of Justice *Instruction Book H*, p. 44, Record Group 60, National Archives.

[2] Marion Johnson, personal communication, June 27, 1955.

[3] Rasch,"Prelude to War," op. cit. [See Chapter 5.]

[4] Rasch, "The Federal Government Intervenes," op. cit. [See Chapter 10.]

[5] Rasch, "The Gory Case of Pierre Buisson," op. cit.

[6] Frank Warner Angel to C. Schurz, October 3, 1878. Records of the Office of the Secretary of the Interior, Appointment Division. Letters Received. Territorial Governors New Mexico 1849–78. Record Group 48, National Archives.

[7] Bess Glenn, personal communications, June 27, 1955, August 2, 1955, December 13, 1955, April 24, 1957, and February 5, 1958. Jane F. Smith, personal communication, July 14, 1954.

[8] Rasch, "Exit Axtell: Enter Wallace," op. cit. [See Chapter 15.]

12.
The Men at Fort Stanton

The English Westerners' Brand Book, April 1961

Through the tapestry of the Lincoln County War runs the blue thread representing the officers and troops of the United States Army stationed at nearby Fort Stanton. The student of these troubles continually reads of their comings and goings—guarding the roads, protecting the county officials, preserving the peace, recovering herds of stolen cattle, pursuing rustlers—but almost never does he become aware of them as individuals. With the single exception of the commanding officer, Lieutenant Colonel Nathan Augustus Monroe Dudley, 9th Cavalry, none of them seems to have been the object of a biographical sketch. And even Dudley's portrait needs refurbishing, as it was drawn before the War Department removed the "restricted" status from certain extremely important documents bearing on his career. Yet, since at least some material about him is available,[1] he shall be ignored here in favour of brief descriptions of his officers, and a curiously mixed assortment they will be found.

Assistant Surgeon **Daniel Mitchell Appel** was born in Pennsylvania October 28, 1854, graduated from Jefferson Medical College in 1875, and entered the Army in 1876. Appel's professional services were in great demand during the Lincoln County War. He tended the wounded after the battle at Blazer's Mill (and was afterwards recalled by George Coe as "Dr. Gordon"[2]) and the Five Days' Battle, as well as on numerous other occasions, and was frequently delegated by Dudley to make investigations and reports of the situation in the county.

With Captains Purington and Blair, he visited Lincoln on July 17,

1878, to investigate the alleged attempted shooting of Private Berry Robinson by the McSween Party. Learning that one of the sheriff's posse, Charles Crawford, was lying wounded on a hillside, Appel and Blair went to assist him, whereupon they came under fire from men in the Montaño house. With Captain Blair, Appel rescued Mrs. McSween, the Ealys, and Miss Gates, together with Ealy's personal property, from the burning McSween home at the height of the Five Days' Battle.

Appel married Miss H. Kate Godfroy, daughter of Frederick C. Godfroy, agent of the Mescalero Apaches, at that agency on February 3, 1879. That summer, he appeared as one of the witnesses at the Dudley Court of Inquiry, where, among other things, he testified that Colonel Hatch had told him he did not believe Governor Wallace could sustain his charges against Dudley.[3]

Later, Appel was transferred to Fort Bayard and was responsible for its conversion to a tuberculosis hospital, winning widespread praise for the procedures which he instituted. After leaving New Mexico, he served as chief surgeon of the Central Department, with headquarters at Chicago. He had experience as a medical supply officer in the Philippines for a number of years, but was in charge of a hospital on the mainland during the Spanish-American War.

By 1914, Appel was the second ranking colonel in the medical corps, and was chief surgeon of the Hawaiian Department. On the night of April 21, he attended a party at the Young Hotel, Honolulu. It was remarked by his friends that he appeared unwell, but was one of the liveliest and most jovial members of the gathering. Appel returned home about 11 p.m. and apparently read in bed for a while before falling asleep. About noon the next day, the Japanese maid entered his room and found him dead. His passing was attributed to heart failure.[4]

Captain **Thomas Blair**, Company H, 15th Infantry. Thomas Blair Nichols was born in Scotland about 1838. He emigrated to the United States in 1861 and dropped the name Nichols. As Blair, he enlisted in the Army in 1865 and won a commission in 1867. At the time of the death of Colonel Gordon Granger, 15th Infantry, in Santa Fe in 1876, Blair was regimental adjutant and accompanied the body east. He was present at the Salt War in San Elizario, Texas, in December, 1877, where his efforts to relieve the besieged Texas Rangers were something less than gallant.[5]

In the fall of 1878, Blair went to Kentucky and married the widowed Mrs. Granger. The happy couple returned to Santa Fe, where Blair assumed command of Fort Marcy. Upon his promotion to captain, he was transferred to Fort Stanton. Perhaps because of his comparatively senior rank, Dudley employed Blair a good deal in investigations of conditions in Lincoln County. He examined the troubles at San Patricio, the murder of Morris Bernstein, and in other ways viewed the fighting from a ringside seat.

A few months later, the American consul at Glasgow forwarded papers charging Blair with bigamy. He emphatically denied the charge, admitting that he was the father of a Mrs. Nichol's children, but denying that he had ever married her. Blair obtained leave to go to Washington to explain the matter. Evidently, his excuses were far from satisfactory, since he was ordered placed under arrest and confined at Governors Island pending trial by court-martial. Blair at first attempted to brazen it out by pleading "not guilty," but the evidence was so overwhelming that he changed his plea to "guilty." He was promptly sentenced to be dismissed from the Army, the order being officially promulgated on March 6, 1879. Blair was released from confinement and promptly departed for Canada, there to disappear into obscurity.[6]

Captain **Henry Carroll**, Company F, 9th Cavalry, was born in New York City on May 20, 1838. After service as an enlisted man, he was commissioned a second lieutenant, 3rd Cavalry, in 1864. He was transferred to the 9th Cavalry in 1867 and immediately found himself fighting Indians in Texas. The highlight of this stage of his career was the attack by 100 men under his command on 300 Indians encamped near the headwaters of the Salt Fork of the Brazos River on September 16, 1869. Twenty-five Indians were killed or wounded, at a cost of three soldiers wounded.

At the outbreak of the Lincoln County War, his company was stationed at Fort Union and was not ordered to Fort Stanton until June 1, 1878. Almost at once, he undertook a very active role in the troubles. He was in hot pursuit of McSween's Regulators following the San Patricio affair and no doubt would have captured them if he had not been recalled when Dudley received word that Congress had forbade the use of troops as a *posse comitatus*. He was later assigned to duty at Roswell, being charged with patrolling the roads between Roswell and Fort Sumner and between Roswell and Seven

Rivers. Early in 1879, he recovered nearly 300 stolen cattle, of which 138 belonged to the estate of the murdered John H. Tunstall,[7] and were turned over to Mrs. McSween.

His loyalty to Dudley appears more than doubtful. While in temporary command of Fort Stanton following the latter's removal, he refused to permit his erstwhile superior to copy official records which were essential to the latter's defence of his actions,[8] and it is noteworthy that he was not called upon to testify at Dudley's Court of Inquiry. His cooperation with Governor Lew Wallace was almost subservient, leading that worthy to request Colonel Edward Hatch, 9th Cavalry, commanding the District of New Mexico, to leave him in command of the fort, since, "His action of late has commended him so greatly that he appears to be the man for the place."[9] Hatch, however, turned the command back to Captain George A. Purington, 9th Cavalry.

During the night of March 19, 1879, Jessie J. Evans and William Campbell, under arrest at Fort Stanton in connection with the murder of Huston I. Chapman, Mrs. McSween's attorney, bribed a recruit known as "Texas Jack" and silently stole away. Texas Jack was soon retaken. The newspapers alleged that this man was from Carroll's company, but a careful review of his muster roll covering this period reveals no deserter who could possibly be the guilty man.

During the Civil War, Carroll had been wounded during operations on Morris Island, South Carolina. Two more wounds were inflicted by the Apaches, but the contemporary accounts of what happened differ so widely that it is almost impossible to reconcile them. Apparently, Carroll was in pursuit of Victorio. On April 6, 1880, he sent Lieutenant Conline and 31 men of the 9th Cavalry to scout ahead of the main body. Late that afternoon, the scouts were attacked by a band of Mescaleros under El Tuerto, also known as Pablo. The Indians withdrew during the night and Conline fell back on Carroll, whom he found at Hembrilla, about 20 miles southwest of Tularosa. The following morning, the troops started up the Membrillo Canyon for water, but were ambushed. Carroll was wounded in the leg and right shoulder. Fighting continued throughout the day and that night. The troops had been without water for two days and their situation became desperate, but the following morning, reinforcements from Major Albert F. Morrow's battalion reached the scene and the Indians moved off to the south. Seven soldiers had been wounded and thirteen horses killed. Only one Indian's body was found; some accounts state it was that of El Tuerto. Carroll's wounds were slow to heal and he went to Arkansas, where his family resided, on six months' sick leave. Ten years later, he was brevetted a major for gallant services in this and previous campaigns against the Indians.

In 1898, Carroll was severely wounded at San Juan Hill, Cuba, during the Spanish-American War, but again recovered, to retire the following year with the rank of brigadier general. He settled in Lawrence, Kansas, but suffered considerably from rheumatism and finally moved to Colorado Springs, Colorado, in hope that a change of climate might benefit him. On February 12, 1908, he died suddenly from blood poisoning, resulting from an ulcerated tooth. His remains were sent to the National Cemetery at Fort Leavenworth, Kansas.[10]

Captain **Casper Hauzer Conrad**, 15th Infantry, was born in Stone Ridge, New York, on March 30, 1844. He enlisted as a private in the 120th New York Volunteer Infantry on August 18, 1862, stating that he was a printer by occupation. He was honorably discharged in 1865, but secured a commission as a first lieutenant, 35th Infantry, in 1867.

Conrad arrived at Fort Stanton on December 2, 1878, so played little part in the troubles which beset that area. He was promoted to major in 1897, and died in the U.S. hospital ship *Olivette*, off Santiago, Cuba, on August 15, 1898. The National Archives possesses a 19-page biography compiled by members of the family.

First-Lieutenant **Byron Dawson**, Company M, 9th Cavalry, was born in Johnson County, Indiana, August 29, 1838. He enrolled in the 3rd Cavalry, 45th Regiment Indiana Volunteers, as a 1st sergeant in 1862, and was promoted to second lieutenant on September 1, 1864. He is described as 5'11" tall, with grey eyes, black hair, and a dark complexion. He was mustered out as a captain and accepted an appointment in the regular army as a second lieutenant, 9th Cavalry, in 1866.

While serving in Texas, he participated in a successful attack against 300 Kiowas and Comanches near the headwaters of the main Brazos River on October 28–29, 1869, and was later brevetted captain for gallantry in this and other actions against the Indians. It was Dawson who found Chapman's body lying in the street at Lincoln, but on the whole, his company appears to have been too busy with the wily Apache to spend much time in Lincoln. This came near costing Dawson his life on September 17, 1879, when, with some 46 men of the 9th Cavalry, he rode into one of Victorio's ambushes near the headwaters of the Las Animas, about 30 miles above Hillsboro, New Mexico, and found himself unable either to advance or to retreat. Later in the morning, a mixed force of soldiers and citizens under Captain Charles D. Beyer, 9th Cavalry, appeared on the scene and supported their fellows. When night fell, the troops withdrew under cover of darkness, having lost several men killed and several others wounded, a large number of horses, the hospital train, and most of the personal baggage of the officers.[11]

Later, Dawson served under General George Crook, in campaigns against the northern Indians. He is to be seen in the photograph of Crook's staff taken at Fort Duchesne, Utah, in 1887 and published in Martin F. Schmitt's edition of Crook's *Autobiography* [University of Oklahoma Press, 1960]. Two years later, Dawson retired. His last years were passed near Indianapolis, Indiana, where he died on December 20, 1913.[12]

Second Lieutenant **James Hansell French**, 9th Cavalry, was born in Philadelphia, Pennsylvania, March 14, 1851, and graduated from the Military Academy on June 17, 1874. Apparently, he earned something of a reputation for being reckless and daring. He was posted to the 9th Cavalry and served in Texas and Colorado until August 31, 1876, when he resigned because of ill health. Two years later, he was reappointed and ordered to Fort Union, New Mexico. He was transferred to Fort Stanton in November, 1878, thus arriving after the worst of the fighting there was over.

However, it took him only to the middle of the next month to involve himself in serious trouble. While aiding Sheriff George W. Peppin in making arrests, French became embroiled in a series of bitter personal clashes with Mrs. McSween's lawyer, Huston I. Chapman, as a result of which Chapman swore out some warrants against him. Dudley promptly placed French under arrest. When he appeared in Lincoln for trial before Justice of the Peace John B. Wilson, Dudley took the precaution of sending Dawson and a detachment of men to protect him from violence. French was acquitted on a charge of feloniously entering the de Guebara [de

Guevara] home and the charge of feloniously entering the McSween house was dismissed. He waived examination on a charge of assault on Chapman and was bound over to the district court. By this time, Dudley had become convinced that the whole thing was part of a conspiracy on the part of Chapman and Mrs. McSween. He appointed a board of officers, consisting of Appel, Conrad, and Dawson, to investigate. They reported that the charges had been inspired by malice and vindictiveness against the officers stationed at Fort Stanton and recommended that no action be taken.[13] Later, the board of officers conducting the Court of Inquiry demanded by Dudley refused to receive any testimony concerning French's conduct on the grounds that the board appointed by Dudley had already taken official action on the matter.[14]

During 1879, French was actively engaged in campaigning against the Apaches. About December 1, he reached Fort Bayard and accompanied Major Morrow on his pursuit of Victorio. On January 17, 1880, Morrow came up with his quarry in the San Mateo Mountains, near Ojo Caliente. In the ensuing fight, French was killed. His body was brought to Santa Fe to be sent to Philadelphia. Somewhat smugly, the *Daily New Mexican* remarked:

> The funderal procession was one of the largest Santa Fe has ever witnessed, and that our citizens took the opportunity of paying their last respects to an officer who gallantly fell at his post, is worthy of commendation and praise....[15]

Second Lieutenant **Charles Elias Garst**, 15th Infantry, was born in Ohio August 21, 1853, and graduated from the Military Academy on June 14, 1876. He played a very minor role in the Lincoln County troubles, although he seems to have spent three weeks in the village in February and March of 1878. During his time at Fort Stanton, he wooed and won the daughter of the post trader, John C. DeLany.

Garst went on leave from the Army on July 12, 1883, still a second lieutenant, and became a missionary to Japan. His resignation from the Army was accepted on January 10, 1884, and he died in Tokyo on December 28, 1898.

Second Lieutenant **Millard Fillmore Goodwin**, Company F, 9th Cavalry, was born in the state of New York on May 25, 1852. He graduated from the Military Academy on June 14, 1872, and saw extensive service on the Texas frontier before being ordered to Fort Stanton. He seems to have been a good soldier—on one occasion, Carroll wrote, "I take pleasure in calling attention to the efficient and agreeable manner in which Lieutenant Goodwin assisted me throughout the toilsome and disagreeable march."[16] The march in question was made while Carroll was assisting Sheriff George W. Peppin in an attempt to arrest the McSween partisans following their fight against the sheriff's posse in the vicinity of San Patricio on June 27, 1878.

Goodwin played a very active role in Lincoln County, being frequently placed in command of troops ordered to assist the sheriff. It seems clear that he had but little use for the McSween faction; on one occasion, after arresting a number of that party for whom Sheriff John N. Copeland had warrants, he suggested that being placed in irons would not hurt Josiah G. "Doc" Scurlock.[17] On June 19, he led troops which surrounded Lincoln while Sheriff George Peppin searched the town. During the Five Days' Battle,[18] he served as Dudley's adjutant, and was later sent in pursuit of the murderers of Morris J. Bernstein. After the murder of Chapman, Goodwin was sent to Lincoln to maintain order, and his troops made an unsuccessful attempt to arrest Billy the Kid and Yginio Salazar. Later, the Kid warned Governor Lew Wallace, "Tell the Commanding Officer to Watch Let Goodwind he would not hesitate to do anything."[19]

Following the Lincoln troubles, Goodwin was transferred to Fort Bayard and participated in the expeditions against the Apaches. He appears to have been with Carroll during the battle with El Tuerto. Goodwin won promotion to first lieutenant, but contracted tuberculosis and was forced to go on sick leave August 1, 1882. On July 19, 1888, he passed away in Yonkers, New York.[20]

William B. Lyon, acting assisting surgeon, is something of an unknown quantity. The National Archives possesses a voluminous file on him, but the expense of having a microfilm copy made would be greater than his role in the Lincoln County troubles appears to justify. He did spend a good deal of time in Lincoln under official orders, and testified at Dudley's Court of Inquiry that the citizens of the village had exhibited especially kind feelings toward that officer.

Lyon evidently had problems of his own, since Hatch recommended on March 19, 1879, that his contract be cancelled, as "he is a person of dissipated habits, and therefore not fit for the position."[21] Lyon apparently left the Army in April, and located in Mesilla,[22] where he soon received an appointment as first lieutenant and adjutant, First Regiment of Militia. Whatever his habits, there was no question regarding his courage. On October 12 of that same year, word was received at Mesilla that the Apaches were prowling around Mason's ranch, some 30 miles from the town, and that immediate help was needed. Five Americans, including Dr. Lyon, and 11 Mexicans immediately set out. Finding no Indians at Mason's, the following morning the party started for Lloyd's ranch, about 17 miles from Colorado, N.M. Some 10 or 12 miles from the ranch, they were ambushed. W.T. Jones, probate clerk of the county, Nepumuseno Barragan, Cleto Sanches, Venceslado Lara, and Pancho Beltran were killed, the others escaping back to Mason's.

W.L. Rynerson, colonel of the First Regiment of Militia, and a large party came to their succour, and then went on to bury the bodies of the fallen. Lyon accompanied them. En route, they found a train apparently from Mexico, with the corpses of ten men scattered around. After burying these and those of Jones and his comrades, they pushed on to the Lloyd ranch, where another five bodies were found. The ranch itself was completely destroyed; every living thing—men, horses, cattle, and chickens—had been killed. The Indians had disappeared without a trace.[23, 24]

In May, 1880, Lyon was appointed deputy collector of customs at Mesilla.[25] He married the daughter of George D. Bowman, of Mesilla, and lived for a number of years in the vicinity of Las Cruces.

Second Lieutenant **Samuel Speece Pague**, Company H, 15th Infantry, was born in Ohio on April 14, 1855, and graduated from the Military Academy June 14, 1876. He went immediately to Fort Stanton, but during the latter part of 1877 and the beginning of 1878 was on duty in Texas in connection with the San Elizario riots. He must have had many fine characteristics, for Lieutenant G.W. Smith described him as "a good and noble boy."[26] At the outbreak of the Lincoln County War, Pague was serving as post adjutant at Fort Stanton. He accompanied Goodwin when he surrounded the village on June 19, but was left in command of Fort Stanton during the Five Days' Battle; hence had no opportunity to observe what transpired in the plaza. At the Dudley Court of Inquiry, Pague testified that Dudley had granted James Dolan permission to have Robert Beckwith buried at Fort Stanton and that Pague himself had read the ceremony over the body. That was the extent of his evidence; the story contained in a recent bit of nonsense by William Lee Hamlin [*The True Story of Billy the Kid*, Caldwell, Idaho, 1959] to the effect that he asked Mrs. McSween some questions which boomeranged on Dudley is simply a fraud on the unwary reader.

In March, 1879, Garst relieved Pague and the latter joined his company at Fort Marcy (Santa Fe). After leaving New Mexico, Pague served in Colorado and Dakota. In 1884, he was promoted to first lieutenant. From 1886 to 1889, he was professor of military science and tactics at Pennsylvania State College, rejoining his regiment upon completion of this tour of duty. In 1895, General Wesley Merritt reviewed the troops at Fort Sheridan. Pague was drunk when he appeared for duty and became abusive toward his commanding officer, Colonel Robert E.A. Crofton. He was arrested and placed in hospital for treatment for alcoholism. He made his escape the next day, appeared at his home, and tried to kill Colonel Crofton, whom he found discussing the situation with Mrs. Pague. A court-martial promptly followed. Considerable speculation resulted when he requested that the court be cleared while he offered his defence. Whatever it was, it was not sufficient to save him; the unfortunate soldier was sentenced to be dismissed from the army.[27] Mrs. Pague then divorced him on grounds of cruelty and returned to her parents' home in Pennsylvania.

Pague obtained employment as a draughtsman in Chicago, but drifted from one job to another, seemingly incapable of holding a position for any length of time. In July, 1899, he registered at the New Era Hotel in Chicago. Rooms were only 15¢, but he was forced to confess that he had but 10¢ to his name and obtained quarters only after the clerk offered to trust him for the other 5¢. On July 8, the unhappy man committed suicide by drinking chloral in the hotel office.[28]

Captain **George Augustus Purington**, Company H, 9th Cavalry, was born in Ohio July 21, 1837. He enlisted in the 19th Regiment Ohio Volunteer Infantry on April 22, 1861, and by the end of the Civil War was a colonel in the 2nd Regiment Ohio Volunteer Cavalry. His record shows that on March 2, 1867, he was brevetted major for gallant and meritorious service in the Battle of the Wilderness, lieutenant colonel for similar actions during the Battle of Winchester, and colonel for identical conduct during the Battle of Cedar Creek—all in all, quite a memorable day in any man's career.

During the winter of 1877 and spring of 1878, Purington was in command of Fort Stanton, and had the questionable pleasure of notifying Colonel Hatch of the outbreak of what was to become known to historians as the Lincoln County War. He stated that he had sent a detachment of troops to Lincoln to prevent destruction of property and loss of life, and requested instructions.[29] Hatch's reply emphasised that troops were not to be used to enforce civil law save by orders of the president of the United States.[30] On April 5, 1878, Purington was relieved of command of the post by Lieutenant Colonel Dudley—and thereby saved from a great deal of trouble.

On June 1, Purington's company was ordered to Roswell to disarm and disband outlaws operating in that area, but it returned to Fort Stanton on June 21, 1878. He wrote the draft of the paper requesting Dudley to go to Lincoln to protect the lives of the women and children, and rode at the head of the column when the troops entered Lincoln during the Five Days' Battle. Command of Fort Stanton again devolved upon Purington when Dudley was summarily removed, and he vigorously defended his superior's conduct at the time of the latter's court of inquiry.

In 1883, Purington transferred to the 3rd Cavalry. His last tour of duty appears to have been as commander of Jefferson Barracks, in St. Louis. He retired from the Army on July 17, 1895, and died at Metropolis, Illinois, on May 31, 1896. His remains were interred at Jefferson Barracks.[31]

Second Lieutenant **George Washington Smith**, Company H, 9th Cavalry, was born in Virginia March 11, 1837. He was commissioned a first lieutenant in the 13th Pennsylvania Volunteer Infantry on August 5, 1861. In due course, he was brevetted major for gallant and meritorious service in the Battle of Chickamauga and lieutenant colonel for similar service during the Atlanta campaign and in the Battle of Jonesboro. At some time during this period, he apparently served under and became friendly with Lew Wallace, the future governor of the territory of New Mexico.

Smith resigned on May 15, 1866, but accepted an appointment as second lieutenant, 9th Cavalry, in 1873. He appears to have seen a great deal of service against the Apaches and won the praise of the Silver City paper[32] for the untiring manner in which he pursued them.

While McSween was hiding out near the Bottomless Lakes in March, 1878, Smith took Dudley's offer of protection to him. McSween accepted, and thus arrived in Lincoln just after the killing of Brady. When the Seven Rivers men under W.H. Johnson descended on Lincoln on April 29, it was Smith and twenty men who were detailed to answer Sheriff John N. Copeland's call for help, and arrested 22 persons. Smith's "good judgement, courage and ability" were officially commended in Dudley's report of the affair.[33]

Smith was with Captain Carroll when he made a scout into Dog Canyon in August, 1878, but had the misfortune to sustain a severe injury to his left ankle when his horse fell. Carroll sent him to the Indian agency to recuperate, and it thus happened that he was present when McSween's desperadoes killed the agency clerk, Morris Bernstein. Smith immediately sent to the fort for assistance and Goodwin and 15 troopers were detailed to pursue the murderers, while Smith was ordered to protect the agency until relieved.

The Lincoln County troubles eventually simmered down, but hostile Indians gave the 9th Cavalry little rest. The year 1880 was introduced at the Mescalero agency by friction between the Apaches and some Mexicans which resulted in the Indians burning seven wagons loaded with hay. Smith and 14 men covered the twenty miles to the scene in an hour and forty-five minutes; his forced march was credited with saving the agency and the lives of those living there.[34]

On August 18, 1881, hostiles attacked the ranches in the vicinity of Lake Valley. The following afternoon, Lieutenant Smith and 19 troopers from the 9th Cavalry, accompanied by George Daly, the superintendent of a local mine, and 20 civilians, took up the trail. They were promptly ambushed in Gavallan Canyon, where Smith, Daly, two soldiers, and two civilians were killed, and a number more were wounded. The command took to the hills, losing about 30 horses and 1,000 rounds of ammunition in the process. When reinforcements arrived, Smith's body was found to have been horribly mutilated and partially burned, although the others had not been touched.

His body was interred at Fort Bayard.[35]

Since most of the officers who played leading roles in the Lincoln County troubles were members of the 9th Cavalry, it might be of interest to review briefly the history of this organisation. The regiment was formed September 21, 1866, at Greenville, Louisiana, with negro enlisted personnel. In 1869, it was distributed to posts in Texas and waged a series of vigorous campaigns against the Indians infesting that area until it was ordered to the District of New Mexico in October, 1875. Here the situation was nearly as bad: fighting was more common than peace and the Army was not always the victor. A particularly severe defeat was suffered from the hands of Victorio at the head of Las Animas Creek on September 18, 1879, but the Ninth had the final word. The regiment served under Crook as his ceaseless campaigns finally brought the Apaches under subjection and accompanied the Buell Expedition into Mexico in the operations that led to the final destruction of Victorio's band.

The contemporary southern New Mexican papers, however, made no secret of their contempt for the fighting ability of the negro troopers, and relations between the Army and the newspaper editors in Silver City, Las Cruces, and Mesilla were generally more than a little strained. Eventually, in fact, the Las Cruces *Thirty-Four* found it expedient to admit that they had "unintentionally done great injustice to the officers and men." They conceded that there was "no reason why the officers of negro regiments should be inferior to others in capacity or gallantry," but remained adamant in their contention that negro troops lacked bravery.[36]

Later in its history, the 9th Cavalry won battle honours in Cuba and in the Philippines. During World War II, it fought in North Africa and was inactivated there on March 7, 1944. In 1950, it was reactivated as the 509th Tank Battalion. At present, its only active element is the 1st Reconnaissance Squadron, 9th Cavalry, an element of the 1st Cavalry Division in Korea.[37, 38]

During the period of the Lincoln County troubles, the regiment was commanded by Colonel **Edward Hatch**. Hatch was born in Bangor, Maine, on December 23, 1832, and attended Norwich University in Vermont for two years. On August 1, 1861, he was appointed captain, Company A, Second Cavalry, Iowa Volunteers. Promotion was both regular and rapid. Hatch became a brevet major general of volunteers on December 15, 1864, for gallant and meritorious service in the battle for Franklin. Mustered out of the volunteer service in 1866, he joined the regular army, and on March 2, 1867, was brevetted a major general for gallant and meritorious service in the battle for Nashville.

After the war, he was stationed in Texas, and those who are familiar with the voluminous Congressional reports on the difficulties along the Mexican border during this period[39, 40] will grant that he could have had no easy time during these years. More germane to this paper is the fact that it was then that he clashed head on with former brevet brigadier general, Lieutenant Colonel Nathan Augustus Monroe Dudley, also of the 9th Cavalry. The cause of their animosity developed from a race riot which took place in Jefferson, Texas, on October 4, 1868, resulting in the lynching of a carpetbagger named George Smith and two of his negro henchmen. A military court was convened to try the members of the mob. During the trial, Hatch accepted the hospitality of the father of one of the prisoners, for which he was severely criticised by Dudley.[41] In 1877, Dudley found himself in command of Fort Union, New Mexico, with Hatch in command of the District. Relations between the two men deteriorated to the point that Hatch asked permission to relieve his subordinate. General John Pope, commanding the Department of the Missouri, replied that if there was something wrong, charges should be prepared.

On November 26, 1877, Dudley was charged with numerous acts of disobedience to lawful commands, disrespect, defamation of character, drunkenness, and other crimes, and placed under arrest. A court-martial agreed that he was indeed guilty of defamation of character and of disrespect to a superior, but held that he was innocent of all other charges. He was sentenced to be suspended from rank and command and to forfeit half of his pay for three months, but when the sentence reached the War Department, the unexecuted portion was remitted.[42]

This must have been a bitter blow to Hatch, and it is probable that he found it a distinct pleasure to grant Governor Wallace's request in 1879 for the removal of Dudley from the command of Fort Stanton. Cynically, he told Dr. Appel that he did not believe the Governor could sustain his allegations. He proved a good prophet: the Court of Inquiry demanded by Dudley delivered the opinion that he had violated neither laws nor orders, and had shown good judgment under exceptional circumstances.[43] Hatch was now about to have his turn at seeing how the shoe fit.

During the Apache outbreak in 1879–1880, he was, of course, in charge of the defence of the territory. If he did anything right, it did not come to the attention of the editors of the great majority of the New Mexican newspapers. By November, 1879, the Las Cruces *Thirty-Four* was demanding that he be removed and that a congressional Committee investigate his management of affairs.[44] In March, 1880, the citizens of the Mesilla Valley held an indignation meeting at Mesilla and complained, "That the campaign instituted by the military authorities...against these Indians has resulted in a complete and disgraceful failure."[45] The people of Grant County met at Silver City on April 23 to request that the president remove Hatch.[46] A second meeting was held there on June 7, in which they adopted resolutions condemning Hatch as "chiefly responsible for these failures on the part of the military and that we consider him wholly incompetent and unfit for the position he holds," and therefore "we demand his removal from this command."[47] The Las Vegas *Optic* got into the act by alleging that Hatch's bungling was responsible for Carroll's defeat.[48] How far these strictures by the citizenry were justified must await a definitive study of the Apache wars, but it requires only a slight effort to imagine the grim amusement with which Dudley must have read the newspapers, while sagely reminding his friends that this was just what he had been telling them all along.

In the midst of these troubles, the harried commander suffered a blow even more severe. While on a visit to Washington, D.C., Mrs. Hatch contracted smallpox and died within two days. We may wonder whether his sorrowful journeying east to attend her funeral was accompanied by any premonition that the days of the 9th Cavalry in New Mexico were numbered. Less than three weeks after he left that ancient city, word [came] that the District of New Mexico had been assigned to General Ranald S. Mackenzie and his 4th Cavalry.

Of all the officers whose careers have been traced in this paper, Hatch was the only one destined to die an accidental death. In March, 1889, he was thrown from his carriage at Fort Robinson, Nebraska, and suffered a fractured hip. He was thought to be recovering uneventfully, but died suddenly on April 11, 1889. With him passed one of the most turbulent, colourful, and exciting periods in the history of the American West.

ACKNOWLEDGMENTS

The author is indebted to a great many people for their help with this article. It is impracticable to attempt to acknowledge all of them, but particular mention must be made of Mrs. Violet A. Silverman, Library of Hawaii; Miss Bonnie-Jean Duncan, Library, University of New Mexico; Louise F. Kampf, Coburn Library, Colorado College; Leonard F. Olliver, adjutant general, United States Military Academy; Victor Gondos, Jr., National Archives and Records Service; Rutherford D. Rogers, New York Public Library; and Donald F. Danker, Nebraska State Historical Society.

NOTES

[1] Rasch, "A Note on N.A.M. Dudley," op. cit.. [See Chapter 14.]

[2] George Coe, *Frontier Fighter*, op. cit., p. 69.

[3] *Proceedings of a Court of Inquiry in the Case of Lt. Col. N.A.M. Dudley*. QQ 1284. Records of the War Department, Records of the Judge Advocate General. In the National Archives.

[4] Honolulu *Pacific Commercial Advertiser*, April 23, 1914; Honolulu *Star-Bulletin*, April 23, 1914.

[5] Walter Prescott Webb, *The Texas Rangers*. (Boston: Houghton Mifflin Co., 1935), pp. 358–362.

[6] Santa Fe *Weekly New Mexican*, December 28, 1878; January 11, February 22, March 8, 15, and 22, 1879.

[7] Rasch, "Prelude to War," op. cit. [See Chapter 5.]

[8] Henry Carroll to His Excellency, The Governor of New Mexico, March 12, 1879. In William Henry Smith Memorial Library of the Indiana Historical Society.

[9] Lew Wallace to General Edward Hatch, March 9, 1879. In William Henry Smith Memorial Library.

[10] Colorado Springs *Gazette*, February 13, 1908.

[11] Santa Fe *Weekly New Mexican*, September 27 and October 11, 1879.

[12] Indianapolis *News*, December 22, 1913.

[13] Philip J. Rasch, "The Murder of Huston I. Chapman," Los Angeles Westerners' *Brand Book*, 8:69–82, 1959. [See Chapter 18.]

[14] *Proceedings of a Court of Inquiry in the Case of Lt. Col. N.A.M.*

Dudley, op. cit.

[15] Santa Fe *Daily New Mexican*, February 27, 1880.

[16] Henry Carroll to Post Adjutant, July 1, 1878. Records of the War Department, Office of the Adjutant General. 1405 AGO 1878. Consolidated File Relating to the Lincoln County War, New Mexico. In National Archives.

[17] M.F. Goodwin to General Dudley, 2 May 1878. Ibid.

[18] Rasch, "Five Days of Battle," op. cit. [See Chapter 9.]

[19] W.H. Bonney to General Lew Wallace [March] 20, 1879. In William Henry Smith Memorial Library.

[20] Westchester [New York] *Times*, July 28, 1888.

[21] Edward Hatch to Assistant Adjutant General, Department of the Missouri, March 19, 1879. Record Group 98. In National Archives.

[22] Las Cruces *Thirty-Four*, April 23, 1879.

[23] Ibid., October 15, 1879.

[24] Ibid., October 22, 1879; Santa Fe *Weekly New Mexican*, October 25, 1879.

[25] Las Cruces *Thirty-Four*, May 26, 1880.

[26] [G.W.] Smith to Lewis Wallace, March 19th [1879]. In William Henry Smith Memorial Library.

[27] New York *Times*, October 23, 27, 30, 31, November 2, 1895; Chicago *Daily Inter-Ocean*, October 24, 1895.

[28] Chicago *Tribune*, July 9, 1899.

[29] Geo. A. Purington to Act. Asst. Adjt. General, February 21, 1878. 1405 AGO 1878, op. cit.

[30] John S. Loud to Commanding Officer, Fort Stanton, N.M., February 27, 1878. 1405 AGO 1878, op. cit.

[31] Bloomington [Illinois] *Pantagraph*, June 3, 1896.

[32] Silver City *Grant County Herald*, July 20, 1877.

[33] N.A.M. Dudley to Lieut. John S. Loud, May 4, 1878. 1405 AGO 1878, op. cit.

[34] Las Cruces *Thirty-Four*, January 7, 21, 28, 1880.

[35] Silver City *New Southwest and Grant County Herald*, August 27, 1881; Las Vegas *Daily Optic*, August 31, 1881.

[36] Las Cruces *Thirty-Four*, November 19, 1879.

[37] Anonymous, "The Ninth Cavalry," Santa Fe *Weekly New Mexican*, November 29, 1879.

[38] D.G. Gilbert to P.J. Rasch, January 18, 1960.

[39] *Report of the Special Committee on Texas Frontier Troubles*. Report No. 343, 44th Congress, 1st Session, February 29, 1876. Washington, D.C.: Government Printing Office.

[40] *Report and Accompanying Documents of the Committee on Foreign Affairs on the Relations of the United States with Mexico*, April 25, 1878.

Washington, D.C.: Government Printing Office.

[41] J.H. Woodard to W. McKee Dunne. In *Proceedings of a General Court Martial Convened at Fort Union, New Mexico*. In National Archives.

[42] Ibid.

[43] *Proceedings of a Court of Inquiry in the Case of Lt. Col. N.A.M. Dudley*, op. cit.

[44] Las Cruces *Thirty-Four*, November 19 and 26, 1879.

[45] Ibid., March 31, 1880.

[46] Ibid., April 28, 1880.

[47] Ibid., June 16, 1880.

[48] Las Vegas *Daily Optic*, cited in Silver City *Grant County Herald*, June 26, 1880.

13.
The Trials of Lieutenant Colonel Dudley

The English Westerners' Brand Book, January 1965

In 1878, Lincoln County, New Mexico, was the scene of ferocious fighting between the partisans of Lawrence G. Murphy, James J. Dolan, and John H. Riley on the one hand and those of John H. Tunstall, Alexander A. McSween, and John S. Chisum on the other. In the course of the war, Tunstall,[1] McSween,[2] and Mrs. McSween's legal adviser, Huston I. Chapman,[3] were slain. Governor Lew Wallace concluded that the conduct of Lieutenant Colonel N.A.M. Dudley, 9th Cavalry, commanding nearby Fort Stanton, had "excited the animosity of parties in Lincoln county to such degree as to embarrass the administration of affairs in that locality,"[4] and asked Colonel Edward Hatch, 9th Cavalry, commanding the District of New Mexico, to remove him. Hatch forwarded his request to Washington, where General William T. Sherman disapproved it, stating bluntly that Dudley was not required to report to the governor, and adding that if the latter wanted him removed, he could prefer charges and the officer would promptly explain his actions to his superiors.[5]

On 4 March 1879, Ira E. Leonard, a Las Vegas lawyer, wrote the secretary of war preferring charges and specifications against Dudley, accusing him of having abetted the murder of McSween and the burning of his home, threatening Justice of the Peace John B. Wilson, permitting the Tunstall store to be robbed, and making slanderous charges against Mrs. McSween. He also accused Lieutenant James Hansell French, 9th Cavalry, of drunkenness on duty, of forcing his way into Mrs.

McSween's house and insulting her, and of threatening and falsely arresting Chapman.[6] Wallace thereupon repeated his request for Dudley's removal, alleging additionally that he was implicated in the murder of Chapman. This time, his plea was successful. On 8 March, Hatch relieved Dudley of his command and ordered him to proceed to Fort Union "to await such action as the Dept. Commander may take upon the allegations preferred by his Excellency the Governor of New Mexico."[7]

As will be shown, Dudley had long been a thorn in Hatch's side; there is evidence in the latter's correspondence with Wallace that it was with a good deal of pleasure that he took this action against his unruly subordinate. Dudley, however, was not the type to accept such decisions passively. He promptly petitioned the adjutant general of the United States Army to appoint a court of inquiry to investigate his actions since assuming command at Fort Stanton. On Sherman's recommendation, Brigadier General John Pope, commanding the Department of the Missouri, on 28 March 1879 issued Special Orders No. 59, constituting the requisite court and directing it to convene at Fort Stanton on 16 April 1879.

This was Dudley's fifth clash with his superiors. With the first, we need be concerned only for the record. In 1861, he was serving as a captain, 10th Infantry. In a court-martial held at Washington, D.C., commencing 7 November 1861, he was charged with "conduct unbecoming an officer and a gentleman" in that he told a deliberate falsehood by stating to Captain A. Pleasonton, 2nd Cavalry, that he had been directed by Captain F.N. Clark, 4th Artillery, to call upon him for a detachment of dragoons to relieve a party of infantry on duty at Marysville, Kansas, 29 September 1861. Dudley was found not guilty. The impression gained from reading the transcript of the proceedings[8] is that the whole thing resulted from a misunderstanding which could have been cleared up in five minutes if Clark had had sufficient common sense to call Pleasonton and Dudley together for a discussion.

The second was the underlying cause of the animosity between Dudley and Hatch. After the Civil War, Dudley was ordered to duty in Texas. A carpetbagger named George W. Smith allegedly "lived with the negroes, and cohabited with them, and treated them as equals, and...for...eighteen months...outraged the moral sentiment of the city of Jefferson."[9] Smith became involved in an altercation with Dick Figures of that city and sought the aid of his negro henchmen. Figures, in turn, called on his friends for assistance. Something of a pitched battle followed, in which the negroes were defeated. Smith sought the protection of the military, who turned him over to the civil authorities. During the night of 4 October 1868, the jail was stormed and the carpetbagger and two negroes, Lewis Grant and Richard Stewart, were lynched. The sentiments of the community are shown in a newspaper account published under the heading "Death of an Infamous Scoundrel":

> In common with the entire community, we deeply deplore the necessity that would cause the people to take the law into their own hands; but all feel that though this particular case may stand condemned in the eyes of the law, yet it had become in the face of fact an unavoidable necessity. The sanctity of home, the peace and safety of society, the prosperity of the country, and the security of life itself demanded the removal of so base a villain.[9]

In May of the following year, Brevet Major General J.J. Reynolds, commanding the Fifth Military District, convened a military court, of which Hatch and Dudley were members. Some thirty citizens were arrested on charges of opposing the authority of the U.S. Government by force and of murdering the three men in question. Ultimately, five were convicted. During the trial, Hatch accepted the hospitality of the father of one of the prisoners, for which he was openly and severely criticised by Dudley.[10] This created a lasting enmity between the two officers.

The next year, Congress cut the size of the Army in half, thus halting promotions. The secretary of war ruled that officers who so desired could apply for transfer to the cavalry to fill vacancies in that arm. In Janaury 1871, Dudley was appointed a major of the 3rd Cavalry and posted to Camp McDowell, Arizona Territory. Under the same ruling, Captain Anson Mills, 18th Infantry, who by his own admission was "likely to be contentious,"[11] Captain Guy V. Henry, 40th Massachusetts Infantry, and First Lieutenant William H. Andrews, 30th Infantry, were granted similar transfers.[12] The three officers promptly clashed with their superior head-on. On the 16th of July, Dudley and Mills became involved in such an acrimonious argument that Dudley ordered the captain to hold no communication with him except in writing or officially, and filed nine charges and twelve specifications against him. Mills promptly preferred charges against Dudley, alleging that on three separate occasions he had been too drunk to perform his duties properly.

General George Crook, commanding the Department of Arizona, ordered the arrest of both officers and convened a general court-martial at Camp McDowell on 23 October. The ensuing trial probably set some sort of a record for legal irregularities. Mills, scheduled to be tried by the same court under charges preferred by Dudley, was a principal witness for the prosecution, Captain Henry served as judge advocate, although Dudley had preferred two specifications of selling government property against him and had requested that he be tried before the same court-martial. Lieutenant William H. Andrews was characterised as "a decidedly unwilling witness," and charges of perjury were preferred against him. Against Lieutenant H.W. Wessells, Jr., a witness for the prosecution, Dudley preferred charges of an unspecified nature. Curiously enough, nearly all of the witnesses for the prosecution were officers; nearly all of those for the defence were enlisted men.

The upshot was that Dudley was found guilty of some of the specifications and sentenced to be suspended from rank for 60 days and to be reprimanded in general orders.[13] In spite of his bitter protests—some of which seem thoroughly justified—Crook duly approved the findings. Years later, Mills wrote,

> McDowell was the most unhappy post at which we ever served. Its commander was of an overbearing tyrannical disposition and was much addicted to drink. The post traders abbetted him and brought about many quarrels between the commander and the officers, so that, in the garrison of five companies, there were few friendships.[14]

Post trader James A. Tomlinson, a witness at this court-martial, was later a witness at Dudley's Court of Inquiry.

When Dudley took command of Fort Union in the winter of 1876–77, he found himself under the jurisdiction of his old enemy, Hatch. About the 15th of February 1877, while a member of a court-martial, convened at Fort Craig, New Mexico, Dudley became involved in a quarrel with an old friend, Lieutenant Colonel P.T. Swaine, 15th Infantry. The details are not known, but the clash was so serious that it interrupted the court and left a lasting bitterness between the two men.

It might be thought that experience would have taught Dudley to be more cautious, but such does not appear to have been the case. Even in Santa Fe itself, he was given to making remarks about Hatch which were, to say the least, indiscreet. There seems to be no record of the direct precipitating incident, but during the fall of that year, Hatch wrote to Brigadier General Pope, requesting permission to relieve Dudley on account of the annoyances he was giving him. Pope replied that Dudley would be the same source of annoyance at any other post and suggested that Hatch prepare charges against him.

At the root of the difficulties were Dudley's clashes with Captain Amos S. Kimball, who held a dual assignment as depot quartermaster, responsible directly to Hatch, and as post quartermaster, responsible to Dudley. This led to difficulties in the chain of command. Tempers grew so heated that finally Kimball bluntly told Dudley that when he passed the fence separating the post from the depot, he had no more authority than an officer from Fort Stanton. On one occasion, the post quartermaster was asked to furnish dry wood to kindle the fires in the officers' quarters. Depot Quartermaster Kimball thereupon instructed Post Quartermaster Kimball not to issue any, as the ricks thereof were needed to hold up the fence around the woodyard. An officer sent by the post commander to investigate found the top of the fence was perhaps two feet away from the ricks and leaning outward. Matters reached a crisis in mid-June 1877, when Hatch authorised the post quartermaster to make certain repairs at the post; Dudley refused to permit him to do so, on the grounds that any such order had to be issued to the post quartermaster through him. Most injudiciously, Dudley made statements to the effect that Kimball was managing his department in a fraudulent manner and that Hatch knowingly allowed such practices to exist. Kimball promptly demanded a thorough inspection, and was cleared of any irregularities.

On 26 November 1877, Hatch "threw the book" at Dudley, as we would say today. He charged him with disobedience to the lawful commands of his superior officer, disrespect to his commanding officer, maliciously attempting to defame Kimball's character, maliciously accusing Assistant Surgeon Carlos Carvallo of theft, of threatening William B. Tipton in an attempt to force him to marry the daughter of one of the officials at the post, and of drunkenness on duty. In all, five charges, comprising 14 specifications, were made. Dudley did not take it gracefully. When notified that he was under arrest, he shook his finger in Hatch's face and exclaimed, "I will make your Depot stink, and will make it red hot for some officers at this Post before you get through with me."[15]

So seriously was the case considered that Captain Chambers McKibbin was sworn in as assistant to the judge advocate, Captain W.S. Tremaine. Dudley retained Thomas B. Catron and William T. Thornton as his counsel. Almost their first act was to protest the appointment of Lieutenant Colonel Swaine as a member of the court on the grounds that he was prejudiced against the defendant. Swaine replied that he was not Dudley's enemy, but felt that his objection should receive favourable consideration. The court thereupon excused him from serving in the case.

The defence repeatedly attempted to prove that Dudley's allegations against Kimball and Hatch were factual, in spite of the judge advocate's objection that the truth of such slanders was no justification for making them since, under the military code, the accused should have preferred charges, or officially brought these matters to the attention of the proper superior officer. The defence further contended that the charges involving Dr. Carvallo were based on a misunderstanding of what the accused had said, and that the visit to the Tipton home was actually a peaceful attempt to suppress a public scandal, involving no threats or disturbance. Dudley specifically denied ever having used language reflecting on his superiors and affirmed that on the occasions when he had been accused of being drunk, he was actually ill.

In effect, the court found Dudley guilty of defaming Hatch and Kimball and of disrespect to a superior, and not guilty of all other charges. Dudley was sentenced to be suspended from rank and command, and to forfeit half of his pay, for three months. One reading the testimony today cannot but feel that he got off very lightly indeed. Hatch must have been bitterly disappointed at the outcome of the trial. Worst yet, on 8 March 1878, the president of the United States, acting on the recommendation of General Sherman and the judge advocate general, remitted the unexecuted portion of the sentence.[16]

Thus restored to duty, Dudley assumed command of Fort Stanton on 2 April 1878. He found Lincoln County in the throes of open warfare between two ruthless combinations of ambitious men, each claiming to be the party of law and order, and that the Army had been directed to support the civil authorities. Unable to decide whether this meant Sheriff William Brady, a Murphy adherent, or Deputy United States Marshal Robert A. Widenmann, a Tunstall employee, Captain George A. Purington, 9th Cavalry, had asked for instructions. Hatch directed him to render assistance to the sheriff, which virtually decided the eventual outcome of the feud.[17] It also involved Dudley in troubles even more serious than those which had beset him earlier.

Following the crushing defeat suffered by McSween's Regulators in the Five Days Battle of July 1878, Mrs. McSween complained to Governor Wallace that Dudley was responsible for the death of her husband and had driven her from the county. Wallace considered these accusations "incredible," but referred the letter to Dudley. Dudley contemptuously ignored the charges, but sent the governor eight affidavits attacking Mrs. McSween's veracity, principles, and morals.[18] On 13 January 1879, Mrs. McSween executed affidavits charging Dudley, Sheriff George Peppin, and Deputy Sheriff Jack Long with the murder of McSween and the burning of the McSween home. Later, she withdrew these and filed a civil suit for libel,[19] demanding $25,000 damages, and a criminal suit for arson,[20] accusing Dudley of burning her home. Shortly afterwards, her lawyer, Chapman, was murdered in Lincoln and the cases were taken over by Leonard.

The Court of Inquiry convened on 2 May 1879, with Captain Henry H. Humphreys, 15th Infantry, as recorder, and promptly decided not to consider Leonard's charges against Lieutenant French, on the grounds that official action had already been taken in this matter.[21] Dudley was defended by Judge H.L. Waldo, since he had had a bitter quarrel with Catron over his refusal to support certain statements which the lawyer had made to Frank Warner Angel during the course of the latter's investigation of affairs in the Territory. Once again, he successfully objected to the presence of Lieutenant Colonel Swaine, which created an unusual situation in that all members of the court as finally constituted were the accused's juniors. Still more unusual was the fact that Leonard, who had prepared the charges, was permitted to serve as an assistant to the recorder. The extent to which Wallace depended upon Leonard to secure a conviction is readily apparent from the correspondence between the two.

First to testify was the governor. He stated that on his arrival at Lincoln, he had found the people in dread of Dudley and so intimidated by him that it was difficult to secure affidavits against alleged murderers who were known to be his friends. He conceded that Chapman, among others, had been trying to revive the feud and admitted he had no personal knowledge of the state of affairs in Lincoln, having relied entirely on information received from others. He complained that Dudley's official despatches had led him to believe that peace and quiet prevailed in the county, and that after issuing his Proclamation of Pardon, he had been surprised and embarrassed by that officer's open letter to the *New Mexican*[22] criticising him for not visiting the county, and reporting five murders and numerous instances of rustling.

Several witnesses testified that Dudley had taken his force to Lincoln and had notified both parties that if it were fired upon, he would return the fire with his howitzer. Justice of the Peace John B. Wilson stated that the colonel had demanded that he issue a warrant for McSween and others in his house on charges of assaulting Private Berry Robinson, with intent to kill. When Wilson objected that a warrant involving a U.S. soldier had to be issued by a U.S. commissioner, Dudley called him a coward and threatened to arrest him and report him to the governor for dereliction of duty. The warrant was then issued and given to Robert Beckwith for service.

At this point, proceedings were thrown into a turmoil by the discovery that the Mesilla *News*[23] had just published official correspondence passing between the governor and the commanding officer of Fort Stanton. An investigation revealed that these papers had been obtained by Dudley for use in his defence, and that officer defiantly proclaimed that he would use such documents "as in my judgment is best calculated to promote my defence…and I do not consider that I am under any restriction in the manner in which I choose to use them…."

Almost at the same time, someone posted a notice in Lincoln threatening that if Leonard did not leave the country, "They would take my scalp and send me to hell."[24] A few nights later, two shots were fired at him as he sat in his office.

Mrs. McSween took the stand a few days later. Her testimony was confused and unimpressive. She stated that she had asked Dudley to protect her home from being burned down and he had replied that he had nothing to do with the matter and was there only to protect the women and children. He added that she had no business having individuals like Billy the Kid and Jim French in her house; that there was a warrant out for McSween; that McSween was resisting the sheriff; and that he would not interfere with that official's performance of his duty. She characterised his manner as abusive and his conduct as brutal, inhuman, and unbecoming an officer, but denied any bitter feelings towards him. When questioned by the court about the affidavit she had executed charging Dudley with the murder of McSween and the burning of her home, she lamely answered: "I made an affidavit but I cannot remember anything contained in it. It was made by my attorney and carelessly read to me. I did not pay much attention to it." On the whole, the testimony of the prosecution's principal witness could have done Dudley little harm, nor her own cause much good.[25]

The prosecution then attempted to prove that Dudley had sent soldiers to help burn the McSween house and had stationed troops in such a position that the McSween partisans outside of the building were prevented from coming to the aid of those within it. Their main witnesses for this were the McSweens' coloured servants, George Washington and Sebrian Bates. Billy the Kid and Jose Chaves y Chaves swore that two or three soldiers had fired at them as they fled from the burning building.

Dr. T.F. Ealy testified that he had had some hard words with Dudley, after which the officer had refused to talk with him, but was forced to admit that, after Mrs. Ealy wrote a note requesting assistance, the officer permitted a group of volunteers to rescue the Ealys' personal effects and to escort Mrs. McSween, Mrs. Shield, Mrs. Ealy, Miss Gates, and the seven Shield children to safety. A number of other individuals also testified, but for the most part their statements were of less direct importance than the foregoing. On 3 June, the prosecution rested its case.

The defence placed Leonard himself on the stand two days later. He admitted that he had no personal knowledge of the facts, as he had only arrived in Lincoln about 4 April 1879, and contended that his only reason for preferring the charges against Dudley "was zeal for the public good"; that he "had no malice or ill will against him," and was serving "without fee or reward." He must have made a bad impression on the court and realised it for, privately, he wrote to Wallace that the court was a bunch of "egotistical damned fools," was making every effort to protect Dudley, and would not permit the prosecution to introduce material relating to the cause and progress of the troubles "but confined us to Dudley's conduct on the day he went to Lincoln."[26] Since the defendant was not in the country during the origin of the troubles, the court's ruling would appear eminently correct. Leonard was no less severe on the civil authorities, simultaneously conducting trials in Lincoln. The conduct of the district attorney was "contemptible" and Judge Bristol was described as "a weak man and one wholly unfit for the present situation."[27] The point of all this became evident when Leonard finally advised Wallace that he had written to certain congressmen asking their aid in having him appointed in Bristol's stead.

Leonard's strictures, of course, had no effect on the progress of the inquiry. As the crisp New Mexican spring turned into the hot summer, the court complained mildly to the department commander of the work involved and the difficulty of obtaining clerical assistance, but continued their labours. Dolan took the stand and flatly denied that Dudley had promised any help to the sheriff. Ex-Sheriff Saturnino Baca swore that Mrs. McSween had threatened to have him and his family killed because she believed him unfriendly toward McSween. He had sought protection from Dudley, and all the prominent citizens in the town felt under obligation to that officer for his actions. Justice of the Peace D.M. Easton described the murder of Andrew L. Roberts by the McSween gang, and ex-Sheriff George W. Peppin testified that he had come to Lincoln to serve warrants for McSween and most of his men, for this and other crimes.

Leonard now began to panic. He wrote to Wallace that he was "thoroughly and completely disgusted" with the proceedings of the court and "had a good notion to show my disgust by abandoning the case and let them have their own way."[28]

A number of witnesses testified to the details of the Five Days' Fight. All denied that the soldiers had participated in any way, Assistant Surgeon Daniel M. Appel alone having been away from the camp at the climax of the fight. It was suggested that many of the posse-men had been wearing "war surplus" clothing and were, consequently, mistaken for troopers. Officers and troopers alike testified that Dudley's purpose in going to Lincoln was purely humanitarian, that he had not aimed his guns at or threatened the McSween house, that his conduct with Mrs. McSween had been scrupulously correct, and that he had in no way aided the sheriff's party. Appel testified that Hatch had told him "he did not think the Governor could sustain his charges" against Dudley. George B. Barber, later the husband of Mrs. McSween, and a number of other citizens averred that the people were grateful to Dudley for having offered them protection and had tendered the officers a complimentary ball to show their appreciation.

On 5 July, Waldo delivered his closing argument, one that must have taken several hours to present. He accused the court of actually being a persecution of his client, sneered at Leonard as "a noble, pure and disinterested philanthropist actuated in his conduct for the good of the world in general and for General Dudley's special good," characterised Wilson as "a stupid ignorant old man," accused Mrs. McSween of perjury, and in general sought to discredit the prosecution's witnesses. He conceded that Dudley was in sympathy with Peppin's efforts to execute the warrants in his possession, but contended that he had been moved by "just enlightened and human motives" and that his conduct had been "more than ordinarily prudent and careful," and proclaimed that the foul conspiracy "concocted by Wallace, Leonard, and McSween" had "ended in utter and ignominious failure....General Dudley comes forth from this feiry [sic] ordeal unscathed. No blemish rests upon his character, no cloud darkens his fame...."

The recorder's summary was far shorter. He argued that Dudley's own evidence showed him to be decidedly friendly to the sheriff's party and equally bitter toward the McSween party. His first act had been to drive out of town the McSween partisans who were in the Montaño house, and he had furnished an escort of soldiers for the sheriff. The killing of McSween constituted murder, and the burning of his home was arson, and every person involved in the affair was equally guilty. He concluded by claiming that all charges made by Wallace had been proven, with the single exception that it had not been shown that Dudley was implicated in the murder of Chapman.

On 8 July, after the usual "careful investigation and mature deliberation," the court found that Dudley "has not been guilty of any violation of the law or of orders," that his actions were "prompted by the most humane and worthy motives and by good military judgment under exceptional circumstances," that none of the allegations made by the governor or by Leonard had been sustained, and that a court-martial was therefore unnecessary.

The file was reviewed by the Bureau of Military Justice, which concluded that there was "no sufficient reason to question the propriety of the conclusion of the Court—the facts proved do *not* call for the trial of Col. Dudley by court-martial."[29] The judge advocate of the Department of the Missouri, however, took violent exception to the findings of the court. He argued that the record showed that Dudley had in fact gone to Lincoln for the purpose of assisting the sheriff's posse and had conducted himself in a strictly partisan manner. General Pope concurred and forwarded the report with the endorsement "the Department Commander disapproves the opinion expressed by the Court of Inquiry."[30] Simultaneously, Pope submitted for consideration another set of charges and specifications against Dudley. The judge advocate general reaffirmed his concurrence in the findings of the court, and—with all due "deference to the Views of Gen. Pope"—expressed the opinion that "it would not be for the public interest to enter into any further investigation of these disorders."[31]

Dudley still had to face trial in the civil courts of the territory. The trial for arson was finallly called before Judge Warren Bristol at Mesilla in November 1879. Mrs. McSween failed to reappear, whereupon the judge ordered her bond of $1,000 forfeited and issued a warrant for her arrest. She finally arrived a week later, accompanied by Bates as a witness, explaining that the delay was due to the failure of Leonard to appear to escort her to Mesilla and to prosecute the charge. The case was heard, beginning 27 November, with U.S. Attorney Sidney M. Barnes, and Judge Simon B. Newcomb as the defence attorneys. Although the indictment was against John Rinney, Peppin, and Dudley, the latter was the only defendant. After three days and two nights of testimony, the jury retired. It returned in three minutes with a verdict of "not guilty," whereupon the spectators in the courtroom burst into spontaneous applause. One may doubt that Mrs. McSween's case was strengthened by the fact that her only supporting witness had been dishonourably discharged from the 9th Cavalry. Barnes wrote the attorney general of the United States that:

> I say to you in confidence that the evidence adduced by Col. Dudley established beyond question his entire innocence of the crime charged...The Evidence developed at his trial and the investigation I have read satisfy me that Col. Dudley had been very badly treated....He is in my opinion a valuable and meritorious officer, and should be sustained by the Government.[32]

"This," commented the Santa Fe *Weekly New Mexican*, "ends a most infamous persecution."[33]

Still outstanding, however, was the plaintiff's libel suit against the officer. Filed on 14 July, it alleged that his communications with Wallace had had the effect of bringing Mrs. McSween

> into public scandal and disgrace among friends neighbours and the public and to cause her to be regarded as a woman of bad character and reputation, and a prostitute, and unworthy of beleif [sic].[34]

The court docket covering the disposition of this cause cannot be found in the records preserved at Carrizozo. Presumably, the case was quietly dropped after the debacle at Mesilla.

Thus cleared by both his military and civilian peers, Dudley was restored to duty as post commander at Fort Union. After extensive service against the Apaches, he was promoted to colonel and transferred to Fort Custer, Montana, where he distinguished himself in operations against Chees-Cha-Pah-Disch, a Crow chief. Eventually, he retired to a peaceful old age, made more enjoyable by his promotion to brigadier general.[35] These facts have not, of course, had the slightest effect on various authors who have not bothered to read the testimony but who have nevertheless been determined to cast him as one of the villains of the piece.

NOTES

[1] Rasch, "Prelude to War," op. cit. [See Chapter 5.]

[2] Rasch, "Five Days of Battle," op. cit. [See Chapter 9.]

[3] Rasch, "The Murder of Huston I. Chapman," op. cit. [See Chapter 18.]

[4] Lew Wallace to Edward Hatch, 7 December 1878. In Mesilla *News*, 22 March 1879.

[5] W.T. Sherman to Secretary of War, 26 December 1878. In Mesilla *News*, 22 March 1879.

[6] Ira E. Leonard to Secretary of War, 4 March 1879. In Proceedings of a Court of Inquiry in the Case of Lt. Col. N.A.M. Dudley, Records of the War Department, QQ1284. In National Archives.

[7] Special Field Orders No. 2, 8 March 1879. Exhibit No. 66, Volume I, Records of the War Department, QQ1284.

[8] Special Orders 129, Hd. Qrs. Army of the Potomac, 4 November 1861. In National Archives.

[9] Jefferson *Times*, quoted in Marshall [Texas] *Republican*, 16 October 1868.

[10] J.H. Woodard to W. McKee Dunn, 9 January 1878. Proceedings of a General Court-Martial Convened at Fort Union, New Mexico, Pursuant to Special Orders No. 195, Department of the Missouri, 29 October 1877. Records of the War Department, Office of the Judge Advocate General. In National Archives.

[11] Anson Mills, *My Story* (Washington, D.C.: Press of Byron S. Adams, 1918), p. 150.

[12] For brief sketches of the careers of Henry and Andrews, see J.W. Vaughn, *With Crook at the Rosebud* (Harrisburg: The Stackpole Co., 1956), pp. 178–179. Mills termed Henry "one of the best cavalry officers I ever knew." Mills, *My Story*, op. cit., p. 407.

[13] Proceedings of a General Court-Martial Convened by Special Order No. 70, Department of Arizona. Records of the War Department, Office of the Judge Advocate General, R.G. 153. In National Archives.

[14] Mills, *My Story*, op. cit.

[15] Proceedings of a General Court-Martial Convened Pursuant to Special Orders No. 195 (cited at note 10).

[16] Ibid.

[17] John S. Loud to Commanding Officer, Fort Stanton, 24 March 1878. In Records of the War Department, Office of the Adjutant-General, 1405 AGO 1878. Consolidated File relating to the Lincoln County War, New Mexico. In National Archives.

[18] N.A.M. Dudley to Actg. Asst. Adj. General, 8 and 9 November 1878. In 1405 AGO 1878.

[19] Cause No. 176, Lincoln County.

[20] Cause No. 298, Lincoln County, renumbered Cause No. 533, Doña Ana County.

[21] Rasch, "The Murder of Houston I. Chapman," op. cit.

[22] Santa Fe *Daily New Mexican*, 14 December 1878.

[23] Mesilla *News*, 17 May 1879.

[24] Ibid.

[25] The account of the inquiry given in Chapter XX of William Lee Hamlin's *The True Story of Billy the Kid* (Caldwell, Idaho: The Caxton Printers, Ltd., 1959) is pure fiction. It does not deserve the attention of anyone interested in the facts.

[26] Ira E. Leonard to Lew Wallace, 20 May 1879. In the William Henry Smith Memorial Library of the Indiana Historical Society.

[27] Mesilla *News*, 17 May 1879.

[28] Ira E. Leonard to Lew Wallace, 13 June 1879. In William Henry Smith Memorial Library.

[29] Ira E. Leonard to Lew Wallace, 6 June 1879. In William Henry Smith Memorial Library.

[30] Bureau of Military Justice to Geo. W. McCrary, 18 August 1879. Records of the War Department, QQ1284.

[31] Jno. Pope, endorsement to report of the Court of Inquiry in the case of Lieut. Col. N.A.M. Dudley, 13 October 1879. Records of the War Department, QQ1284.

[32] Sidney M. Barnes to Charles Devens, 4 December 1879. Records of the War Department, QQ1284.

[33] Santa Fe *Weekly New Mexican*, 6 December 1879.

[34] Civil Cause 176, Lincoln County, N.M.

[35] Rasch, "A Note on N.A.M. Dudley," op. cit. [See Chapter 14.]

14.
A Note on N.A.M. Dudley

Brand Book of the Los Angeles Corral of the Westerners, 1949

One of the most interesting occurrences in the Lincoln County War was the curious conduct of Lt. Col. N.A.M. Dudley, U.S. Army, at the time of the Three [Five] Days' Battle. In view of the prominent role played by this individual in New Mexican affairs during the turbulent years of 1878–79, it seems odd that the various books devoted to his period have made so little mention of his career. The full story of his activities in connection with the Lincoln County troubles must await a definitive biography, material for which is not available here on the West Coast, but in the meantime, the following brief note may be found of interest by students of the Lincoln County War.

Nathan Augustus Monroe Dudley was born at Lexington, Massachusetts, on August 20, 1825, fifth in the family of nine born to John and Ester Eliza Smith Dudley. He was educated in the public schools of Roxbury, a suburb of Boston, and early evinced an inclination toward military service by joining the Massachusetts Militia, becoming the brigade and division inspector of state troops in 1844. On November 12 of the following year, he married Elizabeth Gray Jowett, at Roxbury. Dudley was a member of the Ancient and Honorable Artillery Company of Boston from 1851 to 1855, during which time he earned his living in commercial pursuits. On March 2, 1855, he was appointed a first lieutenant in the 10th U.S. Infantry. Shortly thereafter, he was ordered to Minnesota, and accompanied [General William Selby] Harney on the Sioux Expedition of 1855. During the period

1857–60, he served under Albert Sidney Johnston on the farcical Utah Expedition.

Dudley seems to have been a capable and efficient officer. He was promoted to captain on May 7, 1861, and his Civil War record was one in which any officer might take justifiable pride. He is mentioned several times in the "War of the Rebellion Official Records of the Union and the Confederate Armies" and the "Official Records of the Union and Confederate Navies in the War of the Rebellion." The highlights of this period of his career may be summarized as follows:

1862 (May 6) Appointed member of high commission to try crimes punishable by death or long imprisonment, Department of the Gulf, New Orleans.
(August 5) Brevetted major for gallant and meritorious service in the battle of Baton Rouge, La. Participated in the siege of Vicksburg.
(November 10) Assigned as acting inspector general, Department of Gulf.

1863 (June 14) Brevetted lieutenant colonel for gallant and meritorious service in the siege of Port Hudson, La. Served as Acting brigadier general.

1864 Participated in Red River Expedition. Authorized to raise a colored cavalry brigade in New Orleans and vicinity.

1865 (January 19) Brevetted brigadier general of Volunteers. Served in defense of Nashville & Chattanooga R.R.
(February 16) Honorably mustered out of the Volunteer service.
(March 13) Brevetted colonel for gallant and meritorious service during the war.
(September 13) Appointed major, 15th U.S. Infantry.

After the Civil War ended, Dudley transferred to the cavalry and he enters upon the scenes of our particular interests with his appointment as lieutenant colonel, 9th U.S. Cavalry, on July 1, 1876. It is a long established policy of the War Department to give out no information of a personal character contained in official records unless the specific purpose for which it is desired is compatible with the public interest. It is further considered that revelation of matters which might cause serious embarrassment to living descendants of the individuals concerned serves no useful purpose.

While such a policy precludes desirable historical research, it appears that late in 1877 or early in 1878, Dudley was tried before a court-martial at Fort Union on charges of "conduct unbecoming an officer," growing out of an over-fondness for liquor. He was acquitted of all charges and shortly thereafter relieved Colonel Purington as commanding officer at Fort Stanton. The important thing about this court-marial is that he was successfully defended by Thomas Benton Catron, United States district attorney, head of the Santa Fe Ring, and president of the First National Bank at Santa Fe, financial backer of Murphy, Dolan & Co.

It thus eventuated that the military forces at Fort Stanton were led by men connected to the Murphy, Dolan & Co. faction by ties of gratitude, friendship, and economics. The original head of the partnership had been Colonel Fritz. Lawrence Murphy and his henchman Sheriff William Brady had both been majors. It would have been strange indeed if the officers at Fort Stanton had not found the company of former brothers-in-arms more congenial than that of the straight-laced McSween, the immigrant Tunstall, or unlicked cubs like the Coe boys and one William H. Bonney. James Dolan and John Riley, Murphy, Dolan & Co. partners, had a profitable side line of lending money to the officers to pay gambling debts contracted at their establishment—known far and wide as "The House" or the "Big Store." The proprietors were piling up a fortune fleecing the government on their contracts to supply beef and flour to the Indians. Obviously, this could not have been done without the connivance of the officers checking the deliveries, who must themselves have been receiving a "cut." Nor should the powerful motive of self-interest be overlooked. The Santa Fe Ring was hand in glove with Territorial Governor Samuel B. Axtell. Any officer considering leaving the Army and settling in this new territory would certainly find it advantageous to be on friendly terms with the dominant clique.

At the beginning of 1878, it must have seemed to Dudley and the other officers at Fort Stanton that every factor indicated it was to their advantage to support the policies of The House, but actually the sands were already running low for this organization. Their government contracts were shortly to be the subject of a revealing investigation by Special Agent Frank Warner Angel, of the Department of Indian Affairs. On February 18, John H. Tunstall was murdered by a posse representing the Murphy interests and the Lincoln County War broke out in open violence. Foreseeing the oncoming storm, Johnny Riley lost his nerve, resigned from the company, and moved to Las Cruces, where he bought the Two Circle Ranch. On February 28, Sheriff Brady wired Catron that A.A. McSween, Weideman [Widenmann], and others had raised a mob to defy the law and requested that Governor Axtell have General [Colonel] Hatch instruct the post commander of Fort Stanton to protect him in the discharge of his official duties. On March 4, George W. McCrary, secretary of war, informed General Sherman that "The military can be ordered to support the civil Territorial authorities in maintaining order and enforcing legal process." Brady had sound grounds for his forebodings; on April 1, he and his deputy, George Hindman, were killed and Billy Matthews [Mathews] wounded from ambush on the main street of Lincoln by a group consisting of Billy the Kid, Henry Brown, Fred Wayte [Waite], John Middleton, Jim French, and possibly others. On April 14, "Buckshot" Roberts, a "headhunter" seeking the reward offered for the murderers of Brady, was himself killed by Charlie Bowdre. Murphy, his health broken by drink and dissipation, soon retired to Santa Fe, where he remained until his death, on October 9, after a lingering illness. Dolan was unable to carry on alone and Catron sent down a representative to take over the business.

Dudley's own actions were not meeting with the approval of the War Department. After studying his reports on the situation, Judge Advocate General W.M. Dunn wrote to Secretary of War McCrary on June 8 that [Dudley had acted "without authority of law." See Chapter 7, p. 102.]

The stage was now set for the famous Three [Five] Days' Battle, which took place on July 17, 18, and 19. Walter Noble Burns' popular but woefully inaccurate *The Saga of Billy the Kid* leads the reader to believe that the Murphy forces had the McSween adherents surrounded and at their mercy. He relates that on July 19, Mrs. Juanita Mills slipped out of the town, fled to Fort Stanton, and implored Dudley to bring his troops and save the women and children by stopping the fighting. Dudley took his troopers to Lincoln, arrayed his guns in front of the McSween home, and told its defenders to cease shooting or he would blow up the building. During the ensuing parley, the house was set afire by Dolan and Andy Boyle. In view of this turn in affairs, Dudley did not carry out his threat, but moved to the eastern end of the town, ordered off Martin Chaves and his partisans, and went into camp, leaving the garrison in the McSween home to be finished off by Dolan and his men during the night. One is left to wonder why the presumably impartial Army authorities took no action against the Murphyites or to actually stop the battle.

So far as can be made out from the conflicting stories, it would appear that the Murphy fighting men did indeed surround the McSween home, but were themselves outflanked by a group of McSween supporters led by Deputy Sheriff Chaves, based on the Ellis house at the extreme eastern end of Lincoln. Outnumbered and caught thus between two fires, the Murphy forces found their position untenable and were forced to call upon their good friend Dudley for aid, which, for reasons that have been detailed above, he found it expedient to furnish.

George Coe has damned the Juanita Mills story as "A gross deception" of which he had never heard until he read it years afterward. Mrs. McSween has testified that she made her way to Colonel Dudley's camp and implored him to stop the fighting. She found him with John Kinney, a notorious desperado and cattle rustler, and George W. Peppin, a tool of The House who was both the sheriff and a deputy United States marshal. All three were drunk and greeted her with abusive language. To Mrs. McSween's demands for protection, Dudley replied that he was there only to provide assistance in case the civil officers required help, and it appeared to him that Marshal Peppin had the situation well under control. The following morning, Kinney and his gang looted the McSween store, while Dudley apparently made no attempt to see that law and order were maintained. In his official report, this veteran of so many sanguinary actions in the Civil War praised the desperate courage displayed on both sides and predicted that such men would not permit the feud to lapse because of the decisive outcome of this one battle.

His own questionable part in this affair did not go unmarked. Later, *The Independent* was to write that:

> The removal of Col. Dudley from the command of Fort Stanton was a wise measure and will be regarded with satisfaction by everyone who desires to see peace restored to the county. Had he been removed a

> year ago it would, in our opinion, have saved a number of lives. Certainly McSween and his companions would not have been butchered as they were had it not been for the presence of Col. Dudley and the troops under his command, and the aid he openly gave to the other party. This act alone did more to cripple and deaden the efforts of the orderly citizens of the county and to alarm and deter peaceably disposed people, than any act ever committed in the county by outlaws....Should Col. Dudley's successor prove to be a man of less prejudices and better judgment it will be fortunate for Lincoln.

A more immediate reaction was President Hayes' replacement of Governor Axtell with Lew Wallace, who arrived in Santa Fe on September 30. Mrs. McSween retained Huston I. Chapman, a Las Vegas lawyer, to represent her interests. On October 24, Chapman wrote to Wallace, charging that he was in possession of facts "which make Col. Dudley criminally responsible for the killing of McSween...." Chapman stated that Dudley had threatened Mrs. McSween and requested the governor to supply a military guard for her. Wallace considered the charge incredible, but forwarded Chapman's letter to General [Colonel] Hatch, commanding the Department of New Mexico. In reply, he received a defiant letter from Dudley, together with affidavits attacking Mrs. McSween's character. Wallace wrote two placating letters in reply, insisting simply that Mrs. McSween was entitled to protection regardless of what her character might or might not be.

On November 14, Governor Wallace issued a proclamation of amnesty which he hoped would bring peace to the countryside, but in December, Chapman again complained that Dudley was persecuting Mrs. McSween. Feeling some action was imperative, Wallace wrote the following carefully worded letter to Hatch on December 7, 1878:

> I am constrained to request that Lieut. Col. N.AM. Dudley, commanding at Fort Stanton, be relieved and an officer of equal rank, ability and firmness be ordered in his place.
>
> In doing this I mean no disparagement of Col. Dudley. Not more than once in a life-time probably, is an officer charged with duty more delicate, and that he has maintained himself so long is the highest and best proof of qualities of exceeding value to the country and the service. It is, however, apparent that he has excited the animosity

> of parties in Lincoln county to such degree as to embarrass the administration of affairs in that locality. The same result may happen to any other gentleman whom you may assign to succeed him, yet in view of the important part the military are called upon to perform in keeping the status there as at present, I think it better that you send to that command a stranger to the people—at least one who has no connection whatever with the feuds that have divided them.
>
> Very Respectfully, Your Friend,

In his private notebook, Wallace summarized Dudley as "Honest. Mortal enemy of Hatch. Talks too much."

Bitter enemies though Hatch and Dudley may have been, Hatch forwarded the letter through the chain of command with an unfavorable endorsement, which recommendation was approved by his superiors, Generals Pope and Sheridan. In transmitting the request to the secretary of war, General Sherman declared flatly that Dudley was "not required to report to, or explain his public acts to the Governor of New Mexico, but will promptly do so to his superiors, including the Secretary of War and the President of the United States if called on." He characterized the request as "unjust" and recommended that it be refused unless Wallace preferred charges against Dudley. The secretary concurred and no action was taken. Emboldened by this official support, Dudley wrote a long letter to the Santa Fe *New Mexican*, attacking Wallace and his proclamation.

On February 18, 1879, Chapman was killed in Lincoln by Jim Dolan, Jesse [Jessie] Evans, and Billy Campbell. Mrs. McSween then hired Judge Ira E. Leonard as her lawyer. On February 24, Leonard wrote Wallace that he had evidence that Dudley owed Dolan money and that Dolan had paid the gunmen who killed Chapman. Wallace persuaded Hatch to arrest the killers without warrants and on March 7 requested that Dudley be removed so that they could be indicted. This time, Hatch complied and ordered Dudley to Fort Union, where he immediately demanded a court of inquiry. Oddly enough, it would appear that up to this time, Dudley and Wallace had never met.

Dolan, Campbell, and Evans were temporarily lodged in the guard house at Fort Stanton. Wallace wrote the commanding officer that he had information that a plan for the escape of the prisoners had been concocted and requested that special precautions be taken. Nevertheless, Campbell and Evans escaped on March 19 and were not heard of again. One cannot but feel that they "knew too much" and their escape was countenanced to preclude the possibility of embarrassment to certain parties resulting from their testimony at a trial. Dolan was indicted for murder but arranged for a change of venue to Socorro County, where he was acquitted in August of that year.

The board of inquiry convened at Fort Stanton on May 8 to consider charges against Dudley of unbecoming conduct and disobedience. Dudley was defended by Territorial Attorney General Judge Henry L. Waldo, a friend of ex-Governor Axtell, while Wallace was aided by Judge Leonard, whom he had designated acting district attorney. The court sat for six weeks. In *Frontier Fighter*, George Coe exults that "Colonel Dudley was court-martialed and thrown out of the United States Army," a statement that is repeated by Donald Davison in *Alias Billy the Kid*. Actually, there is not a grain of truth in this allegation. The board proved decidedly partial to a brother officer harassed by a group of civilians and rendered the following opinion:

> In view of the evidence adduced the court is of the opinion that Lieut. Colonel N.A.M. Dudley, 9th U.S. Cavalry has not been guilty of any violation of law or of orders that the act of proceeding with his command to the town of Lincoln on the 19th of July 1878, was prompted of the most humane and worthy motives and of good military judgment under exceptional circumstances.
>
> The Court is of the opinion that none of the allegations made against Lieut. Colonel Dudley of His Excellency the Governor of New Mexico or of Ira E. Leonard have been sustained and that proceedings before a court martial are therefore unnecessary.

Upon review of the case in Washington, the judge advocate general recommended approval of the findings of the court of inquiry substantially as expressed in the board's opinion, adding the remarkable comment that it appeared that Wallace was "mistaken in his impression that the feelings entertained by the community at Lincoln, in the spring of 1879, toward Col. Dudley, were of a hostile character." The recommendation was then approved by the secretary of war, although Dudley did receive a reprimand for minor misconduct.

Dudley, however, still had to face charges filed against him in the civil courts. The district court had convened at Lincoln on April 14, 1879. A grand jury issued numerous indictments in connection with the Lincoln County troubles, one of which charged Dudley with arson. Mrs. McSween struck back at her enemy by filing a suit for $25,000 for slander. Here too Dudley won an acquittal, and was thus exonerated of all charges, civil and military.

Thus officially vindicated, Dudley resumed his duties in the field with the 9th Cavalry. For the next few years, his attention was fully occupied with the pressing problems of Indian fighting. Victorio had just gone on the war path. On September 14, 1879, ten miners and ranchers were killed near Hillsboro, N.M. Dudley took up the pursuit and was unfortunate enough to find the Apaches at the head of Las Animas Creek on September 18. Four companies of the 9th were present, but in the day long fighting that followed, Victorio won a convincing victory. During the night, the troopers withdrew from the field. Fighting between the Apaches and the 9th Cavalry continued literally for years. Dudley served under Crook on his campaigns against the Apaches and had the satisfaction of commanding the cavalry on the Buell Expedition into Mexico, where the Army cooperated with Mexican forces in operations that led to the destruction of Victorio's band on October 14 of the following year. The gauge of battle was then picked up by the ancient Nana, who finally retreated to Mexico in August of 1881. In 1882, Chato [Chatto], Nachite [Naiche], and Loco spread a trail of death and destruction through Arizona, New Mexico, and Western Texas. They were corralled in May of 1883, but the uneasy peace that followed lasted barely two years, for on May 17, 1885, Geronimo and his followers fled from the San Carlos Reservation, presaging the outbreak of one of the worst of the southwest Indian troubles.

Dudley's life during this period must have been anything but an easy one, but it was rewarded on June 6, 1885, by promotion to colonel and assignment to command the 1st Cavalry, stationed at Fort Custer, Montana, as replacement for Colonel Grover, deceased. In the fall of 1887, Chees-Cha-Pah-Disch (Sword Bearer), a Crow chief, and his followers became disaffected. Their actions culminated in an attack on the agency buildings on the night of September 30. On November 4, Colonel Dudley led a force made up from the 1st Cavalry, 7th Cavalry, and 3rd Infantry to arrest the malcontents. The following day, Dudley demanded the Indians' surrender, but the

Crows replied with an attack on the troops. This was repulsed and in the ensuing battle, Sword Bearer was killed. Discouraged by the loss of their leader, the Indians surrendered and were sent to Fort Snelling.

On August 20, 1889, Dudley was retired by operation of law (Sec. 1 Act, June 30, 1882) and returned to his boyhood home of Roxbury to spend his declining years. One more honor was still to be bestowed upon the old warrior: on May 25, 1904, he accepted promotion to the rank of brigadier general under the provisions of the Act of April 23, 1904. Apparently, he took little part in the affairs of his community, for the Roxbury Branch of the Public Library of the City of Boston advises its files contain no record of his activities during this period. On April 29, 1910, Dudley followed Murphy, Brady, McSween, The Kid, Wallace, Victorio, Nana, and many another old friend and enemy before whatever Court of Inquiry on the other side demands an accounting of our actions. He was survived by a grandson, Nathan W. Dudley, of Philadelphia, and a granddaughter, Mrs. Harry E. Stevens. Funeral services were held at Dudley Street Baptist Church, Roxbury, on May 2 at 2 p.m., and his body was interred at the Arlington National Cemetery.

A chronological account of this kind affords little opportunity to assess a man's character, yet it seems safe to say that Dudley possessed in full measure both the failings and the virtues of his fellows. He was hard drinking, prejudiced, and obstinate, but he was also a competent officer and a first class fighting man.

Note: The writer would like to acknowledge his indebtedness to Mr. Edward H. Redstone and Mr. Alan H. Smith of the Public Library of the City of Boston for their courteous assistance in compiling the above data.

15.
Exit Axtell: Enter Wallace

New Mexico Historical Review, July 1957

During the 1870s, the federal government was deluged with complaints about the political and economic conditions in Lincoln County, Territory of New Mexico. In 1878, the outcries attained such a volume that they could no longer be ignored. Frank Warner Angel, a New York attorney, was appointed a special agent, representing both the Department of the Interior and the Department of Justice, and sent to the territory to examine and and report on the situation. Unfortunately, his original instructions cannot be located in the National Archives.[1] It is evident from his letters that his assignment included the investigation of the killing of John H. Tunstall and of the charges which had been preferred against Frederick C. Godfroy, agent of the Mescalero Apaches; Thomas B. Catron, United States district attorney; Samuel B. Axtell, governor of the territory; and the surveyor general.

His task proved to be no easy one. In one report,[2] he [complained that he "was met by every opposition possible." See Chapter 10, p. 142.] Angel reached the conclusion that Tunstall had been murdered in cold blood, recommended the removal of Axtell[3] and suggested that Godfroy be permitted to resign.[4] His action in regard to Catron is not known, since the report which he submitted and Catron's subsequent letter of resignation cannot be located in the files of the National Archives.[5, 6]

Less than a month after Angel visited Lincoln, the plaza erupted into five days (July 15–19, 1878) of fighting between the friends of the deceased Tunstall, led by Alexander A. McSween, and the partisans of Lawrence G. Murphy, James J. Dolan, and John H. Riley. Angel had arrived home in August and had obtained permission from Attorney General Charles Devens to remain with his family while preparing his reports. However, on August 17, he was suddenly ordered to proceed to Washington immediately to present a brief report to President Rutherford B. Hayes.

Angel's description of affairs in New Mexico apparently convinced the president that Axtell must be replaced as governor of New Mexico. At the suggestion of Postmaster General Tyner, himself from Indiana, Secretary of the Interior Carl Schurz offered the position to Lewis Wallace, of Crawfordsville, Indiana, a son of David Wallace, one time governor of that state. Wallace, a former Civil War major general and member of the military commission which had tried persons accused of implication in the assassination of President Lincoln, was at this time fifty-one years of age and thoroughly bored by his law practice. He had been a loyal worker for the election of Hayes and had hoped for an appointment as minister to Italy, Spain, Brazil, or Mexico in return for his services.[7] However, excited by the prospect of adventure and wealth on the frontier, he accepted the proffered post. On September 4, Schurz sent him an order suspending Axtell as governor and appointing Wallace as his successor.

On September 13, Wallace reported to Schurz for instructions. About two weeks later, he left Crawfordsville for Santa Fe. The Indianan traveled by way of the Atchison, Topeka & Santa Fe to Pueblo, Colorado, by narrow gauge to Trinidad, and thence by buckboard to Cimarron, New Mexico, where he rested a few days as the house guest of Frank Springer. The citizens of Cimarron, who had hailed the news of Axtell's removal with a 50 gun salute, gave the new governor an enthusiastic welcome. He was tendered a reception at the home of Judge Lee and was the subject of a highly laudatory article in the local paper.

Wallace arrived at Santa Fe on Sunday evening, September 29, where his reception was considerably more restrained than it had been at Cimarron. The *Rocky Mountain Sentinel*[8] noted that his appearance was a surprise and disappointment to quite a number of those who had hoped that Axtell's removal would not be consummated. On Monday afternoon, the new governor took the oath of office from Associate Justice Samuel G. Parks, of the territorial supreme court. The following day, he sent Axtell a note informing him that he had qualified. Enclosed was the order of suspension. Accompanied by U.S. Marshal John E. Sherman and Judge Henry L. Waldo, Wallace then called upon Axtell in person. To save the discredited official all humiliation possible, Wallace requested that there be no public ceremony at his inauguration, and granted his predecessor two weeks time in which to move out of his official residence, El Palacio del Gobernador. Asked about the Lincoln County troubles, he stated that he would go there at once, and "if peace and quiet are not fully restored in that county within the next sixty days I will feel ashamed of myself." To Schurz he wrote, "As to Lincoln County, I shall go to see the people immediately."[9]

The state of affairs in Lincoln County was dark indeed. With neither posse nor troops to assist him, Sheriff George W. Peppin was completely powerless. The result was chaos. Bands of armed men roamed the country, rustling, stealing, burning property, abducting and raping women, and openly defying the sheriff to arrest them. On September 6, Joe Bowers and Sam Smith, of the McSween faction, had run off all of Charles Fritz's horses while they were being herded by his sons only six hundred yards from his house,[10] but their crime was minor indeed compared with those of the Wrestlers.[11] This marauding band was led by John Selman,[12] alias John Gunter, who was afterwards to win a dubious sort of fame by shooting John Wesley Hardin in the back.[13] Alleged to be included in the gang were Thomas Selman, alias "Tom Cat," Charles Snow,[14] alias Johnson, Reese Gobly [Gobles], V.S. Whittaker, John Nelson, Robert Speaks [Speakes], Gus Gildea, James [John W.] Irvin, William Dwyer, and one [John] Collins.[15] On a sweep through the county during the latter part of September, they burned the Coe ranch house at Tinnie, after first stealing everything of value.[16] They wrecked Hoggins' Saloon (the old Murphy Brewery) near Lincoln, abused his wife and sister, and seriously injured a man named Sheppard when he remonstrated against their treatment of the women.[17] On the Hondo, they wantonly murdered two boys, Clato and Desiderio Chaves, and a crazy boy named Lorenzo Lucero.[18] Stealing what horses they could find, they proceeded to the Martin Sanchez [Sanches] ranch and killed his fourteen year old son, Gregorio. A few nights later, they raped two women.[19] Not long afterwards, it was reported that the bodies of Reese Gobly

[Gobles], James [John W.] Irvin, and "Rustling Bob" [Bryant] had been found on the Pecos, presumably murdered by their fellows.

In one of his reports of their depredations, Lieutenant Colonel Nathan Augustus Monroe Dudley,[20] commanding Fort Stanton, begged, "I respectfully and earnestly ask in the name of God and humanity, that I may be allowed to use the forces at my command to drive these murderers, horse-thieves and escaped convicts out of the country."

Following the rape of the two women, he sent Captain Henry Carroll out with twenty men to provide protection for the citizens. Colonel Edward Hatch, commanding the District of New Mexico, immediately notified him that his action was in violation of orders and instructed that Carroll be recalled at once.[21]

Sherman informed Wallace that he had warrants for residents of Lincoln County but was powerless to execute them due to the condition of affairs there.[22] Judge Warren Bristol telegraphed from Mesilla that it was impossible to hold court in Lincoln County.[23] Probate Judge Florencio Gonzales, Justices of the Peace John B. Wilson, George Kimble [Kimbrell], Nicolas Torres, J. Gregorio Trujillo, and County Commissioners Saturnino Baca and Francisco Romero y Luna [Romero y Lueras] petitioned for protection under the terms of the Treaty of Guadalupe Hidalgo, warning that the force of the outlaws was stronger in the county than was that of the law-abiding citizens.[24] Dudley wrote that "ten murders have been reported within the last fifteen days. No man, woman, or child is safe in the county outside of the shadow of the Military."[25]

Terrified for their very lives, even the citizens who had taken no part in the Murphy-Dolan-Riley-Tunstall-McSween troubles found it necessary to move elsewhere. The Las Vegas *Gazette* reported:

> Six wagon loads of emigrants from North and South Spring in Lincoln County,[26] passed through town Tuesday going north. They were driven out by the lawless element of the section. They had tried hard to take no part in the contest and preferred to leave rather than to take either side. About twenty horses had been taken from them. A deputy sheriff rode up and demanded that they take up arms and go with them and fight. This they refused to do and loaded up and left the country. They left their houses, lands, standing crops, gardens and everything pertaining to comfortable homes. They will seek

> employment on the railroad. No new country can well afford to lose so industrious and law abiding class of people.[27]

In spite of the *Gazette*'s warning, the troubles continued. The Beckwiths, the Pierces, William [Thomas B.] Powell, and Lewis Paxton fled the county. Saturnino Baca remained, but was forced to seek refuge at Fort Stanton. The post offices at Roswell, Seven Rivers, and Lloyd's Station were abandoned.[28] The settlement of Antelope, near Roswell, was deserted, and a steady stream of families flowed out of the territory.[29]

In the midst of all these troubles, Lawrence G. Murphy, one of the men most responsible for their existence, was called before the tribunal which passes final judgment on a man's deeds. Broken in health and in power, the former dictator of Lincoln County died of "general debility" at Santa Fe on October 20, 1878.[30] Unfortunately, his death did nothing to calm the storm which his life had raised.

President Hayes had issued the following:

PROCLAMATION

> *Whereas*, it is provided in the laws of the United States, that whenever by reason of unlawful obstructions, combinations or assemblages of persons, or rebellion against the authority of the government of the United States, it shall become impracticable in the judgment of the President to enforce by the ordinary course of judicial proceedings, the laws of the United States within any state or locality, it shall be lawful for the President to call forth the militia of any or all the states, and to employ such parts of the land and naval forces of the United States as he may deem necessary to enforce the faithful execution of the laws of the United States, or to suppress such rebellion in whatever state or territory thereof the laws of the United States may be forcibly opposed or the execution thereof forcibly obstructed; and
>
> *Whereas* it has been made to appear to me, that by reason of unlawful combinations and assemblages of persons to arms, it has become impracticable to enforce by the ordinary course of judicial proceedings the laws of the United States within the Territory of New Mexico, and especially within Lincoln county thereof, and that the laws of the United States have been therein forcibly opposed, and the execution thereof forcibly resisted; and
>
> *Whereas*, the laws of the United States require that whenever it

> may be necessary in the judgment of the President to use the military force for the purpose of enforcing the faithful execution of the laws of the United States he shall forthwith by proclamation command such insurgents to disperse and retire peacefully to their respective abodes within a limited time. Now therefore I, RUTHERFORD B. HAYES, President of the United States, do hereby admonish all good citizens of the United States, and especially of the Territory of New Mexico, against aiding, countenancing, abetting or taking part in such unlawful proceedings, and I do hereby warn all persons engaged in or connected with such obstruction of the laws to disperse and return peaceably to their respective abodes on or before noon of the thirteenth day of October, instant.
>
> *In Witness* whereof I have hereunto set my hand and caused the Seal of the United States to be affixed. Done at the City of Washington this seventh day of October in the year of our Lord eighteen hundred and seventy-eight, and of the Independence of the United States the one hundred and third.

The next day, Secretary of War George W. McCrary issued a general order instructing the general commanding the Military Department of the Missouri to inform the proper military officer that after the 13th of October, he would disperse by force all unlawful combinations or assemblages within the Territory.[31]

Wallace at once advised Secretary of State W.M. Evarts that "I shall go down to Lincoln immediately that I can get conveyance and escort the better to report the effect of the Proclamation and the manner in which it is observed."[32] Before he could start, it was rumored that Juan Patrón's gang had shot two men and hung another somewhere between Lloyd's Station and Fort Sumner.[33] Sixty-five horses belonging to a group of Jicarilla Apaches under the care of Agent Jack Long camped on the reservation less than a mile from Fort Stanton were run off on October 12. A week later, five thousand sheep were stolen from the grazing region just north of Lincoln; the three Mexican herders were believed to have been killed.

Wallace seems to have been acting on the assumption that if left to themselves, the people of Lincoln County would reach a peaceful solution of their problems. Now his patience was exhausted. In placing the situation before Schurz, he stated:

> My judgment is that to refer the matter to the civil authorities is

> childish. Read again what Judge Bristol said about juries in Lincoln county, observe the petition of officers of the county given above. So, too, putting the military at my order or that of Sheriffs is but a half way measure. We cannot act without process; while courts must sit surrounded by bayonets, and juries deliberate in dread of assassination. In fact there is nothing to be done but make war upon the murderous bands. When prisoners are taken, let them be sent before a military commission, appointed to sit continuously at Fort Stanton. In other words, martial law for the counties Lincoln and Doña Ana. The proclamation in quickest time possible.[34]

Apparently, Schurz disapproved of this request, for on October 26, the governor asked Hatch for military assistance in maintaining law and order in Lincoln and Doña Ana counties.[35] Hatch at once instructed Dudley to furnish assistance to the U.S. marshal and territorial sheriffs and deputies in making arrests upon proper writs, in pursuing thieves, and in protecting the mails.[36] Reinforced by additional troops from Fort Union, Dudley ordered the detachment at Tularosa, under Lieutenant Millard F. Goodwin, to cooperate with the authorities in that area,[37] and sent a detachment under Captain Carroll to take station at Roswell for the protection of the citizens there.[38] Goodwin was ordered to maintain patrols along the highway between South Fork, La Luz, and Dog Canyon; Carroll was instructed to divide his command, part to patrol the road between Roswell and Fort Sumner, part the road between Roswell and Seven Rivers.

The president's proclamation and the action of the troops seem to have had the effect of causing many of the depredators to leave the territory, although Guadalupe Grejada made an affidavit that John Jones, Thomas Johnson, and one Calamo, heading for Texas with a party of some fifteen other men, had paused long enough to kill three Mexicans and seize their wagons and horses.[39]

For a few weeks, however, things remained generally quiet. Wallace, perhaps overly anxious to claim success in pacifying the county, then issued a proclamation of his own:

PROCLAMATION BY THE GOVERNOR

> For the information of the people of the United States, and of the citizens of New Mexico in especial, the undersigned announces that the disorders lately prevalent in Lincoln County in said Territory,

have been happily brought to an end. Persons having business and property interests therein, and who are themselves peaceably disposed, may go to and from that County without hinderance or molestation. Individuals resident there, but who have been driven away, or who, from choice, sought safety elsewhere, are invited to return, under assurance that ample measures have been taken, and are now and will be continued in force, to make them secure in person and property. And that the people of Lincoln County may be helped more speedily to the management of their civil affairs, as contemplated by law, and to induce them to lay aside forever the divisions and tends which, by national notoriety, have been so prejudicial to their locality and the whole Territory, the undersigned, by virtue of authority in him vested, further proclaims a general pardon for misdemeanors and offenses committed in the said County of Lincoln against the laws of the said Territory in connection with the aforesaid disorders, between the first day of February, 1878, and the date of this proclamation.

And it is expressly understood that the foregoing pardon is upon the conditions and limitations following:

It shall not apply except to officers of the United States Army stationed in the said County during the said disorders, and to persons who, at the time of the commission of the offense or misdemeanor of which they may be accused, were, with good intent, resident citizens of the said Territory, and who shall have hereafter kept the peace, and conducted themselves in all respects as becoming good citizens.

Neither shall it be pleaded by any person in bar of conviction under indictment now found and returned for any such crimes or misdemeanors, nor operate the release of any party undergoing pains and penalties consequent upon sentence heretofore had for any crime or misdemeanor.

In witness whereof I have hereunto set my hand and caused the seal of the Territory of New Mexico to be affixed.

Done at the city of Santa Fe, this 13th day of November, A.D. 1878.

To Schurz he wrote: "The trouble is ended now"; of Evarts he enquired, "Do you not think me entitled to a promotion?"[40]

The Army had found their duty of assisting the peace officers both delicate and distasteful. In addition, Dudley was anxious to start training his men for the trouble which he foresaw would soon commence with the Apaches. He promptly asked his superior whether the governor's proclamation was sufficient authority for him to suspend action,[41] but warned that it had the effect of bringing back into the county some noted outlaws, including Jim French and Josiah G. "Doc" Scurlock,[42] and that Sheriff George W. Peppin and his deputies did not consider it safe to leave Fort Stanton to make arrests without a military escort.[43]

Almost simultaneously with the issuance of Wallace's proclamation, a band of thieves stole part of Pat Coghlan's cattle from Three Rivers. They were pursued by Lieutenant Goodwin's force, who recovered part of the cattle and captured Jake Owens and H.J. Bassett, both of whom claimed to have been cowboys for John Riley, Frank Wheeler, John W. Irving [Irvin], and H.J. [Charlie] Moore.[44] Coghlan, however, suddenly developed a convenient illness and was unable to appear to testify against them when the case was called before Justice John B. Wilson. Catron's brother-in-law and local representative, Edgar A. Walz, however, presented himself before the court and volunteered the information that Coghlan had informed him that he had not lost a single head of cattle! The prisoners were perforce turned loose. That same afternoon, a Mexican was killed about a mile from the Fritz home.[45] A few days later, the bodies of Irving [Irvin] and Moore were found near the White Sands. Who had shot them was never discovered.

Aggravating although these things may have been to Dudley, it is likely that he was more concerned over his own troubles with Mrs. Sue Ellen McSween's lawyer, a man named Chapman.

Huston I. Chapman was from Portland, Oregon. He had accidentally lost one arm in his youth, but being of a vigorous, aggressive nature, had obtained a position as a civil engineer on the Atchison, Topeka & Santa Fe Railroad, specializing in bridge construction. He left the railroad in September, 1878, to open a law office in Las Vegas. Within a few weeks, he was retained by the widow of Alexander McSween and adopted her cause with the burning zeal of a born fanatic.

In October, Chapman had written to Governor Wallace that

> I am in possession of facts which make Col Dudley criminally responsible for the killing of McSween, and he has threatened, in case Martial law was proclaimed that he would arrest Mrs. McSween and her friends immediately. Through fear of his threat Mrs. McSween left Lincoln and is now visiting here, until such time as

> she may with safety return to her home.[46]

Wallace forwarded a copy of this letter to Colonel Hatch, with the comment that

> Candidly speaking, the accusations therein against Col. Dudley strike me as incredible; at the same time, it is apparent that Mrs. McSween...is alarmed; wherefore...I respectfully request a special safeguard for her....
> You will further oblige me by calling Col. Dudley's attention to this letter....The charges preferred by Mr. Chapman seriously affect his fitness for the very delicate duty.[47]

Dudley's reply was anything but the retort courteous. He declined to comment on Chapman's charges, but sent Hatch eight affidavits, obtained from Saturnino Baca, George W. Peppin, Jack Long, John Priest, Francisco Gómez, Lieutenant G.W. Smith, Lieutenant Samuel S. Pague, and Assistant Surgeon D.M. Appel, attacking Mrs. McSween's veracity, principles, and morals, requesting that they be laid before the governor to demonstrate the character of the principal complainant against him.[48] Some of the material in these documents is of a nature which could not be printed here. In forwarding the papers to Wallace, Hatch commented that "The safeguard for Mrs. McSween is not, under the circumstances necessary."[49] In this decision, Wallace concurred, and his request for a safeguard was withdrawn. Later, he explained that his action was not due to the nature of the affidavits but because he was convinced that the precautions ordered by Hatch made special protection for her unnecessary.[50]

Chapman called on Wallace and over the governor's protests insisted that he would press charges against Dudley before the next meeting of the grand jury. After he left, Wallace drew out of his desk the preliminary version of his proclamation of pardon for the Lincoln County feudists and thoughtfully inserted the clause regarding Army officers, with the object of protecting them from harassment by Mrs. McSween and her lawyer. To Dudley he wrote, "I had a good reason for that by the way which I shall explain when I see you."[51]

Unfortunately for the governor's good intentions, in a long "Open Letter,"[52] Dudley, with the endorsement of his officers, rejected the pardon for himself and his command, contending that as they had committed no illegal acts, they could not be pardoned, and severely criticized Wallace for his failure to visit Lincoln to investigate the five murders, the rapes, and the horse and cattle thefts that had recently taken place. Injudiciously, he referred to the "eight long affidavits" and characterized Mrs. McSween as "a notoriously bad woman."

Intemperate though his language was, his attitude could be attributed to the delicate sense of honor which military men have always professed. Wallace contented himself with writing the officers at Fort Stanton a mild note inviting them to call upon him so that he might show them that "the clause of which you complain was even more than a kindness to such of you as were on duty in Lincoln county during the disorders there,"[53] and informed Schurz that he was deliberately staying away from Lincoln in order to avoid provoking jealousy and bad feeling.[54]

Perhaps Wallace's forebearance stemmed from the fact that only the previous week, he had requested that Dudley be relieved from command of Fort Stanton, as "he has excited the animosity of parties in Lincoln County to such a degree as to embarrass the administration of affairs in that locality."[55] Dudley's superiors, however, unanimously disapproved the request. General of the Army William T. Sherman noted in his endorsement that Dudley was not required to explain his public acts to the governor, but would promptly do so to his superiors if Wallace would prefer charges against him.[56]

Chapman repeatedly addressed Wallace, insisting in increasingly abusive language that the governor must visit Lincoln in person. Dudley, he wrote, was "a whiskey barrel in the morning and a barrel of whiskey at night....His conduct has become a reproach to the military service of the country and an insult to every officer who tries to maintain the dignity of his position."[57] Failing to receive satisfaction from Wallace, he finally challenged him directly by organizing a mass meeting of the citizens of Lincoln on December 7

> for the purpose of expressing their sentiments in regard to the outrages committed in this county, and to denounce the manner in which the people have been misrepresented and maligned; and also to adopt

> such measures as will inform the President of the United States as to the true state of affairs in Lincoln County.[58]

To the governor himself, Chapman wrote contemptuously:

> The people of Lincoln County are disgusted and tired of the neglect and indifference shown them by you, and next week they intend holding a mass-meeting to give expression to their sentiment, and unless you come here before that time you may expect to be severely denounced in language more forcible than polite....
>
> I am now preparing a statement of facts for publication, which, I am sorry to say will reflect upon you for not coming here in person, for no one can get a correct idea of the outrages that have [been] committed here by quietly sitting in Santa Fe and depending on drunken officers for information.[59]

Fortunately for the peace and quiet of Lincoln, Chapman's meeting met with the disapproval of Isaac Ellis, Ben Ellis, Jose Montaño, and others of the cooler heads among the McSween partisans. As a result, it seems to have gone off without disturbance of any kind. Wallace jubilantly informed a reporter that when he

> reached his post of duty he found the Territory in a state of anarchy and confusion....
>
> By systematic management, with the assistance of the national authorities, who placed at his disposal the United States troops stationed in the Territory, he has brought about a state of profound peace, and he says New Mexico is...free from turmoil and anarchy today....[60]

The governor was soon to learn that he had committed a strategic blunder which a former major general should have avoided: he had fatally underestimated Chapman's ability to create trouble.

NOTES

[1] Report by Marion Johnson, with Thad Page, to P.J. Rasch, July 28, 1955.

[2] Frank Warner Angel to C. Schurz, October 3, 1878. Record Group 48,

Records of the Office of the Secretary of the Interior, Appointment Division, Letters Received, Territorial Governors, New Mexico, 1849–78. National Archives.

[3] Frank Warner Angel to Charles Devens, Undated Report, Department of Justice. National Archives.

[4] Frank Warner Angel to C. Schurz, October 2, 1878. Record Group 75, Records of the Bureau of Indian Affairs. National Archives.

[5] Bess Glenn to P.J. Rasch, August 2, 1955.

[6] Bess Glenn to P.J. Rasch, December 13, 1955.

[7] Irving Wallace, *"Ben-Hur" Wallace*. Berkeley: University of California Press, 1947, p. 136.

[8] Santa Fe *Rocky Mountain Sentinel*, October 2, 1878.

[9] Lew Wallace to C. Schurz, October 1, 1878. The William Henry Smith Memorial Library of the Indiana Historical Society.

[10] N.A.M. Dudley to Act. Asst. Adjutant General, District of New Mexico, September 7, 1878. Records of the War Department, Office of the Adjutant General, File 1405, AGO, 1878. National Archives.

[11] It seems likely that "Wrestlers" is a mistaken rendition of the word Rustlers.

[12] Selman was killed by U.S. Deputy Marshal George Scarborough in El Paso, Texas, on April 5, 1896. See State of Texas vs. Geo. A. Scarborough, Cause No. 1945. Also El Paso *Daily Times*, April 7, 1896.

[13] See State of Texas vs. John Selman, Cause No. 1874. Also El Paso *Times*, August 20, 21, 22, 1895.

[14] Charles Snow was one of the Clanton gang of rustlers wiped out by Mexicans in Guadalupe Canyon on August 13, 1881. See Phil Rasch, "A Note on Buckskin Frank Leslie," in 1954 *Brand Book*, Denver Posse of the Westerners, Boulder, Colorado: Johnson Publishing Company, 1955, p. 208.

[15] See Causes 272, 273, 275, 276, 327, 328, 329, and 330, Lincoln County, New Mexico.

[16] Coe, *Frontier Fighter*, op. cit., p. 106.

[17] N.A.M. Dudley to Acting Asst. Adjt. General, District of New Mexico, September 28, 1878. File 1405, AGO, 1878.

[18] N.A.M. Dudley to Asst. Adjt. General, District of New Mexico, September 29, 1878. File 1405, AGO, 1878.

[19] N.A.M. Dudley to Act. Asst. Adjt. General, District of New Mexico, October 3, 1878. File 1405, AGO, 1878.

[20] For a brief biography of this individual, see Rasch, "A Note on N.A.M. Dudley," op. cit. [See Chapter 14.] Since that account was written, the War Department has removed a great deal of very important material about Dudley from the classified list. His actions at Lincoln need to be re-

evaluated in the light of this newly-available material.

[21] Loud to Comdg. Officer, Fort Stanton, October 8, 1878. File 1405, AGO, 1878.

[22] John Sherman, Jr., to Lew Wallace, October 4, 1878. William Henry Smith Memorial Library of the Indiana Historical Society.

[23] Bristol to Sherman, October 4, 1878. The William Henry Smith Memorial Library of the Indiana Historical Society.

[24] Florencio Gonzales *et al.* to Lew Wallace, October 8, 1878. The William Henry Smith Memorial Library of the Indiana Historical Society.

[25] N.A.M. Dudley to Lewis Wallace, October 10, 1878. The William Henry Smith Memorial Library of the Indiana Historical Society.

[26] This apparently refers to the Mormon settlers who had been welcomed by John Chisum a few years earlier. For the background of this settlement, see Rasch, "The Pecos War," op. cit. [See Chapter 3.]

[27] Las Vegas *Gazette*, August 17, 1878; quoted in Cimarron *News and Press*, September 29, 1878.

[28] N.A.M. Dudley to Act. Asst. Adjt. General, District of New Mexico, October 19, 1878. File 1405, AGO, 1878.

[29] Daniel Dow, Robert Steward, and August Kline to Commander at Fort Stanton, October 1, 1878. File 1405, AGO, 1878.

[30] Santa Fe *New Mexican*, October 26, 1878.

[31] Geo. W. McCrary to Wm. T. Sherman, October 8, 1878. File 1405, AGO, 1878.

[32] Lew Wallace to W.M. Evarts, October 9, 1878. Record Group 59, General Records of the Department of State, Miscellaneous Letters.

[33] N.A.M. Dudley to Act. Asst. Adjt. General, District of New Mexico, October 10, 1878. File 1405, AGO, 1878.

[34] Lew Wallace to C. Schurz, October 14, 1878. The William Henry Smith Memorial Library of the Indiana Historical Society.

[35] Lew Wallace to Edward Hatch, October 26, 1878. File 1405, AGO, 1878.

[36] John S. Loud to Commanding Officer, Fort Stanton, October 27, 1878. Exhibit No. 1, Vo. No. 3, Court of Inquiry convened by S.O. 59, Head Quarters, Department of the Missouri, March 28, 1879. National Archives.

[37] N.A.M. Dudley to M.F. Goodwin, November 3, 1878. Exhibit No. 3, Vol. No. 3, Court of Inquiry convened by S.O. 59.

[38] S.S. Pague, Special Orders No. 130, November 4, 1878. Exhibit No. 2, Vol. No. 3, Court of Inquiry convened by S.O. 59.

[39] M.P. Corbett to Judge Blacker, Nov. 9, 1878. State of Texas *Adjutant General's Reports*, 1870–1881, pp. 6–8.

[40] Quoted in McKee, op. cit., p. 145.

[41] N.A.M. Dudley to Asst. Adjt. General, District of New Mexico, December 6, 1878. Exhibit No. 7, Vol. No. 3, Court of Inquiry convened by S.O. 59.

[42] N.A.M. Dudley to Acting Assistant Adjt. General, District of New Mexico, November 30, 1878. Exhibit No. 23, Vol. No. 1, Court of Inquiry convened by S.O. 59.

[43] N.A.M. Dudley to Acting Asst. Adjt. Gen., District of New Mexico, December 7, 1878. File 1405, AGO, 1878.

[44] N.A.M. Dudley to Acting Assist. Adjt. General, November 23, 1878. Exhibit No. 5, Vol. No. 3, Court of Inquiry convened by S.O. 59.

[45] N.A.M. Dudley to Acting Assist. Adjt. General, December 3, 1878. Exhibit No. 6, Vol. No. 3, Court of Inquiry convened by S.O. 59.

[46] H.I. Chapman to Lew Wallace, October 24, 1878. Exhibit No. 4, Vol. No. 1, Court of Inquiry convened by S.O. 59.

[47] Lew Wallace to Edward Hatch, October 28, 1878. File 1405, AGO, 1878.

[48] N.A.M. Dudley to Actg. Asst. Adjt. General, November 7, 1878, and November 9, 1878. File 1405, AGO, 1878.

[49] John S. Loud to Lew Wallace, November 13, 1878. File 1405, AGO, 1878.

[50] Testimony of Lewis Wallace, P. 9 Court of Inquiry convened by S.O. 59.

[51] Lew Wallace to N.A.M. Dudley, November 30, 1878. Exhibit No. 26, Vol. No. 1, Court of Inquiry convened by S.O. 59.

[52] Santa Fe *Weekly New Mexican*, December 14, 1878; Mesilla *News*, December 21, 1878.

[53] Lew Wallace to N.A.M. Dudley *et al.*, December 16, 1878. William Henry Smith Memorial Library of the Indiana Historical Society.

[54] Lew Wallace to C. Schurz, December 21, 1878. William Henry Smith Memorial Library of the Indiana Historical Society.

[55] Lew Wallace to Edward Hatch, December 7, 1878. P. 9 Court of Inquiry convened by S.O. 59.

[56] W.T. Sherman to the Secretary of War, December 26, 1878. Pp. 11–12 Court of Inquiry convened by S.O. 59.

[57] H.I. Chapman to Lew Wallace, November 25, 1878. Exhibit No. 24, Vol. No. 1, Court of Inquiry convened by S.O. 59.

[58] Quoted from copy of placard with N.A.M. Dudley to Acting Asst. Adjutant General, December 9, 1878. File 1405, AGO, 1878.

[59] H.I. Chapman to Lew Wallace, November 2, 1878. Exhibit No. 25, Vol. No. 1, Court of Inquiry convened by S.O. 59.

[60] Denver *Tribune*, January 30, 1879.

16.
The Governor Meets the Kid

The English Westerners' Brand Book, April 1966

In 1878, Lincoln County, New Mexico, was torn by a feud between the partisans of Lawrence G. Murphy, James J. Dolan, and John H. Riley and those of John H. Tunstall, Alexander A. McSween, and John S. Chisum.[1] In the fighting, both Tunstall[2] and McSween[3] were killed. The widowed Mrs. McSween retained attorney Huston I. Chapman to protect her interests. Shortly after accusing the commanding officer of Fort Stanton, Lieutenant Colonel N.A.M. Dudley, 9th Cavalry, of complicity in the killing of McSween and the burning of his home, Chapman was himself murdered.[4]

Colonel Edward Hatch, 9th Cavalry, commanding the District of New Mexico, and Lew Wallace, governor of the territory of New Mexico, hurried to Lincoln. Hatch and Dudley had been bitter personal enemies for years; Wallace, still smarting over the consequences of the battle of Shiloh, apparently saw a chance to pay off old scores against the Regular Army, and was determined to place the blame for the entire affair on the shoulders of Dudley, whom he had never met. And even as Hatch and Wallace rode south together, yet another of Dudley's self-appointed enemies was seeking his undoing.

Ira E. Leonard, a Las Vegas lawyer, wrote Secretary of War George W. McCrary, forwarding a long newspaper account of the death of Chapman and making serious charges against Dudley and Second Lieutenant James H. French, 9th Cavalry. He alleged:

1. That Dudley had assisted a band of outlaws in killing McSween and burning his house.

2. That he had compelled Justice of the Peace John B. Wilson to issue warrants for McSween and others, under threat of ironing and imprisonment.
3. That he had permitted the Tunstall store to be plundered of $6000 worth of goods.
4. That he had procured wicked men to make base and slanderous charges against Mrs. McSween.
5. That he had refused to buy corn from David Easton after the latter refused to make an affidavit against the character of Mrs. McSween.
6. That he had published an open letter in which he made false and malicious charges against Mrs. McSween, and which was intended to foment trouble in Lincoln County.
7. That he had sent Lieutenant French to Lincoln, that French had become drunk and had insulted and abused Mrs. McSween, Chapman, John N. Copeland, and other citizens.

He urged that these charges be investigated, and, if they were sustained, the officers concerned be punished.[5]

Hatch and Wallace arrived at their destinations late on the afternoon of 5 March 1879, Hatch going to Fort Stanton and Wallace proceeding to Lincoln. A public meeting was held in the village, after which Wilson, Juan B. Patrón, Martin Sanchez [Sanches] (father of the murdered Gregorio Sanchez [Sanches]), Ben Ellis, James A. Tomlinson, James Jabalicoe (Jasper Coe?), and a few other McSween supporters visited the governor in his room at the Jose Montaño house to complain of Dudley's conduct. Hatch himself ignored his subordinate, other than to order him to send a patrol to report to the governor for such duty as he might require.

Reassured by the presence of the troops, the citizens of Lincoln gave a ball, to which the officers at Fort Stanton and their ladies were sent bids by the Committee on Invitations, composed of George B. Barber, A.J. Ballard, and Jose Montaño. Dudley was too seasoned a campaigner to be deluded by superficial courtesies. He had expressed his opinion of the inhabitants of Lincoln in his report on the 28 February conference with them:

> Knowing these people so thoroughly and having been so repeatedly trifled with by them, I disliked having any intercourse with them, but on reflection I accepted their invitation, and went to the Plaza for the

> first time in seven months....It was a repetition of the meetings of last May and June, when the McSween clique passed the most complimentary resolutions eulogizing the actions of the Post Commander and the troops in giving them protection, at that time all the arrests were being made from the *Dolan and Riley* faction. As soon as a change of Sheriffs was made and men were arrested belonging to the other party, then the troops changed in their estimation, and became partisans and murderers, and no doubt a similar change will take place in their views, if the troops interfere with their friends.[6]

They were now engaged in proving his point. An invitation to a fete became a sardonic gesture when those arranging the affair were actively seeking his removal.

Whatever his faults—and they were many—Dudley was not unintelligent. He realised that his enemies had him surrounded and were making every effort to bring him down. His anxiety and uncertainty are evident in the letter which he now sent to Hatch:

> I am unofficially informed that his Excellency the Governor, intends to remain some time in Lincoln County, and that the District Commander proposes to soon leave for Fort Bliss. I respectfully request that I may be furnished with additional instructions before your departure, in regard to furnishing troops to make arrests, preserve the peace &c in Lincoln and Doña Anna Counties.
>
> Letters of instruction of Oct 27th 78, which has not been changed or modified in any way, does not authorise the Comdg Officer of the Post of Fort Stanton to send the troops under his command in pursuit of Criminals charged with crimes, except when called upon by the Sheriff of the County, his deputies, or the U.S. Marshall [sic] or his deputies, and one of these civil functionaries to be present with the posse.
>
> Two detachments are now out after alleged criminals, having no warrants or civil officer with them. I have the District Commanders instructions to protect me in both these cases, but, after he leaves, I may be called upon to furnish troops in the same manner by his Excellency the Governor. No officer can afford to take the responsibility of complying with such requests in the face of the positive Military orders now covering these delicate duties.
>
> I do not wish to be understood as wishing to throw any obstacle in his Excellency having every assistance the troops can give him. On the Contrary, I will strip the garrison down to a Corporals Guard,

> and then go myself, in charge of a similar command, to aid him in capturing every outlaw and criminal he can locate, but I cannot, with the experience I have had, and the Knowledge I possess of these people, put myself in a position to be charged with a violation of well defined orders and instructions.
>
> If it is the intention for the Governor to use the Troops as he may see fit, a written order to this effect will be all that is necessary, and the District Commander can rest assured he will have no occasion to find any fault with the promptness with which each case will be met by the writer.[7]

Hatch promptly issued Special Field Orders No. 2, relieving Dudley from command of Fort Stanton and ordering him to Fort Union "to await such action as the Dept. Commander may take upon the allegations preferred by his Excellency the Governor of New Mexico."[8] The allegations in question had been preferred in a letter from Governor Wallace:

> I have the honor to repeat the request made on a former occasion that Lt. Col. N.A.M. Dudley be relieved of the command of Fort Stanton.
>
> This is done upon conviction that he is so compromised by connection with the troubles in this county that his usefulness in the effort now making to restore order is utterly gone. The intimidation under which really well disposed people are suffering, and which prevents my securing affidavits as the foundation of legal proceedings against parties already in arrest, results in great part from fear of misdirection of authority by him.
>
> It is with the greatest possible regret I add, if I am to believe the information which has come to me, the dread referred to is not irrational. In justice to Col. Dudley, and that he may take such course as he deems best to have an investigation with a view to his exoneration, and also that you may take such action as your sense of duty may suggest under the circumstances, I will state in general terms that it is charged here that Lt. Col. Dudley is responsible for the killing of McSween and the men who were shot with that person; that he was an influential participant in that affair, and yet is an active partisan. I have information also, connecting him with the more recent murder of H.I. Chapman; to the effect that he knew the man would be killed, and announced it the day of the night of the killing, and that one of the murderers [William Campbell] stated

> publicly that he had promised Colonel Dudley to do the deed. I am informed that another man [Charles Scase] was driven in fear of life from Lincoln to Fort Stanton; that a band of armed men followed him there, and hunted for him about the Trader's Store, avowing a purpose to kill him; that the party pursued appealed to Col. Dudley to give him protection, but was turned away, and escaped with difficulty; that there was no investigation of the affair by Col. Dudley, and that the would-be murderers were not interrupted in their hunt, which was repeated through two days, but were permitted to leave at their leisure, and within a night or two after engaged in the killing of Chapman in the town of Lincoln.
>
> I beg to say distinctly that I make you this statement as information come to me in a manner to make the giving the statement and the request which precedes it matters of official duty. You will greatly favor me by furnishing Lt. Col. Dudley a copy of this communication.[9]

Hatch attributed Dudley's troubles to the fact that he had constantly been under the influence of liquor. He wrote to his superiors, "From the evidence now in the possession of the Governor, he seems warranted in making these serious charges,"[10] but to Assistant Surgeon Daniel M. Appel he cynically expressed the opinion that the governor could not sustain his allegations.[11] Upon learning that Dudley had been relieved, Wallace called a meeting of the citizens of Lincoln. The burden of his talk with them was that "the best day's work that ever was done for the citizens of Lincoln or Lincoln County had been done that day, and that was the removal of General Dudley."[12] Be that as it may, it is to the eternal discredit of Hatch and Wallace that they would conspire to remove an officer of long and meritorious service on hearsay evidence, much of which was to be proven false, without affording him even an opportunity to speak in his own defence.

On receiving Hatch's order, Dudley immediately demanded that he be furnished with a copy of the charges against him and the names of the witnesses to them. He pointed out that he had never so much as seen Wallace, much less been afforded a chance to answer any of the complaints made against him. Hatch forwarded the communication to Wallace, who returned it with an endorsement that was irrelevant, immaterial, and inconsequential: "Lieut Colonel Dudley will excuse me if I decline to give him any advice."[13] Hatch forwarded this answer to Dudley, with the additional information that he could not give the matter his personal attention, since he was leaving early in the morning! He might have added that he and the governor were attending a dinner at the post and would be there all night. Justly enraged at Wallace's senseless affront, Dudley stiffly returned the paper with a curt note that he had not asked for any advice and his orders did not require him to do so; hence, he could only conclude that the governor's endorsement was meant for some other communication.

He petitioned Hatch to be allowed to remain at the post long enough to secure affidavits and make copies of official papers, but the colonel insisted that he leave promptly, in spite of the fact that Dudley would have to be back in Lincoln by 2 April to attend court. Dudley was an extremely difficult person with whom to deal and had long been a thorn in Hatch's side. Nevertheless, the facts are that he had acted strictly in accordance with Hatch's orders and had kept him fully advised of every move he made and of every item of interest which came to his attention. His repeated requests for instructions had been ignored and he had been required to take actions in conflict with his written orders. Hatch's failure to support his subordinate was not in keeping with the best traditions of the service and reflected no credit upon him as an officer or as a man.

With the military at his command and with President Hayes' approval of his proceeding under the proclamation of 7 October 1878, Wallace took swift and perhaps not altogether legal action to clean up the situation in Lincoln and Doña Ana Counties. A militia company—inelegantly known to the citizens as the governor's Heelflies[14]—was organised, with Juan Patrón as captain, Ben H. Ellis as first lieutenant, and Martin Sanches, alleged murderer of Gabriel Basiel, as second lieutenant. A hint of where the governor's sympathies lay may be gleaned from the fact that included in its roster were Fernando Herrera, Martin Chaves, Jose Chaves y Chaves,[15] Yginio Salazar, George Washington, Florencio Chaves, Jose Maria Sanchez, and other McSween fighting men. Under Wallace's personal direction, they galloped hither and thither across the countryside, busily engaged in accomplishing relatively little.

After a futile attempt to arrest Billy the Kid and Tom O'Folliard at Las Tablas, the military were kept more than busy. They were ordered to visit all cattle camps, seize any unbranded cattle, and arrest the asserted owners. Justice of the Peace John B. Wilson was reminded that he had no authority to issue writs of habeas corpus and was urged to ignore any steps taken in the interests of the prisoners. Wallace furnished Captain Henry Carroll, 9th Cavalry, with a long list of men who were to be arrested immediately and held in the guardhouse at Fort Stanton.[16,17] It has not been possible to account satisfactorily for all of these individuals, but their names and the charges against most of them can be chronicled:

1. John Slaughter. Wanted for the murder of Barney Gallagher at South Spring, New Mexico, in October 1876. His role in Lincoln County has been detailed elsewhere.[18] He went on to become the famous sheriff of Tombstone and to die peacefully in his San Bernardino Ranch on 15 February 1922.

2. Andrew Boyle. Wanted for stealing R.B. Sagely's horses in the fall of 1877. He died 14 May 1882.

3. John Selman. Wanted for the murder of Gregorio Sanches, Clato Chaves, Desiderio Chaves, and Lorenzo Lucero in September 1878.[19] Selman fled to Texas. He became a constable in El Paso and earned a dubious sort of fame by shooting John Wesley Hardin in the back. He was himself killed by George Scarborough on 5 April 1896.[20]

4. Tom "Tom Cat" Selman. Wanted on the Selman charges.

5. Gus Gildea. Wanted on the Selman charges. Gildea removed to Arizona, took up a ranch in the Dragoon Mountains not far from Tombstone, and died in bed 9 August 1935.[21]

6. James Irwin [John W. Irvin]. Wanted on the Selman charges. His body is said to have been found on the Pecos.[22]

7. Reese Gobles. Wanted on the Selman charges. His body is said to have been found with that of Irwin [Irvin].[23]

8. "Rustling Bob." Wanted on the Selman charges. His body was found on the Pecos, presumably killed by his own party.[24]

9. Robert Speaks [Speakes]. Wanted on the Selman charges and for the murder of one Beatty near Albuquerque in the fall of 1878. A man by this name enlisted in the Texas Rangers at [Fort] Stockton, Texas, in August 1880, but was discharged when it was found that he was under an indictment.[25]

10. The Pilgrim. Wanted on the Selman charges.

11. John Beckwith. Accused of stealing Tunstall cattle. He was killed by John Jones on 26 August 1879.[26]

12. Hugh [Henry] M. Beckwith. Wanted for the murder of his son-in-law, William H. Johnson, at the Beckwith Ranch on 17 August 1878. Beckwith went to Texas and is said to have been beaten to death in 1892.[27]

13. James French. Wanted for the murder of Bill Williams, alias Andrew "Buckshot" Roberts, at Blazer's Mill on 4 April 1878. His end is not certain; he may have been the man shot at Catoosa, Indian Territory, during an attempted robbery in the autumn of 1895.[28]

14. Josiah G. Scurlock. Wanted on the French charge. He died at Eastland, Texas, on 25 July 1929.[29]

15. Charles M. Bowdre. Wanted on the French charge and for the murder of Sheriff William Brady at Lincoln on 1 April 1878. He was shot by Sheriff Pat Garrett at Stinking Springs on 22 December 1880.

16. William H. Bonney. Wanted on the Bowdre charges. He was shot by Garrett at Fort Sumner on 14 July 1881.

17. Henry Newton Brown. Wanted on the Bowdre charges. Brown had already left New Mexico. He became sheriff at Caldwell, Kansas, and was killed by a mob on 30 April 1884 when breaking jail after his arrest for murder and attempted bank robbery.[30]

18. John Middleton. Wanted on the Bowdre charges. He had left New Mexico with Brown. Middleton lived in Kansas for some time, but eventually disappeared.

19. Fred Waite. Wanted on the Bowdre charges. Waite had left New Mexico with Brown and Middleton and returned to his home on the Washita in the Indian Territory.

20. Jacob B. Mathews. Wanted for the murder of John H. Tunstall. Mathews became a prominent citizen of New Mexico and was postmaster at Roswell when he died on 3 June 1904.[31]

21. Jessie J. Evans. Wanted for the Tunstall murder. The last record of Evans is his escape from the Texas State Penitentiary at Huntsville, Texas, on 23 May 1882.[32]

22. James J. Dolan. Wanted for the Tunstall murder. Dolan played a prominent role in New Mexican history of the time and died at his Feliz Ranch—the old Tunstall place—on 26 February 1898.[33]

23. George Davis (alias Tom Jones). Wanted for the Tunstall murder and for the murder of the Pholis (Feliz) family near Lamotte

in October, 1878. He was killed by Texas Ranger Sergeant E.A. Seiker [Edward A. Sieker, Jr.] about 18 miles north of Presidio del Norte, Texas, on 3 July 1880.[34]

24. ——— Rivers. Wanted for the Tunstall murder. The identity of this individual is uncertain.

25. Juan Patrón. Wanted for the Tunstall murder. He was killed by Michael E. Maney at Puerto de Luna, New Mexico, on 9 April 1884.[35]

26. John A. Jones. Wanted for the Pholis (Feliz) murder and for the murder of William Riley on the Peñasco in 1875 or 1876, and for the murder of a man in Kinney County, Texas. He was killed by Bob Olinger in Pierce Canyon on 29 August 1879.[36]

27. James Perry Jones. Wanted for the Pholis (Feliz) murder and for the murder of a man in Kinney County, Texas. Died at Rocky Arroyo on 5 February 1930.

28. William Marcus Jones. Wanted for the Pholis (Feliz) murder. Died 17 March 1950.

29. Marion Turner. Wanted for the Pholis (Feliz) murder.

30. Heiskell Jones. Wanted for the Pholis (Feliz) murder.

31. Caleb Hall (alias Collins). Wanted for the Pholis (Feliz) murder.

32. William B. [Thomas Benton] "Buck" Powell. Wanted for the killing of Yopp about the end of December, 1876.[37] Powell died at his Peñasco ranch 31 August 1906.

33. James Hyson (James M. Highsaw). Wanted for the killing of Richard Smith at Loving's Bend of the Pecos River on 28 March 1877.[38]

34. Jake Owens. A rustler.

35. Joseph Hill, alias Olney. Wanted for the murder of a deputy sheriff in Burnettown [Burnet], Texas.

36. Frank Wheeler. A horse thief. Killed by Sam Perry in July, 1879.[39]

In rapid succession, Slaughter, Dolan, Campbell, Mathews, Evans, Owens, and one of the Jones boys were arrested. Joe Bowers, Scurlock, and Chris [Charles] Morsner soon followed. If not martial law, this was in effect indistinguishable from it. To Wallace's dismay, however, the prisoners' lawyer, Sidney Wilson, demanded writs of habeas corpus. The governor complained to Secretary of the Interior Carl Schurz that he was placed in the dilemma of either turning his prisoners loose or ignoring the court's order.

Wallace was especially anxious to arrest Billy the Kid,[40] who, as a member of the McSween faction and a witness to the murder of Chapman, might be a source of evidence against both Dudley and the Dolan party. He must have been both surprised and pleased to receive the following letter from him:

> I have heard that you will give one thousand $ for my body, which I can understand, it means alive as a witness. I know that it is as a witness against those that murdered Mr. Chapman. If it was arranged so that I could appear at court, I could give the desired information, but I have indictments against me for things that happened in the last Lincoln County War, and am afraid to give up because my enemies would kill me. The day Mr. Chapman was murdered I was in Lincoln at the request of good citizens to meet J.J. Dolan, to meet as friends, so as to be able to lay aside my arms and go to work.
>
> I was present when Mr. Chapman was murdered and know who did it, and if it were not for those indictments, I would have made it clear before now.
>
> If it is your power to annul those indictments, I hope you will do so, so as to give me a chance to explain.
>
> Please send an answer by bearer.
>
> I have no wish to fight any more, indeed I have not raised an arm since your proclamation. As to my character I refer you to any of the citizens, for the majority of them are my friends and have been helping me all they could. I am called Kid Antrim, but Antrim is my stepfather's name.[41]

Wallace replied as follows:

> Come to the house of old Squire Wilson (not the lawyer) at nine (9) o'clock next Monday night alone. I don't mean his office, but his residence. Follow along foot of the mountain south of the town, come in on that side, and knock at the east door. I have authority to exempt you from prosecution, if you will testify to what you say you know.
>
> The object of the meeting at Squire Wilson's is to arrange the matter in a way to make your life safe. To do that the utmost secrecy is to be used. *So come alone.* Don't tell anybody—not a living soul—where you are coming or the object. If you could trust Jesse Evans, you can trust me.[42]

By "Squire Wilson," Wallace meant Justice of the Peace John B. Wilson,[43] a McSween supporter who was living just east of the courthouse. The reference to Evans is an unsolved mystery. On the night of the 17th, Wilson and Wallace sat in the jacal, tense and expectant. Just after midnight, a knock was heard on the door. As Wallace[44] long afterwards recalled the scene, he answered: "Come in."

The door opened and the Kid entered. In his right hand was a revolver; in his left, a Winchester. "I was to meet the governor here at midnight. It is midnight; is the governor here?"

Wallace rose to his feet and held out his hand.

"Your note gave promise of absolute protection," said the outlaw warily.

"I have been true to my promise," replied the governor. "This man," pointing to Wilson, "and myself are the only persons present."

The revolver was returned to its holster, the rifle was lowered, and the visitor dropped into a chair. Wallace lost no time in stating his proposition.

"Testify before the grand jury and the trial court and convict the murderer of Chapman and I will let you go scott-free with a pardon in your pocket for all your own misdeeds."

The Kid listened in silence and thought for several minutes before replying, "Governor, if I were to do what you ask, they would kill me."

"We can prevent that," answered the governor. He then unfolded a plan whereby the Kid was to be seized while asleep. To this the Kid agreed, but made two stipulations: he was to pick the men who were to effect his capture and he was to be ironed while in confinement in order to protect his reputation as a desperate man.

The plans nearly went awry on 19 March when Evans and William Campbell, who were held in the guardhouse at Fort Stanton on a charge of murdering Chapman, bribed their guard, a recruit known as "Texas Jack," and the three men fled from the fort. Wallace posted a $1,000 reward for their recapture. The deserter was soon retaken,[45] but Evans and Campbell made good their escape, presumably going to Arizona with Slaughter's herd.[46] The Kid's uncertainty over the effect of Evans' escape on his own situation is reflected in the note which he immediately sent to Wilson:

> Please tell you know who that I do not know what to do, now as those Prisoners have escaped to send word by bearer, a note through

> you it may be that he has made different arrangements if not and he still wants it the same to send: William Hudgins [Hudgens] as Deputy to the junction tomorrow at three oclock with some men you know to be all right. Send a note telling me what to do, do not send soldiers.[47]

Wallace was quick to reassure him:

> The escape makes no difference in arrangements.
>
> To remove all suspicion of understanding, I think it is better to put the arresting party in charge of Sheriff Kimball [Kimbrell], who will be instructed to see that no violence is used.
>
> This will go to you tonight. If I don't get other word from you the party (all citizens) will be at the junction by 3 o'clock tomorrow.[48]

The note was sent to Wilson, to be forwarded to the Kid. That he cannot have been far away is shown by the fact that he replied the same day:

> I will keep the appointment I made, but be Sure and have men come that You can depend on I am not afraid to die like a man fighting but I would not like to be killed like a dog unarmed. tell Kimbal to let his men be placed around the house and for him to come in alone: and he can arrest us all I am afraid of is that in the Fort we might be poisoned or killed through a window at night, but you can arrange that all right. tell the Commanding Officer to Watch Let Goodwind [Lieut. Goodwin] he would not hesitate to do anything there Will be danger on the road of Somebody Waylaying us to kill us on the road to the Fort.
>
> You will never catch those fellows on the road Watch Fritzes, Captain Bacas ranch and the Brewery, they will either go to Seven Rivers or to Jicarillo Mountains they will stay around close untill the scouting parties come in give a Spy a pair of glasses and let him get on the mountain back of Fritzes and watch and if they are there there will be provisions carried to them it is not My place to advise you but I am anxious to have them caught, and perhaps know how men hide from Soldiers, better than you please excuse me for having so much to say and I still remain Your Truly
>
> W.H. Bonney
>
> P.S.
>
> I have changed my mind Send Kimball to Gutierres just below San Patricio one mile because Sanger and Ballard are or was great

> friends of Commels [Campbell's]. Ballard tole me yesterday to leave for you were doing everything to catch me. it was a blind to get me to leave tell Kimball not to come before 3 oclock for I may not be there before.[49]

The plans were executed without a hitch. On 21 March, Sheriff Kimball [Kimbrell] and his posse brought in the Kid and Tom O'Folliard. They were placed in the home of Juan Patrón, under the guard of Deputy Sheriff T.M. Longworth. Having pledged their word not to escape, they were at first allowed a good deal of freedom, but were shortly transferred to the Lincoln County jail. To Wallace's amazement, he found that the Kid was regarded by the townsfolk as something of a hero. We may suspect that for the first time the governor began to appreciate the complexities of the problem which he had undertaken to solve. The baffled feeling with which this cultured eastern gentleman viewed these strange and violent folks of the western frontier is clearly reflected in a letter which he wrote to Schurz:

> To still further weaken my confidence in juries as instruments of the law in this county, I have been forced to take account of the fact that everybody of any force or character has in some way been committed to one side or the other in the recent war, and is yet all alive with prejudices and partialities. A precious specimen nicknamed "The Kid", whom the Sheriff is holding here in the Plaza, as it is called, is an object of tender regards. I heard singing and music the other night; going to the door I found the minstrels of the village actually serenading the fellow in his prison. So, speaking generally, the prisoners are good brave boys according to the side on which they have been fighting. These prejudices and partialities are as certain to follow jurors into the box the day of the empannelling as that day will come. Either the verdicts will be acquittal or there will be no verdict....I see...nothing to be hoped except from martial law.[50]

That same day, he wired President Rutherford B. Hayes, asking that Lincoln and Doña Ana Counties be placed under martial law. This suggests that Wallace had serious doubts as to the legality of the orders he had issued, in particular, perhaps, the one for troops to visit every cattle camp in the county, seize all the cattle whose legitimate ownership could not be proved, and arrest those in charge of them. The cattle were to be turned over to Probate Judge Florencio Gonzales for delivery to John Newcomb, cattlekeeper for the county.[51] In the course of executing this order, Captain Henry Carroll, 9th Cavalry, had recovered 138 head of cattle belonging to the Tunstall estate. George Taylor also wrote to President Hayes, his cousin, telling him that the governor could not accomplish much without military support.[52]

Wallace himself visited the outlaw and permitted him to give an exhibition of his skill with the revolver and the rifle. More seriously, on the 28th, he had a long and important talk with Bonney concerning the situation in the county. It has lately been the fashion to describe the Kid as "a moronic little killer," or by some other similar term. However, the notes which Wallace kept on his conversation with the Kid, and which are still preserved in the William Henry Smith Memorial Library of the Indiana Historical Society, clearly show that he was a keen observer, fully posted on events occuring within the area. Billy was a psychopathic personality, but to refer to him as "moronic" is to display a complete ignorance of the facts.

Wallace arranged for Leonard to assist in prosecuting the prisoners. Mortally offended by his introduction into the trials, District Attorney William L. Rynerson did his best to hinder the prosecution. He flatly refused to cooperate with the governor's plan to grant Bonney immunity in exchange for turning state's evidence and told the prisoners that the district attorney was simply a figurehead—Leonard was the man whom the governor had selected to see them punished. Perhaps it was a result of his attitude that the outlaws posted a notice stating that if Leonard did not leave the country, they would take his scalp and send him to hell. On the night of 24 April, an attempt was made to assassinate the lawyer by firing into the house where he was living with Taylor. One McPherson, a deputy sheriff whom Leonard had brought to Lincoln with him, was also shot at, the bullet grazing his forehead.

Judge Warren E. Bristol, Leonard complained, was "a weak man and one wholly unfitted for the present situation." He had issued writs of habeas corpus upon such flimsy pretexts that it appeared that he "stood in fear of the desperate characters that curse this country instead of the boldness and determination to bring them to justice, and seemed interested only in getting away." The Dolan party, he alleged, was part and parcel of the Santa Fe Ring, and the people would never feel secure as long as Bristol was there to execute the laws.[53] There were probably good grounds for Leonard's complaint. Bristol had earned the enmity of the entire McSween faction by his charge to the jury when McSween was on trial for embezzlement, and may well have wished himself anywhere but in Lincoln. Rumours that he was slated to be killed were rife. The judge domiciled at Fort Stanton during the trial, going to Lincoln and back under the protection of a strong military escort. At the same time, the surviving evidence suggests that Wallace may have promised Leonard his assistance in securing a federal judgeship as the reward for his services, and the lawyer may well have been interested in creating a vacancy for himself by securing Bristol's removal.[54]

The grand jury, under Foreman Isaac Ellis, convened on 17 April. In a long charge to it, Bristol commented that "the experiment of redressing wrongs and grievances in Lincoln County by violence—by the rifle and revolver—by the shedding of blood" had been "pretty thoroughly tested" and had not paid. He warned that if judicial proceedings were rendered ineffectual, the only remedy would be martial law.[55] The county had a voting population of 150; the grand jury returned nearly 200 indictments—over 100 of them for murder. All of the latter were against members of the Dolan party; not one was found against members of the McSween faction. Practically every member of the sheriff's posse during the Five Days' Battle[56] was indicted, and about twenty-five men were accused of the murder of Frank MacNab.[57] Nearly all of them pled the governor's amnesty of 13 November 1876[58] and were discharged. Dolan, accused of the murder of Chapman, was admitted to bail in the sum of $3,000 and granted a change of venue to Socorro. A true bill was returned against Marion Turner and John Jones for the murder of McSween.[59] John Kinney, George Peppin, and Dudley were charged with the burning of McSween's home. Dudley took a change of venue to Doña Ana County and was eventually the only defendant in the cause. Neither Scurlock nor the Kid were indicted. Charges against O'Folliard of stealing Fritz's horses were dismissed. Eighteen persons charged with murder or grand larceny were brought before the court, but only two criminal cases were finally tried: Lucas Gallegos was sentenced to two years imprisonment on a charge of murdering his nephew, and Dan Dedrick was acquitted on a charge of attempted murder. Three alleged horse thieves, John Hudgens, Tobe Hudgens, and Robert Henry, escaped from the sheriff. Perhaps the most exciting event during the entire session occurred when Eli Gray, one of the militia-men, accidently shot and killed himself.

Once more, disgruntled citizens circulated a petition asking for Bristol's removal. On the whole, however, Wallace was probably satisfied. He informed Schurz that the Dolan and the McSween factions were dead as organisations. His amnesty proclamation, he said, had had exactly the effect intended—it had sheared off the past and let everybody start afresh. To have attempted to prosecute all the causes found by the pro-McSween grand jury would have accomplished little but further impoverish the already bankrupt county. Fear of the troops had caused the outlaws to flee from Lincoln and Dona Aña Counties, and he no longer recommended the imposition of martial law.[60]

Judge Bristol informed Captain George A. Purington, 9th Cavalry—whom Hatch had placed in command of Fort Stanton in spite of Wallace's request that the post be assigned to Captain Henry Carroll, 9th Cavalry—that the governor's amnesty proclamation had virtually abrogated the right to employ troops and that no measures could legally be taken under it. Purington thereupon refused to furnish military assistance without further instructions, and advised his superiors that peace and quiet reigned, that the militia company should be able to render such assistance as the civil officers might require, and that there was no further need for troops at Roswell or Lincoln.[61]

In the meantime, however, the governor had been confronted with other pressing business. Upon being relieved and ordered to Fort Union, Dudley had telegraphed directly to the adjutant general of the Army and requested that a court of inquiry be ordered to investigate his conduct. On the recommendation of General William T. Sherman, Brigadier General John Pope, commanding the Department of the Missouri, was instructed to convene such a court. Dudley promptly informed Wallace that he would be served with a subpoena to appear before the court. The executive had thereupon returned to Santa Fe to make his preparations for the inquiry. One of them was to arrange for the appointment of Leonard to assist the judge advocate in conducting the prosecution.

ACKNOWLEDGEMENTS

The writer is indebted to Miss Caroline Dunn, librarian, William Henry Smith Memorial Library of the Indiana Historical Society; Watt P. Marchman, director, Hayes Memorial Library; Miss Gertrude Hill, Miss Ruth Rambo, Mrs. Edith McManmon, and Mrs. Elma A. Medearis, of the Library of the Museum of New Mexico, for their assistance in the preparation of this paper.

NOTES

[1] Philip J. Rasch, "War in Lincoln County," in English Westerners' *Brand Book*, 6:2–11, July 1964. [See Chapter 7.]

[2] Rasch,"Prelude to War," op. cit. [See Chapter 5.]

[3] Rasch, "Five Days of Battle," op. cit. [See Chapter 9.]

[4] Rasch, "The Murder of Huston I. Chapman," op. cit. [See Chapter 18.]

[5] Ira E. Leonard to Secretary of War, 4 March 1879. In Proceedings of a Court of Inquiry in the Case of Lt. Col. N.A.M. Dudley, Records of the War Department, QQ 1284. In National Archives.

[6] N.A.M. Dudley to Acting Asst. Adjutant Genl., Dist. New Mexico, 21 February 1879. Exhibit No. 43, Volume No. 1, QQ 1284.

[7] N.A.M. Dudley to Edward Hatch, 7 March 1879. Exhibit No. 65, Volume No. 1, QQ 1284.

[8] Edward Hatch, Special Field Orders No. 2, 8 March 1879. Exhibit No. 66, Volume No. 1, QQ 1284.

[9] Lew Wallace to Edward Hatch, 7 March 1879. Exhibit No. 1, Volume No. 1, QQ 1284.

[10] Edward Hatch to Assistant Adjutant General, Department of the Missouri, 8 March 1879. QQ 1284.

[11] Testimony of D.M. Appel. QQ 1284.

[12] Testimony of Allen J. Ballard. QQ 1284.

[13] Lew Wallace, 9 March 1879. Endorsement of N.A.M. Dudley to Edward Hatch, 9 March 1879. Exhibit No. 68, Volume No. 1, QQ 1284.

[14] This was a term of contempt which had been applied to the Texas State Troops during Reconstruction Days.

[15] Chaves y Chaves later became a policeman in Las Vegas, N.M., affiliated with the notorious La Sociedad de Bandidos de Nuevo Mexico, and was sentenced to be hanged for his part in the murder of Gabriel Sandoval. This was commuted to life imprisonment, and he was eventually paroled in

1 February 1909. He died at Milagro, N.M., 17 July 1923.

[16] Lew Wallace to Henry Carroll, 11 March 1879. In Lew Wallace Collection, William Henry Smith Memorial Library of the Indiana Historical Society.

[17] Lew Wallace to H. Carroll, 14 March 1879. In Lew Wallace Collection.

[18] Philip J. Rasch, "John Slaughter in Lincoln County," in *Corral Dust*, III:9–10, June 1958.

[19] Rasch, "Exit Axtell: Enter Wallace," op. cit. [See Chapter 15.] See also Causes Nos. 270, 272, 273, 275, 276, Lincoln County District Court Records.

[20] State of Texas vs. Geo. A. Scarborough, Cause No. 1945. See also El Paso *Daily Times*, 7 April 1896.

[21] Tombstone *Epitaph*, 15 August 1935.

[22] Statement of the Kid, made Sunday night, 28 March 1879. In Lew Wallace Collection.

[23] Ibid.

[24] Ibid.

[25] C.L. Nevill to John B. Jones, 8 August 1880. Transcript in Webb Collection, University of Texas Library.

[26] Philip J. Rasch and Lee Myers, "The Tragedy of the Beckwiths," in English Westerners' *Brand Book*, 5:1–6, July 1963.

[27] Ibid.

[28] Frank L. Van Eaton, *Hell on the Border* (Fort Smith: Hell on the Border Publishing Co., 1953), pp. 282–83.

[29] Philip J. Rasch, Joseph E. Buckbee, and Karl K. Klein, "Man of Many Parts," in English Westerners' *Brand Book*, 5:9–12, January 1963. [See *Trailing Billy the Kid*, Chapter 13.]

[30] Rasch, "A Note on Henry Newton Brown," op. cit.

[31] Santa Fe *New Mexican*, 4 June 1904.

[32] Philip J. Rasch, "The Story of Jessie J. Evans," in *Panhandle-Plains Historical Review*, XXXIII:108–121, 1960.

[33] Santa Fe *New Mexican*, 2 March 1898.

[34] Philip J. Rasch, "The Mystery of George Davis," in English Westerners' *Brand Book*, 14:2–5, July 1962.

[35] Philip J. Rasch, "The Murder of Juan Patrón," in Potomac *Corral Dust*, V:20–21, July 1960. [See Chapter 21.]

[36] Rasch and Myers, "The Tragedy of the Beckwiths, op. cit.

[37] Rasch, "The Pecos War," op. cit. [See Chapter 3.]

[38] Ibid.

[39] *Mesilla Valley Independent*, 12 July 1879.

[40] For studies of the background of this individual, see Rasch and

Mullin, "New Light on the Legend of Billy the Kid," op. cit.; Rasch and Mullin, "Dim Trails—The Pursuit of the McCarty Family," op. cit.; Rasch, "The Twenty-One Men He Put Bullets Through," op. cit.; Rasch, "A Man Named Antrim," op. cit.; Rasch, "More on the McCartys," op. cit.; Rasch, "Clues to the Puzzle of Billy the Kid," op. cit.; Rasch, "And One Word More," op. cit.; Philip J. Rasch, "The Bonney Brothers," in *Frontier Times*, 39:43 et seq., January, 1965. [All are included in *Trailing Billy the Kid.*] Also W.E. Koop, *Billy the Kid: The Trail of a Kansas Legend,* op. cit.

41 W.H. Bonney to General Lew Wallace, 13 March [1879]. From photostat at Old Lincoln County Memorial Commission.

42 Lew Wallace to W.H. Bonney, 15 March 1879. In Lew Wallace Collection.

43 A John B. Wilson had been commissioned a justice of the peace in Hamilton County, Illinois, in 1826, 1829, and 1831. He was commissioned quartermaster of the 13th Odd Battalion on 2 January 1847, but this unit saw no action in the Mexican War. There is some evidence that this man was the Wilson of Lincoln County, but it is rather tenuous.

44 Indianapolis *The World*, 8 June 1902.

45 According to the Mesilla *Independent* for 29 March 1879, "Texas Jack" was a member of Captain Carroll's company. Captain Carroll was in command of Company F, 9th Cavalry. His Muster Roll for the period 25 February 1879 to 30 April 1879 does not reflect a desertion and recapture on the dates appropriate to "Texas Jack's" career.

46 Rasch, "John Slaughter in Lincoln County," op. cit.

47 W.H. Bonney to Friend Wilson, 20 [March] 1879. In Lew Wallace Collection.

48 Lew Wallace to W.H. Bonney, 20 March 1879. In Lew Wallace Collection.

49 W.H. Bonney to General Lew Wallace 20 [March] 1879. In Lew Wallace Collection.

50 Lew Wallace to Carl Schurz, 31 March 1879. In Lew Wallace Collection.

51 Lew Wallace to C. Schurz, 21 March 1879. In Lew Wallace Collection.

52 George Taylor to R.B. Hayes, 4 April 1879. In the Hayes Memorial Library.

53 Ira E. Leonard to Lew Wallace, 20 May 1879. In Lew Wallace Collection.

54 Philip J. Rasch, "The Would-Be Judge—Ira E. Leonard," in Denver Westerners' *Roundup*, XX:13–17, July 1964. [See Chapter 19.]

55 Rasch, "Exit Axtell: Enter Wallace," op. cit. [See Chapter 15.]

[56] Rasch, "Five Days of Battle," op. cit.

[57] Rasch, "War in Lincoln County," op. cit.

[58] Lew Wallace to Carl Schurz, 11 June 1879. In Lew Wallace Collection.

[59] Cause No. 300, County of Lincoln, New Mexico.

[60] Ira E. Leonard to Lew Wallace, 13 June 1879. In Lew Wallace Collection.

[61] Geo. A. Purington to Acting Asst. Adjutant General, District of New Mexico, 15 June 1879. Records of the War Department, Office of the Adjutant-General, 1405 AGO 1878. Consolidated File Relating to the Lincoln County War, New Mexico. In National Archives.

17.
Gunfire in Lincoln County

The English Westerners' Brand Book, April 1967

In July, 1878, the village of Lincoln, N.M., was the scene of a five-day pitched battle between the supporters of James J. Dolan and John H. Riley on the one hand and the Regulators, led by Alexander A. McSween, on the other. The latter suffered a decisive defeat. McSween was killed, his house burned, the store which he owned in partnership with John H. Tunstall looted, and the Regulators destroyed as an effective fighting force.[1] At the April, 1879, term of court, the grand jury found nearly 200 indictments—over 100 of them for murder. All of the latter were against members of the Dolan-Riley faction. Practically all of the accused invoked the amnesty which had been proclaimed by Governor Lew Wallace in November, 1878, and were discharged.[2]

The Regulators broke up as an organized party. Henry McCarty, better known as Billy the Kid, and Josiah G. "Doc" Scurlock, becoming bored with life in the county jail, took their departure during the night of June 17, 1879. Robert A. Widenmann, fearing to return to Lincoln, left for London to visit the Tunstall family. The Coes left the county. In May, Frank, mistaken for his cousin George, was arrested in Santa Fe on a charge of complicity in the murder of Al "Buckshot" Roberts. He was later discharged when his identity was established. Jim French was reported[3] killed in a quarrel over the division of stolen stock.[4] Wallace wrote to Secretary of the Interior Carl Schurz, "the old factions known respectively as the

'Murphy-Dolan' and the 'McSween' are dead as organizations," but warned that a "confederacy of outlaws and their friends" (known as the Black Knights) remained a disturbing element. He requested that all troops (except Captain Carroll and Lieutenant Dawson) who had been stationed at Fort Stanton during the troubles be relieved, so that the civil authorities would be supported by men not involved in local hates or friendships.[5] Jesse James was alleged to have been a guest at Las Vegas Hot Springs from July 27 to July 29, and to have discussed with Billy the possibility of their joining forces. If so, nothing came of it.[6] The military had a failure to report in August when Captain L.H. Rucker, 9th Cavalry, and a detachment of troops assisted the sheriff in surrounding a cabin about six miles below Lincoln in an effort to capture the Kid. As he had done in his youthful days in Silver City, Billy climbed up the chimney and made his escape.

Elsewhere in the county, disagreements continued to be settled by resort to gunplay. In July, one of the Black Knights, William "Babe" Gronso, stole a number of mules and horses from the Casad family. He was overtaken at Lloyd's ranch and the animals recovered. Later, Frank Wheeler boasted of having "fixed" Babe, whereupon he was killed by Sam Perry. Other accounts say that Gronso was actually eliminated by a party of Mexicans, and Wheeler was shot in an argument over the money he had received from the sale of some of Perry's cattle.[7, 8] Whatever the truth, the Las Cruces *Thirty-Four* unfeelingly suggested that honest folk would sleep more soundly if Perry would now die of remorse.[9]

John M. Beckwith went into partnership with John A. Jones in the cattle business, but is alleged to have registered their joint brand in his own name. Furious, Jones began to complain that Beckwith had stolen his cattle, and threatened drastic action if he did not pay for them. When he told Milo Pierce that he was going to kill his partner, Pierce replied, "Well, John, you [know] that if you do that you will have to kill me too, don't you?" That seemed to end the conversation, but matters came to a head on August 26, when the two partners met near Joe Nash's chozo in the mouth of Pierce Canyon. When Jones upbraided Beckwith and insisted that he be paid for his share of the cattle, the latter went for his gun. The move was fatal for him. The newspapers of the time gave what appears to be a simple and straightforward account of the affair, but nothing in

Lincoln County was either simple or straightforward. For reasons which are no longer apparent, the grand jury later indicted Marion Turner, as well as Jones, for the murder.

Three days after the shooting, Jones started out to give himself up to a justice of the peace. As he rode up to Pierce's rock house in Pierce Canyon, the rancher himself was reclining on a couch talking with Bob Olinger, one of Beckwith's employees. As Jones made his appearance, Pierce remarked, "He's coming to kill me and I will have to kill him."

"I'll do it," answered Olinger. "Just lie still."

As Jones came in the door, Olinger grabbed for the rifle he was carrying. The gun went off, hitting Pierce in the hip. Olinger shot Jones, and Pierce was placed in a wagon and taken to Fort Stockton for medical treatment. When the news reached Governor Wallace, he reported to Secretary of the Interior Carl Schurz:

> ...one "Jim Beckwith" was shot and killed by one "Tom Jones" and that "Jones" was then killed by one "Olinger", to which, as the three are amongst the most bloody of the "Bandits of the Pecos", all the good people cried "Amen."[10]

But week after week during that spring, summer, and fall, the commanding officer at Fort Stanton, Captain George A. Purington, 9th Cavalry, continued to report to his superiors that nothing of importance had occurred in the civil affairs of the county. As Wallace remarked, "I venture to suggest that the military in that quarter are not of the opinion that the killing of outlaws by outlaws is of importance to justify official mention."[11]

That fall, Charles Fritz and Emilie Scholand took another step in their long legal battle to recover the Fritz insurance money. On September 29, Sheriff George Kimball [Kimbrell] served a writ of *sciri facias* on Mrs. McSween. The document averred that McSween had promised to pay the plaintiffs $10,000, but had failed to do so. Since McSween's death had been suggested in open court and his wife had been appointed his executrix, the plaintiffs demanded that she be summoned before the October term of district court to show cause why her name should not be substituted for that of her husband and judgment rendered against her.

In October, the Kid, Scurlock, Tom O'Folliard, Charles Bowdre, and two Mexicans rounded up 118 head of John S. Chisum's cattle, alleging that he owed them $600 each for services rendered during the Lincoln County War. The herd was driven to Alamogordo and sold to Colorado beef buyers, but was afterwards recovered by its owner.[12] Scurlock decided to break off with the gang, and moved his family to Potter County, Texas.[13] The Kid himself disappears from the records for a period. It may have been about this time that he delivered some rustled cattle to Patrick Shanly [Shanley] at McMillanville and spent a month there with his old schoolmate, Pat Rose.[14]

In November, all of the Lincoln County cases taken to Socorro County on change of venue, including that of Dolan for the killing of Mrs. McSween's lawyer, Huston I. Chapman,[15] were dismissed by Judge Parks. On the 22nd of that month, a party of men spent the night carousing in Lincoln. All departed the following morning with the exception of Dick Hardman (or Hardeman), alias Dick Turpin, who shattered the Sunday quiet by firing his revolver promiscuously and pointing it at objecting citizens. When the disturber of the peace was arrested, he became abusive and made loud threats about what he would do when released. Since Lincoln had no jail, he was locked up in a back room of the Patrón building, under the custody of Deputy Sheriff Tom Longworth. Some time during the night, a band of men rushed into the building and shot the prisoner five or six times, killing him instantly.[16] About a month later, James McDavin [McDavis] killed a Mexican at Patos Spring,[17] and someone shot Allen J. Ballard in the back. There is reason to believe that this was a case of mistaken identity, but the fact that he recovered was little less than miraculous.

The editor of the Las Vegas *Daily Optic* drily commented, "If a Lincoln county man would call us a liar, we would consider the source and pass on, provided it did not in the least degree interfere with his wishes in the matter. We're a timid fellow sometimes."[18]

Billy himself returned to public view in January, 1880, when he killed Joe Grant at Fort Sumner. According to Garrett, Grant was anxious to kill the Kid and gain a reputation as a gunman. Billy heard this boasting, but kept his own counsel. On the 10th of January, a number of men were drinking in Bob Hargrove's saloon. Grant, drunk and vicious, snatched a fine pistol from Jack Finan's scabbard. The Kid examined it admiringly, noticed it had only three cartridges in the chambers, set it so that the hammer would fall on an empty one, and returned the weapon to Grant. A little later, the would-be badman suddenly pointed the pistol at the Kid and pulled the trigger. The revolver failed to fire, of course, and a bullet from Billy's own weapon promptly crashed into Grant's brain.[19] Presumably, Garrett obtained this account from Barney Mason, an eye-witness who was a relative by marriage, and it has at least a reasonable relationship to the facts. However, when Milnor Rudulph [Rudolph], the postmaster at Sunnyside (near Fort Sumner), asked the Kid what had occasioned the trouble, he replied, "Oh, nothing; it was a game of two and I got there first,"[20] which is not very enlightening.

February saw the good work continued. The Kid, Billy Wilson,[21] Mose Dedrick, Pas Chavez {Paz Chaves], Yginio Salazar, and one More stole 48 head of horses from the Mescalero Indian Reservation, and traded them off up and down the Pecos. They then rustled 54 beef cattle near Los Portales and sold them to Tom Cooper at White Oaks for $10 a head.[22] Probably, these were the animals which Cooper then sold to Pat Coghlan for $12 each, although the going price was $25 to $27. Coghlan butchered most of them to fill a government beef contract at Fort Stanton, but was eventually brought to trial and fined $150.[23] Bob Olinger[24] killed a man named Frank Hill, but the details have not survived.[25] Later in the month, four men entered the grocery store owned by Will Hudgens, located halfway between Lincoln and Fort Sumner, and proceeded to help themselves to its stock. Deputy Sheriff Longworth, Ben Ellis, Bill Ellis, Thomas Tillotson and a man named Paul took up posts on the surrounding house tops. They shot and fatally wounded Johnny Mace, who had stolen stock from one of the possemen, and obtained the surrender of Dan Lemons and two men named Scruggs and Oates. Lemons was turned over to Olinger for delivery to Fort Stockton, where a reward of $500 had been posted for his apprehension. He escaped en route, but there were strong hints that his escape from earthly trials was of a permanent nature. Scruggs broke out of the county jail and disappeared. As the month ended, Pas Chavez [Paz Chaves] was found suspended from a cottonwood tree,[26] and the mutual aid society at Seven Rivers dispatched Juanito Mes, said to have been a desperate character,[27] to whatever reward awaited him.

Indian troubles were so bad that spring that the June term of court was canceled. Among those killed by the Apaches were Bill and Sam Smith and one of Mrs. Brady's sons. Such matters were all but forgotten, however, when gold was discovered at White Oaks. For a time, Lincoln was almost depopulated as its citizens joined in the rush to the mines. When the town was laid out and its officers elected, James S. Redman (Redmond) was chosen president; G.W. Gaides, treasurer; Dolan, John Hudgens, Samuel R. Corbett [Corbet], and a Mr. Hubbs, directors.

Unfortunately, it did not take the new town long to fall into the evil ways of the old one. On the 31st of May, Joseph Askew (Asque) and Virgil Cullom became intoxicated and shot up the town. Indignant citizens returned the fire, shattering Askew's right arm and knocking him from his horse. The constable sent Joel Fowler and Dan Riverhouse in pursuit of Cullom. They met him returning to the village; Fowler promptly put a slug from his Winchester through the man's right lung, fatally wounding him. Askew, however, recovered and later became a prominent member of John Kinney's gang of rustlers.[28]

(Such goings-on were of little interest to the military. On February 3, General Edward Hatch, commanding the District of New Mexico, reported that civil affairs had been peaceable since July, 1879, and that the governor had been authorized to call out 1,000 militia if needed. He therefore urged that the troops be relieved of the responsibility for peace and order in Lincoln County, especially as every soldier was needed to deal with the Indians.[29] General John Pope, commanding the Department of the Missouri, heartily concurred.[30] The secretary of war referred the matter to the Department of State and was informed that he had the authority to issue the orders necessary to restore normal civil conditions in the county.[31] On February 28, Hatch directed the commanding officer at Fort Stanton to cease all military action under the president's proclamation and to terminate the conditions established by it. Thereafter, the troops took no part in civil affairs in the county.)

Meanwhile, Will Hudgens had run into Fowler's saloon and asked for a gun so that he could help make the arrests. Two pistols were available, but Alex Colvin claimed they belonged to him and his partner and refused to permit Hudgens to use them. Will thereupon told him in plain language that he was no better than the men who had shot up the town. Shortly afterwards, I.T. McCray appeared on the scene, warned Hudgens that an insult to Colvin was an insult to him, and asked if he wanted to fight. Assuming he meant with fists, Hudgens moved to take off his gun belt. As he did, McCray jerked his pistol and fired, but had the poor judgment to miss. Hudgens immediately drew his own weapon and shot his assailant through the heart. The man continued to fire, however, and some unidentified friend of Hudgens' put a bullet through McCray from the rear. Colvin later told the victor that McCray had killed a U.S. marshal in the Cherokee Nation and that there was a price of $1,600 on his head.[32] Hudgens was tried in due course and acquitted on grounds of self-defense.[33]

The good burghers of Lincoln were not to be overshadowed by their upstart neighbor. A youth named Stone was killed in the village by "One Armed Joe" Murphy about this same time. Murphy was arrested and jailed. He attempted to escape, was wounded by the jailor, and recaptured. The next morning, it was found that someone had put a bullet through his head during the night. On July 3, a young man named Harriman (or Harrison) became intoxicated in the village, committed some offense, and was locked up. That night, a mob stormed the jail and riddled him with bullets. A deputy sheriff was rumored to be an accessory to the crime. In any event, he appears to have been handy with his pistol and to have killed several men, which had made him decidedly unpopular with the lawless element of the community. On the night of the 4th, another mob surrounded the jail and killed the deputy. The following evening, a third mob broke into the jail and lynched one of the prisoners. Who he was is not recalled. "They talk of such matters down there very casually," said the informant of the *New Mexican*, "and seemed to think it all right. I did not wish to meddle in the affair, so did not ask many questions about it."[34]

Wallace reported to Schurz that there was "a somewhat unsettled condition of affairs in Lincoln county, signalized by several atrocious murders." He blamed this state of affairs on the fact that no court had been held in the county for two successive terms. His proposed remedy was to have Ira E. Leonard appointed to the judgeship in the 3rd Judicial District.[35] In view of the decided antipathy existing between Leonard on the one hand and many of the most powerful citizens, the Army officers, and the outlaws on the other,[36] this scarcely seems a recommendation which would have led to peace and quiet.

Only a little later, however, one of The Boys received his just desserts at the dour hands of the Texas Rangers. About 5 o'clock on the evening of May 18, 1880, August Gross and Jesse Graham, known in Lincoln County as George Davis, alias Tom Jones, walked into Keesey's barroom at Fort Davis, Texas, and announced that the drinks were on them. As the eager citizens bellied up to the bar, Jessie J. Evans, Albert "Bud" Graham, and Charles Groves Graham robbed the Sender & Siebenborn store, as well as two customers who had the misfortune to be on the premises. A few nights later, a posse led by Francis Rooney captured Bud. Meanwhile, Governor O.M. Roberts had ordered detachments of Texas Rangers to the scene. On their arrival, the officers learned that the robbers were members of a gang of about twenty men led by John Selman, who had earlier left a trail of theft, arson, and rapine behind him in Lincoln County.[37] They thereupon resorted to strategy. Graham was transferred to the Fort Davis jail and Selman appointed jailor, so that both men could be kept under surveillance. Unfortunately, Sheriff T.A. Wilson got drunk and announced that he was going to fire Selman and release Graham. This forced the Rangers to place Selman under arrest.

The Rangers were informed that the rest of the outlaws had been seen in the vicinity of Presidio del Norte, about a hundred miles to the north. Sergeants L.B. Caruthers and E.M. Seiker [Edward A. Sieker, Jr.], with Privates George R. Bingham, Sam A. Henry, D. Thomas Carson, and Richard R. Russell, immediately started for that area, guided by Deputy Sheriff Cleto Herredia. About 1 o'clock on July 3, they came in sight of their quarry. The gang fled into the Chinati Mountains, barricaded themselves in Pinto Canyon, and opened fire on their pursuers. Bingham was killed in the first volley. Seiker [Sieker] in turn shot Jesse Graham, whereupon Evans, Gross, and Charles Graham surrendered.

The prisoners were lodged in the Bat Cave jail at Fort Davis, a dungeon blasted out of solid rock under the floor of the sheriff's office and covered over the top by heavy timbers. Entrance and egress were through a trap door. No ray of light penetrated to the cell. In August, Texas Ranger Lieutenant C.L. Nevill wrote to Adjutant General John B. Jones:

> The prisoners are getting very restless I have a letter they wrote to a friend of Evans in New Mexico calling himself Billy Autraum to cause their rescue, and to use his words he was "in a damned tight place only 14 rangers here any time, ten on a scout and only four in camp now" and that Antrum and a few men could take them out very easy and if he could not do it now to meet him on the road to Huntsville as he was certain to go. I understand this man Antrum is a fugitive from some where and a noted desperado. If he comes down and I expect he will, I will enlist him for a while and put him in the same mess with Evans & Co.[38]

The following month, he returned to the subject:

> Since writing to you on 2nd inst I have been informed that there is a party made up in Lincoln County N.M. headed by one Billy Antrum alias Kid, for the purpose of releaseing Jesse Evans and his gang if so they may be here in a day or two. The information is from a reliable source.[39]

In view of the publicity the Kid has received since his death, it is interesting that Nevill apparently had never heard of him. Obviously, Billy could not have received Evans' letter. Whether he even knew that his old friend was in custody and whether he would have made any attempt to rescue him if he did are simply matters for speculation. About the time the Ranger made his reports, Billy and his henchmen, known as the Los Portales gang, were busily engaged in stealing cattle from John Newcomb at Agua Azul, from a Mexican at Fort Sumner, and from various other individuals in Lincoln County.[40] If he ever made an effort to organize a party to aid Evans, it has been lost to history. The Kid was very careful about endangering his own skin and, to this writer at least, it seems highly unlikely that he would have wanted any part of tangling with the Rangers.

As it was, Evans stood trial and was sentenced to the state penitentiary at Huntsville. On May 23, 1882, he made his escape from a contractor to whom he had been leased. For all practical purposes, his story ends there, although there are rumors about his being recognized in one place or another.[41] Selman later escaped from jail and sought refuge in San Pablo, Mexico. Eventually, he returned to the States and earned a dubious sort of fame by shooting John

Wesley Hardin in the back in El Paso on August 19, 1895. In turn, he was himself shot by George Scarborough on April 5, 1896.

At the November term of court, Mrs. McSween submitted a statement of her actions as administratrix of the Tunstall estate. Her account shows that she had collected $976.00 from the sale of Tunstall cattle but had expended $842.45 in doing it. She had received $574.33 in rent for the store which he had owned jointly with McSween, but had spent $572.00 for repairs. In addition, she had paid H.I. Chapman $146.00 for his work in connection with the Tunstall ranch and the same amount for his services in regard to the store.[42] If Tunstall's father had ever had any serious hope of recovering at least part of his investment, it must have vanished when this report reached him. Her final report, filed March 6, 1883, showed that the expenses of settling the estate had exceeded its value by some $502.46. One reason was that Leonard had been paid $600.00 for his legal assistance. It is difficult to escape the suspicion that the estate was deliberately looted.

Charles Fritz and his sister fared a little better. On November 12, 1881, he obtained a judgment in the district court in the sum of $3,300.00. The sheriff levied on the Tunstall-McSween store. Fritz bought it at public auction for $1,870.00, and rented it to Dolan. This closed the case in the public courts.[43] Years afterwards, Mrs. McSween told Dolan's daughters that the Fritz insurance money had gone to build the McSween home and stock the Tunstall-McSween store.

In November, 1880, the Los Portales gang was reported to be at Blake's Saw Mill, near White Oaks. Deputy Sheriff William Hudgens summoned a posse consisting of Constable John Longworth, George Neil, John Hudgens, James Carlyle (alias Jim Bermuda), Redman, J.P. Eaker, James W. Bell, and William Stone. The officers trailed the gang to Coyote Springs. In an exchange of fire, the horses ridden by the Kid and by John Hudgens were killed. The rustlers made a successful escape, the posse apparently being more interested in collecting the loot which they left behind them than in pursuing the thieves.

On the night of the 23rd, some of the gang brazenly rode into White Oaks. They took a pot shot at Redman, who was lounging in front of Will Hudgens' saloon, but missed. Carlyle and Bell fired at them as they galloped out of town, but with no better aim. Longworth, the Hudgens brothers, Bell, Carlyle, Eaker, James

Watts, John Mosby, James R. Brent, J.P. Langston, Ed Bonnell, W.G. Dorsey, and Charles Kelley followed the Kid, Billy Wilson, and Dave Rudabaugh[44] to the Greathouse and Kuck [Kuch] ranch, about 40 miles northeast of White Oaks, which was operated in part as a lodging house for travelers. The posse surrounded the house during the night. About daylight, Joe Steck, a teamster employed at the ranch, came out to the corral to hitch up his team. He was seized by the lawmen, who sent him back into the house with a note demanding surrender of the three outlaws. The rustlers laughed at the idea, returning a reply inviting the leader of the posse to come in and talk with them.

Carlyle is said to have been a schoolmate of Wilson's. Probably for this reason he was chosen to represent the posse. He made some objection to going into the house, but was finally persuaded to do so when Jim Greathouse offered himself as a hostage for his safety. Unfortunately, Carlyle became somewhat under the influence of liquor, got involved in an argument with his hosts, and about 2 o'clock in the afternoon jumped out of a window. His body hit the ground with three bullets in it. The posse returned the fire for a time, but was suffering intensely from exposure, hunger, and thirst. Hudgens finally withdrew it to Jerry Hocradle's ranch, about fifteen miles away, where Greathouse was released. The following day, Steck and Kuck [Kuch] returned to the ranch and buried Carlyle.[45] The trio of murderers made their way north to Anton Chico, where they appear to have been supplied with horses by Greathouse. Once mounted, they rode south to Las Cañaditas, where they were joined for Tom O'Folliard,[46] Charles Bowdre, and Tom Pickett.[47]

Greathouse was loud in his protestations that he had not known who his guests were and had furnished them accommodations just as he would have done for any travelers. Others, however, took a dim view of his self-proclaimed innocence. A posse had been raised at Lincoln by Deputy Sheriff John Hurley to reinforce the White Oaks officers. It met the latter at Hocradle's, learned what had transpired, rode on to Greathouse and Kuck's [Kuch's], burned the place to the ground, and returned to Lincoln. Kuck [Kuch] was so terrified that he left the area and did not return until 1884. By that time, his former partner was dead, having been shot by Fowler late in 1881, when the latter suspected him of stealing his cattle.[48]

Wallace promptly informed Schurz, "I have reason to believe

that a new trouble has broken out in Lincoln county....I will...go down there myself if necessary."[49] Apparently irked by the unfavorable press notices he had received, the Kid wrote the governor a long letter setting forth his version of what had occurred:

Fort Sumner
Dec 12th 1880
Gov Lew Wallace

Dear Sir

I noticed in the Las Vegas Gazette a piece which stated that, Billy the Kid, the name by which I am known in the Country was the Captian of a Band of Outlaws who hold Forth at the Portales. There is no such organization in Existence. So the Gentleman must have Drawn very heavily on his Imagination. My business at the White Oaks the time I was waylaid and my horse Killed, was to see Judge Leonard who has my case in hand. he had written to me to Come up, that he thought he could get Everything Straightened up

I did not find him at the Oaks & should have gone to Lincoln if I had met with no accident. After mine and Billie Wilsons horses were Killed we both made out way to a Station, forty miles from the Oaks kept by Mr Greathouse. When I got up next morning the house was Surrounded by an outfit led by one Carlyle, Who came into the house and demanded a Surrender I asked for their Papers and they had none. So I Concluded it amounted to nothing more than a mob and told Carlyle that he would have to Stay in the house and lead the way out that night. Soon after a note was brought in Stating that if Carlyle did not come out inside of five minutes they would kill the Station Keeper (Greathouse) who had left the house and was with them. In a Short time a Shot was fired on the outside and Carlyle thinking Greathouse was Killed Jumped through the window. breaking the Sash as he went and was Killed by his own Party they thinking it was me trying to make my Escape.

the Party then withdrew.

They returned the next day and burned an old man named Spencer's house and Greathouses also.

I made my way to this Place afoot and During my absence Deputy Sheriff Garrett Acting under Chisums orders went to the Portales and found Nothing. on his way back he went by Mr. Yerbys ranch and took a pair of mules of mine which I had left with Mr Bowdre who is in charge of Mr Yerbys Cattle. he (Garrett) claimed that they were Stolen and even if they were not he had a right to confiscate any outlaws property.

> I have been at Sumner Since I left Lincoln making my living Gambling the mules were bought by me the truth of which I can prove by the best Citizens around Sumner J.S. Chisum is the man who got me into Trouble and was benifited Thousands by it and is now doing all he can against me There is no Doubt but what there is a great deal of Stealing going on in the Territory and a great deal of the Property—is being taken across the Plains as it is a good outlet—but so far as my being at the head of a Band there is nothing of it in Several Instances I have recovered Stolen Property where there was no chance to get an Officer to do it.
>
> one instance for Hugo Zuber Postoffice Puerto De Luna, another for Pablo Aualla Same Place.
>
> if Some impartial Party were to investigate this matter they would find it far Different from the impression put out by Chisum and his Tools.[50]

Wallace was not impressed. Two days later, he issued a proclamation offering $500 reward for the capture and delivery to the sheriff of Lincoln County of William Bonny, alias "The Kid." From then on, it was simply a question of time.

NOTES

[1] Rasch, "Five Days of Battle," op. cit. [See Chapter 9.]

[2] Philip J. Rasch, "The Governor Meets the Kid." English Westerners *Brand Book*, Vol. 8, No. 3, April 1966. [See Chapter 16.]

[3] George A. Purington to Acting Asst. Adj't General, District of New Mexico, June 21, 1879. In Record Group 98, Letters Received, District of New Mexico, 1879. In National Archives.

[4] A Jim French was killed during the robbery of Reynolds & Company's general store at Catoosa, Oklahoma, in the autumn of 1895. (S.W. Harman, *Hell on the Border*. Fort Smith, Arkansas: Hell on the Border Publishing Co., reprinted 1953, pp. 282–283.) Ramon F. Adams treats them as a single individual in the index to his *Six-Guns & Saddle Leather*, but this writer has been unable to determine whether anything more than a coincidence in names exists.

[5] Lew Wallace to C. Schurz, June 11, 1879. In Wallace Collection, William Henry Smith Memorial Library of the Indiana Historical Society.

[6] Philip J. Rasch, "Jesse James in New Mexico Folklore." New York Westerners *Brand Book*, 4:62–64, 1957.

[7] Mesilla *Independent*, July 12, 1879.

[8] Las Cruces *Thirty-Four*, July 16, 1879.

[9] Ibid.

[10] Rasch and Myers, "The Tragedy of the Beckwiths," op. cit.

[11] Lew Wallace to C. Schurz, September 15, 1879. In Wallace Collection, William Henry Smith Memorial Library.

[12] Garrett, *The Authentic Life of Billy, the Kid*, op. cit.

[13] Rasch, Buckbee, and Klein, "Man of Many Parts," op. cit. [See *Trailing Billy the Kid*, Chapter 13.]

[14] Rasch, "Clues to the Puzzle of Billy the Kid," op. cit. [See *Trailing Billy the Kid*, Chapter 7.]

[15] Rasch, "The Murder of Huston I. Chapman," op. cit. [See Chapter 18.]

[16] Santa Fe *Rocky Mountain Sentinel*, December 25, 1879.

[17] R.T. Swaine to Act. Asst. Adjt. Genl Dist of New Mexico, December 22, 1879. In Record Group 98, Fort Stanton Document File, 1879–1880. In National Archives.

[18] Las Vegas *Daily Optic*, February 22, 1881.

[19] Garrett, op. cit., pp. 86–88.

[20] Las Vegas *Daily Optic*, January 9, 1880.

[21] For an account of this individual, see Philip J. Rasch, "Amende Honorable: The Life and Death of Billy Wilson." *West Texas Historical Association Year Book*, XXXIV:97–111, October, 1958. [See *Trailing Billy the Kid*, Chapter 8.]

[22] Garrett, op. cit., pp. 90–97.

[23] Raton *New Mexico News and Press*, May 6, 1882.

[24] For an account of this individual, see Philip J. Rasch, "The Olingers, Known yet Forgotten." Potomac *Corral Dust*, VIII:1 *et seq.*, February, 1963.

[25] Cimarron *News and Press*, March 11, 1880.

[26] Ibid., March 18, 1880.

[27] Las Cruces *Thirty-Four*, March 10, 1880.

[28] Philip J. Rasch, "The Rustler War." *New Mexico Historical Review*, XXXIX:257–273, October, 1964.

[29] Edward Hatch to Assistant Adjutant General, Department of the Missouri, February 3, 1880. Letters Sent, District of New Mexico, 1880. Record Group 98. In National Archives.

[30] John Pope to Adjutant General of the Army, February 10, 1880. Letters Sent, Department of the Missouri. In National Archives.

[31] Wm. H. Evarts to Alexander Ramsey, February 3, 1880. In National Archives.

[32] Las Vegas *Daily Optic*, June 7, 1880.

[33] Ibid, June 21, 1880.

[34] Grand County *Herald* (Silver City, N.M.), July 3, 1880; Santa Fe *Weekly New Mexican*, July 19, 1880.

[35] Lew Wallace to C. Schurz, July 23, 1880. In Wallace Collection, William Henry Smith Memorial Library.

[36] Philip J. Rasch, "The Would-Be Judge—Ira E. Leonard," op. cit. [See Chapter 19.]

[37] Philip J. Rasch, "Chaos in Lincoln County." Denver Westerners *Brand Book*, 18:150–173, 1963. [See Chapter 6.]

[38] C.L. Nevill to John B. Jones, August 26, 1880. In Walter Prescott Webb Collection, University of Texas.

[39] C.L. Nevill to John B. Jones, September 5, 1880. In Walter Prescott Webb Collection, University of Texas.

[40] Garrett, op. cit., pp. 90–97.

[41] Rasch, "The Story of Jessie J. Evans," op. cit.; Rasch, "The Mystery of George Davis," op. cit.

[42] In the Matter of the Estate of John H. Tunstall Deceased. Probate Court Files, Lincoln County, N.M., November 6, 1880.

[43] Ted Raynor, "Folk Lore Corner." Lordsburg *Liberal*, December 2, 1955.

[44] For an account of this individual, see F. Stanley, *Dave Rudabaugh, Border Ruffian*. Denver: World Press, Inc., 1961.

[45] White Oaks *Lincoln County Leader*, December 7, 1889.

[46] For an account of this individual, see Philip J. Rasch, "The Short Life of Tom O'Folliard." Potomac Westerners *Corral Dust*, V:20–21, July, 1960. [See *Trailing Billy the Kid*, Chapter 11.]

[47] For an account of this individual, see Philip J. Rasch, "He Rode with the Kid—The Life of Tom Pickett." English Westerners *10th Anniversary Publication*, 1964, pp. 11–15. [See *Trailing Billy the Kid*, Chapter 14.]

[48] Philip J. Rasch, "Alias 'Whiskey Jim.'" *Panhandle-Plains Historical Review*, XXXVI:103–114, 1963.

[49] Lew Wallace to C. Schurz, December 7, 1880. In Wallace Collection, William Henry Smith Memorial Library.

[50] William Bonney to Lew Wallace, December 12, 1880. In Wallace Collection, William Henry Smith Memorial Library.

18.
THE MURDER OF HUSTON I. CHAPMAN

CORRAL DUST, POTOMAC CORRAL OF THE WESTERNERS, JULY 1960

In July, 1878, the placita of Lincoln, New Mexico, was the scene of a five day battle between the partisans of James J. Dolan, Lawrence G. Murphy, and John H. Riley, and those of Alexander A. McSween and John Chisum. The latter were decisively defeated, McSween being killed.[1] The widowed Mrs. Sue Ellen McSween promptly employed a fiery, one-armed Las Vegas lawyer, Huston I. Chapman, to defend her interests and to aid her in obtaining vengeance. In a series of letters and personal interviews with Lew Wallace, newly appointed governor of the territory, Chapman demanded that the governor come to Lincoln to investigate the situation in person. Hoping to avoid stirring up old troubles, Wallace steadfastly refused.[2] Chapman thereupon cast about for some other opportunity to embarrass the civil and military authorities of Lincoln County. An excuse to vent his venom against the officers at Fort Stanton was soon furnished by the rash actions of a young second lieutenant of the 9th Cavalry, James Hansel [Hansell] French.

Sheriff George W. Peppin had advised Lieutenant Colonel N.A.M. Dudley, 9th Cavalry, commanding Fort Stanton, that he had warrants for fifteen individuals, and requested that he be furnished with sufficient military force to effect their arrest. Fourteen of these warrants were for McSween partisans: Charles Bowdre, Josiah G. Scurlock, John Scroggins, Stephen Stevens [Stephens], George Coe, Frank Coe, William Bonney,[3] alias William Antrim and Billy the Kid, Eusabio [Eusebio] Sanchez, Antonacio Martinez, Francisco Berrerra [Fernando Herrera], Jasper Coe, Ignacio Gonzales, John

Middleton, Fred Waite, and Henry Brown.[4] One was for Frank Rivers, a Dolan henchman. The sixteenth was for an ordinary cattle rustler: Charles Morsner, alias Griss. None of the wanted men were taken.

When the district court convened at Lincoln on December 13, Peppin "made an official demand for a Guard to protect him from violence and being killed by well known murderers, while in attendance in his official capacity in the Probate Court."[5] French, with seventeen men, was detailed to this duty. Peppin deputized the officer and gave him warrants for Scurlock, Jim French, and several other individuals, suggesting that they might be found at Masimiano de Guebara's [Maximiano de Guevara's] house. Failing to locate any of the men there, French sent Privates Shannon Keton and Louis Horton to the residence of Mrs. McSween (the former Saturnino Baca home), while he and Trumpeter George Washington visited the house of John N. Copeland, the former sheriff. There French arrested a Mexican boy he found bearing a pistol and went on to Mrs. McSween's. Upon his arrival he found that the two privates had arrested Chapman. Neither of them knew the lawyer and they had assumed that he was one of the men for whom the lieutenant had warrants.

After the Mexican boy had been questioned and his pistol confiscated, he was dismissed. Chapman then demanded, "What right have you to arrest me?"[6]

"Chapman," answered the officer, "I didn't arrest you."

"Well, your men did."

"If my men arrested you, it is a mistake of mine and I am responsible for it."

As Chapman became increasingly abusive, the officer added, "By God, Sir, if I have any authority I'll show it to you. I'm a better lawyer than you are." With that, he commenced to look though the warrants which he had received from the sheriff.

"That may be, but you have a poor way of showing it," snapped the lawyer.

"Lieutenant French," interjected Mrs. McSween, "if you have a warrant for Mr. Chapman, show it to him and he will go with you."

"Mrs. McSween, shut your mouth," was the retort discourteous.

French got out of his chair and walked over to Chapman. "If you will allow me, I will give you an understanding in this thing."

"It is no use to allow you. You have acted ungentlemanly with me. You are a scoundrel!" roared Chapman, shaking his finger under the lieutenant's nose.

If Chapman was presuming upon the fact that he had but one arm, he had misjudged his man. The officer removed his belt, overcoat, and blouse. Calling to one of the troopers to tie one arm behind him, he warned, "You have been insulting me all day. Now business ends and if you want anything out of me, take it."

"For God's sake, Lieutenant," screamed Mrs. McSween, "do not have any trouble in my house." With that, she succumbed to a fit of hysterics, culminating in a fainting spell.

Chapman exclaimed, "Now you must get out of this house! We have had enough of it! Look at that woman! Look what you have done! Now get out of here!"

French dressed and with some of his men made a patrol of the plaza. Chapman ran to the house of the doctor. Both going and returning, he was challenged by the troopers, but was allowed to pass.

During the night, James A. Tomlinson brought Copeland to French's quarters. He stated that the ex-sheriff had just shot a boy named Johnny Mace in a bar room brawl and had demanded the protection of the military. The next morning, Chapman and Sidney Wilson, another attorney, requested permission to see Copeland privately, which French refused to permit.

"Damn you," shouted Chapman, "I'll talk with him if I like to."

"You can't speak to him at all," replied the officer. "You leave this room. Here is the door. Get outside of it as quickly as you can! I am on duty and don't want any trouble with you."

The lawyer stepped outside. "Come out here," he challenged. "Step outside. I'm not afraid of you."

Again French eagerly offered to fight him with one hand tied behind his back, but this time Sheriff Peppin intervened. He ordered Chapman to leave and not to come back, warning that he was trying to start trouble and if he kept on, he was liable to do it. Chapman demanded French's arrest, and the sheriff and the attorney exchanged bitter words. At intervals during the day, further courtesies were exchanged, Chapman calling French a "damned skunk" and a "damned fool," but Peppin was able to prevent an actual fight. Later, the officer commented that, "Only for the coolness and authority of the sheriff I would have arrested this man or done an act of personal violence to him which I might have regretted."[7] Nevertheless, on French's return to Fort Stanton, Dudley placed him under arrest.

Chapman, as lawyer for de Guebara [de Guevara], brought a charge of feloniously entering a house against French, and Chapman and Mrs. McSween accused him of felonious entry and of assault. When French was ordered to appear before Justice of the Peace John B. Wilson, Dudley sent First Lieutenant Byron Dawson, 9th Cavalry, with a detachment of men to protect him from violence and to bring Mace back to the post, since Will H. Hudgens had made an affidavit that a mob was said to be forming to lynch Mace and his nurse, John Hurley.[8] French was acquitted on the first charge and the second was dismissed. On the third, he waived an examination and was bound over to appear before the district court. After receiving the officers' reports, Dudley wrote to Colonel Edward Hatch, commanding the District of New Mexico, "I begin to believe with others that it is a conspiracy on the part of Chapman, the notorious Mrs. McSween, and others to blackmail Lieut French."[9]

The colonel appointed a board of officers, composed of Captain C.H. Conrad, 15th Infantry, Lieutenant Dawson, and Assistant Surgeon Daniel M. Appel, to investigate the incident. French's statement of the affair grandiloquently alleged that he was the victim of a conspiracy by

> Chapman...[and] his Mistress Mrs. McSween...not only to ruin me but through me to injure the Army, especially that part of it at Fort Stanton...The military and civillians should be a fraternity. Here they are as inimical as the red and white roses, and knowing this I demand personally and for the sake of the army that the military authorities fully sustain me in every particular. If I do not prove to them that I am innocent of all imputations, then, let them desert me.[10]

His brother officers did not desert him. They disregarded allegations that the lieutenant had been under the influence of liquor and reported that the statements of Chapman, Mrs. McSween, and de

Guebara [de Guevara] were unworthy of credence. They recommended that no action be taken, as the charges had been inspired by malice and vindictiveness against French and all of the officers stationed at the fort. Dudley concurred in their recommendation. He issued an order forbidding Chapman, Sam Wortley, Copeland, Jim French, Scurlock, Antrim, Bowdre, Brown, George Coe, and Frank Coe to set foot on the reservation except to obtain their mail. At the same time, he forbade the soldiers to visit Lincoln until order and peace were again restored.

Governor Wallace seems to have been oblivious to the situation. Smugly, he wrote Secretary of the Interior Carl Schurz,

> An individual by the name of Chapman went to the plaza (town of Lincoln) and tried to get up a disturbance, but failed. The burthen of his plaint was that I had not visited the town to get the truth there instead of at the Fort. On the other hand, Dudley's grief is that I did not come to the Fort to get the truth there. Now as the two places town and fort were centers of the two factions, it was not possible for me to go to either without provoking jealousy and bad feeling, so I stayed away from both, and am well satisfied that I did so.
> Today I am going down the country to be gone a few days.[11]

He might better have devoted the time to his official duties.

Two days after Christmas, James J. Dolan, Jacob B. Mathews, and John Long sought sanctuary at the Fort, complaining that they were unable to return to their business in safety due to the presence of outlaws in Lincoln. Ominously, Dolan wrote to Wallace,

> Your friend (Chapman) appears to be the only man in this County who is trying to Continue the old feud. I and Many of our Citizens feel Confident that if this man was silenced, the trouble would End... I have learned Enough since I returned here that should I remain in this County, may fate will be that of Major Brady and others. I only intend remaining until such time as I can Straighten up my business to the interests of my Creditors, and as per Agreement with them. It makes me and my friends feel Mighty Sore, that we are compelled to leave our homes and business, which we are Compelled to do, or put ourselves on Equal footing with the outlaw And assassin.[12]

It is difficult to comprehend how Wallace could fail to recognize that Chapman, like John Henry Tunstall before him,[13] had been sentenced to death. Yet if he appreciated the gravity of the situation, his actions gave no sign of it.

Tension continued to mount as other members of Peppin's posse during the Five Days' Battle encountered their own troubles. John Kinney was indicted for the murder of Isabel [Ysabel] Barela, but took a change of venue to Grant County and was found not guilty. John H. Riley had Jim McDaniels arrested for horse theft. Marion Turner complained to the governor that he had been arrested on suspicion of cattle theft, insulted and shot at by the military. Sam Perry was arrested on charges of horse stealing, but was later found not guilty.

At the time, New Mexican justice was at best a capricious jade. William Smith, charged with assault with intent to kill one Waldo, was tried before a justice of the peace, found guilty, and fined $2.50. Gregorio Baldonado was charged with selling a sack of tobacco for five cents and trading another for a box of matches and a jack-knife, found guilty, and sentenced to six months in jail. Tired of waging the unequal battle, Sheriff George Peppin submitted his resignation and on January 1, 1879, was succeeded by George Kimball [Kimbrell].[14]

For the moment, Chapman was busy with the details of probating McSween's estate. Isaac Ellis and Jose Montaño had been appointed appraisers, and in January, 1879, submitted a report evaluating the estate at $1,853.50 in personal property, $1,910.00 in real estate, $10,023.21 in collectable notes and accounts, and $771.76 in uncollectable notes and accounts.

Once these court details were out of the way, Chapman appeared before Justice John B. Wilson and swore out a warrant charging Dudley with complicity in the murder of McSween. He then started for Santa Fe to procure orders from Colonel Edward Hatch, commanding the District of New Mexico, for the surrender of Dudley. In Las Vegas, Ira E. Leonard, another attorney, persuaded him to drop the matter. However, David P. Shield, Mrs. McSween's brother-in-law and himself a lawyer, accompanied Chapman to the capitol. There Shield demanded that Wallace and Hatch furnish him with copies of certain affidavits Dudley had submitted regarding Mrs. McSween,[2] explaining that both Dudley and McSween were Masons and he desired to lay the matter before the Masonic order for investigation. Both officials refused his request. Wallace stated that the existing situation made it improper for him to be connected even indirectly with any prosecution of Dudley, and Hatch advised that official papers could not be made available without the express permission of the secretary of war.

Wild with rage, Chapman set out in the return trip to Lincoln, vowing that he would place the matter before the secretary of war and demand an investigation. Leonard and other friends in Las Vegas endeavored to dissuade him from proceeding to the plaza, warning that he would be in constant danger of his life. Chapman admitted that he feared violence, but reaffirmed his determination to bring Dudley and French to justice, regardless of the personal danger which might be involved.[15]

Meanwhile, Dudley and the governor had become embroiled in yet another controversy. Captain Henry Carroll, 9th Cavalry, stationed at Roswell, had informed his superior that Special Constable Emil Powers had demanded a military posse, and had requested instructions. Dudley replied that under the existing instructions, only sheriffs, U.S. marshals or their deputies were entitled to such assistance, but asked Hatch for a confirmation of this. Wallace insisted that this aid should be extended to all civil authorities, and requested Hatch to direct Dudley to furnish it. Hatch forwarded Wallace's letter to Major General John Pope, commanding the Department of the Missouri. Pope disapproved of Wallace's request, but forwarded it to Washington for a decision. In due course, the secretary of war ruled that "the military forces of the United States must not be used to the extent asked for by the Governor of New Mexico."[16]

Noting that Wallace had given a glowing description of the situation in Lincoln County to a Denver *Tribune* reporter,[17] Dudley drily suggested that since affairs were in such good order, the troops should be withdrawn from Roswell and held in readiness to meet the Indian outbreak which he expected to occur that spring. However, Second Lieutenant George W. Smith, 9th Cavalry, and his company were sent to Roswell to relieve Carroll. Indicative of the tension existing between the citizens and the military is the fact that Carroll was ordered to stop outside the plaza, close up his detachment, and under no circumstances to permit an enlisted man to enter either a house or a store in Lincoln.

On February 11, the day before Chapman left Las Vegas for Lincoln, Mrs. McSween appealed to Dudley for aid in recovering 275 head of cattle belonging to the Tunstall estate which had been run off by Robert Speakes and other parties. Dudley politely assured her that upon proper representation by the sheriff, he would furnish every assistance in his power, and requested the commanding officer at Fort Bliss, Texas, to take steps to prevent the thieves from crossing into Mexico. To Hatch, however, he wrote that it was "farsical" for Mrs. McSween to call upon him for assistance after having asked the governor for a safeguard against him and having sworn out a writ charging him with the murder of her husband. He suggested that the real reasons for her request was that she hoped it would be refused so that she would have an opportunity to accuse him of partisan action.[18] The cattle were afterwards recovered by Captain Carroll. It was found that 138 of them were from the Tunstall estate, and these were turned over to Mrs. McSween. Most of the balance were Hunter & Evans property, which Carroll reported had been driven off by John Jones, Jim Jones, Tom Jones, alias George Davis (said to have been a brother of Jessie Evans), and Tom Cochran [Cochrane], and given Marion Turner's brand.[19]

On the morning of February 18, Dudley was shown a letter from William Bonney to one of the Dolan faction, "wanting to know whether they proposed peace or fight &c."[20] The Dolan men agreed to meet representatives of the McSween faction that evening. Bonney, accompanied by Joe Bowers[21] and Yginio Salazar, spent the day loafing in the village. According to Walz,[22] negotiations were commenced with the Kid and his supporters sheltered by one thick adobe wall and Evans and his henchmen concealed behind another. Finally, Walz was successful in getting the two leaders to meet and shake hands in the middle of the street. Some hard words were exchanged and Evans threatened to kill the Kid on the spot. Bonney replied that they had met for the purpose of making peace and that he did not care to open negotiations with a fight, but that if they would come at him three at a time, he would whip the whole damn bunch.[23]

In spite of this inauspicious beginning, the two sides finally concluded a peace treaty. It was agreed that neither party would kill any member of the other one without first giving notice of having withdrawn from the agreement; that all persons who had acted as friends to either party were included in the treaty and were not to be molested; that neither party should appear nor give evidence against the other in any civil prosecution; that neither officers nor soldiers were to be killed for any act previous to that date; that each group would give the individual members of the other party every aid in their power to resist arrests on civil warrants, and that if arrested they would try to secure their release; that any member of either faction failing to carry out this compact should be killed on sight by either party.[24] The reconciled enemies then had dinner at the Ballard home, after which they made a tour of the bars, singing, ringing cowbells, and firing guns to celebrate the peace. During the festivities, they visited the home of Juan B. Patrón. For some reason, Campbell announced that he was going to kill their host, but his friends managed to dissuade him from carrying out his threat.

Early that evening, Chapman arrived from Las Vegas and put his horses in Mrs. McSween's corral. As he was suffering from a severe attack of neuralgia, he went to a neighbor's to obtain a bread poultice. While returning, he met Dolan, Evans, the Kid, Walz, Salazar, Bowers, Tom O'Folliard, Billy Mathews, George Van Sickle, James Redman, William Campbell, and others of the celebrants. Campbell halted Chapman, punched the muzzle of his pistol against the lawyer's breast, and asked, "Who are you and where are you going?"

"My name is Chapman and I am attending to my business."

"Then you dance!"

"I do not intend to dance for a drunken crowd. Am I talking to Mr. Dolan?"

"No," interrupted Evans, "but you are talking to a damned good friend of his."

At this point, Dolan, who was very drunk, fired his pistol, allegedly into the ground. Campbell immediately shot Chapman. The lawyer received two wounds, either of which would have been fatal. As he fell, he cried, "My God, I am killed."

It is interesting to note that Chapman's murder occurred just a year after that of Tunstall, and that he is said to have fallen midway between the spots where Brady and Hindman were killed. For all practical purposes, his death marked the end of the Lincoln County

War, although the troubles which followed in its wake were far from settled. No doubt it was a great comfort to Chapman's parents later to read Walz's considered opinion: "There was really no malice in this shooting. Life was held lightly down there in those days...."[25]

Unruffled by the shooting, the revelers proceeded up the street to the Cullum eating house, Campbell exclaiming, "I promised my God and General Dudley that I would kill Chapman and I have done it. I am going to the post to kill Charley Scase. I promised General Dudley that I would not kill Scase in the post, but now I am going to kill him wherever I find him."

Scase, an employee at the Mescalero Apache Indian Reservation, had earned Dudley's enmity by complaining to Wallace that Campbell and his gang had threatened his life, and that when he had fled to Fort Stanton, Dudley not only refused him protection but permitted his pursuers to search the post for him at their leisure. The facts seem to be that Dudley had assigned him a bed in quarters occupied by colored troops. This was unacceptable to Scase and that night, he left the fort.

An hour after the killing of Chapman, Campbell gave Walz a pistol and asked him to place it in the murdered man's hand to make it appear that he had fired the first shot. This Walz refused to do. The Kid then agreed to do it, but instead rode out of the village.

Later, at Dolan's trial for the murder of Chapman, Mathews, Van Sickle, Redman, and Walz testified that they were in abject fear of Campbell and were afraid to express the least disapprobation of his killing Chapman. In New Mexican folklore, this is explained by the statement that Chapman was actually Jesse James. The story seems to have started with a letter that George Taylor, a grandson of Cynthia Birchard, the sister of President Rutherford B. Hayes' mother, wrote to the president. Taylor, a resident of Lincoln at the time, stated,

> A few weeks ago a lawyer by the name of Chapman who was settling up the estates of McSween and Tunstel was shot and killed by Dolan who had returned and two desperate outlaws Evans and Cambell.
> Cambell is Jesse James, Governor Wallace and man by the name of McPherson who knows him say.[26]

Wallace unquestionably believed this to his dying day,[27] but the little known about Campbell indicates that he could not have been James. Wallace was advised that Campbell had killed "three men in the buffalo country in cold blood."[28] This does not fit in with anything known about James. The fact that Billy the Kid wrote the governor that "Sanger and Ballard are or was great friends of Camels"[29] suggests that he may have been in the area for some time. For what it is worth—and that is probably very little—Burns[30] reported that he was a Texan named Ed Richardson. A Lincoln tradition has it that he was actually a man named Hines, who had once been a member of the James gang, but there appears to be no evidence to support this theory. It has been determined by Breihan[31] that Jesse at one time traveled under the alias of William Campbell, and it is possible that the whole story rests on a simple case of confusion in names. Breihan[32] at least is sure that it has no foundation in fact.

Meanwhile, Kimball [Kimbrell] had hurried to Fort Stanton to obtain a posse of soldiers to enable him to arrest the Kid and Salazar. Twenty men were furnished, under the command of Lieutenant Dawson. Accompanied by Acting Assistant Surgeon W.B. Lyon, they arrived at Lincoln at 11:30 p.m. Several houses were searched without finding any sign of the outlaws. During the search, the troops found the body of Chapman. The clothing was burning when he was discovered; one account has it that the clothes had been soaked with whiskey and then set afire. As a result, the body was badly disfigured. When Dawson informed Justice Wilson of the finding of the corpse, the Justice replied that he was aware that Chapman had been killed, but he had been unable to obtain assistance in moving the remains. The soldiers then took the body up to the courthouse.

The village was thrown into a frenzy of fear over the possibility that Chapman's murder presaged an outbreak of the old troubles. Kimball [Kimbrell] requested that a detachment of troops be posted in the plaza, supporting his request with a petition signed by every citizen in the town. Second Lieutenant Millard F. Goodwin, 9th Cavalry, and a detachment of men were sent to Lincoln in answer to this plea. Mrs. McSween offered the Tunstall building for their use, but Goodwin preferred to use two rooms placed at their disposal by Jose Montaño.

Wilson wrote Dudley a friendly letter stating that he was throwing the charges against him out of court and suggesting that they be friends and let bygones be bygones. Dudley replied in kind, and, after considerable hesitation, accepted the invitation of the citizens to visit Lincoln and discuss the situation with them. Entering the plaza for the first time in seven months, he was met by some twenty men, who expressed their desire for military protection. In reply, Dudley sternly told them that under the existing regulations, the troops would continue to aid the sheriff in keeping the peace and making arrests, but warned that it was time that they organized a home guard to protect themselves and ceased to expect the military to be at their every call. Fining men like William Smith $2.50 for attempted murder would not scare off desperadoes who had killed from three to six men each, he added.[33] When Wilson requested the loan of arms and ammunition to equip such a home guard, he was informed that there were no arms available at Fort Stanton for the purpose and that in any event only the secretary of war could authorize such a loan.

At the sheriff's request, Goodwin furnished a posse of six soldiers to accompany him to San Patricio in an endeavor to arrest the Kid and Salazar, but the search proved fruitless.

Dudley's reports to Colonel Hatch were not well received. He was warned that there was no authority for his furnishing troops upon the petition of citizens, and was directed to withdraw them.[34] Dudley vigorously retorted that his instructions directed him to dispose of his troops "as you may deem best to preserve the peace," and pointed out that they had been furnished only upon the legal demand of the sheriff,[35] which was strictly in accordance with his orders.[36]

It is easy to imagine the dismay that must have swept over Wallace as he read Dudley's reports. All his glowing descriptions of the happy state of affairs in Lincoln, all his hopes of promotion and honor seem dashed upon the rocks of this officer's statements. As in the dark aftermath of the Battle of Shiloh, the Regular Army had interposed between him and his dreams of glory. Rudely jarred out of the complacency with which he had contemplated the situation, Wallace took the unjust but perhaps natural course of writing Schurz a bitter letter placing the blame on Dudley:

> One H.I. Chapman, lawyer, was assassinated in front of the court House in Lincoln the night of the 18th inst. producing a sensation amounting to panic in the town. A request was sent to Col. Dudley, at

> Fort Stanton, for troops to protect the lives and property. The affair seems to have stopped with the murder of Chapman; yet Col Dudley went over in person, carrying with him the equivalent of two Companies. He also took a Gatling gun. Upon his own showing, a sergeant with a patrol would have been sufficient. The effect of his ridiculous action will be, I fear, to throw the people into a state of unnecessary alarm.
>
> The outlaws have always run to the mountains, in my judgment the only way to get at them was by untiring use of the troops and Indian scouts. The plan was submitted to General Hatch, commanding the District of New Mexico, and he has approved and entered heartily into it. He will go with me and in person direct the movements of the troops. I will rely greatly upon his judgment and energy. Accordingly I will leave for Lincoln tomorrow....[37]

Dudley might have objected that the affair stopped with the murder of Chapman precisely because he took the action which he did, and Hatch might have commented that the reference to him was actually something less than the whole truth. Wallace had indeed asked the colonel to prepare for the proclamation of martial law; the officer, considerably less disturbed over the situation than was the governor, had routinely forwarded the request to his superiors, noting:

> This communication is forwarded merely as an expression of the Governor's opinion of the condition of affairs in Lincoln Co. Should the emergency arise referred to, it will be quite time to make arrangements to meet the same.
>
> No information at these H'D'q'rs that Martial Law is to be declared in Lincoln Co.—a power not vested in the officer of the Governor.[38]

In due course, grim old General William Tecumseh Sherman added his endorsement:

> Respectfully submitted to the Hon Secretary of War. The Governor of a Territory has no power to declare martial Law nor to do any act which incidentally changes the Status and duties of Army officers. If the President declares Martial Law, he can order what steps he adjudges necessary in the premises, even naming the officer who is to be entrusted with the execution of the terms of the Proclamation.

> The Governor should be notified that he should absolutely exhaust his Civil power and report his inability to protect life and property.[39]

The news that Hatch and Wallace were proceeding to Lincoln must have been received with mixed emotions by Dudley. Certainly, a consultation of senior Army and territorial officials with the man on the spot was long past due, but both of these men—one of whom he had never even met—were his avowed enemies. Such a conference could scarcely fail to be most unpleasant.

ACKNOWLEDGMENTS

The writer is indebted to Miss Gertrude Hill, Miss Ruth Rambo, Mrs. Edith McManmon, and Mrs. Elma A. Medearis, of the Library of the Museum of New Mexico; Miss Caroline Dunn, librarian, William Henry Smith Memorial Library of the Indiana Historical Society; Watt P. Marchman, director, Hayes Memorial Library; Colonel W.J. Morton, librarian, U.S. Military Academy; William S. Wallace, archivist, New Mexico Highlands University; and Carl W. Breihan for their assistance in collecting the data for this paper. The material concerning the alleged implication of Jesse James in the killing of Chapman originally appeared in Philip J. Rasch, "Jesse James in New Mexico Folklore," New York Westerners *Brand Book*, 4:62–64, 1957.

NOTES

1 Rasch, "Five Days of Battle," op. cit. [See Chapter 9.]

2 Rasch, "Exit Axtell: Enter Wallace," op. cit. [See Chapter 15.]

3 For studies of the background of this individual, see Rasch and Mullin, "New Light on the Legend of Billy the Kid," op. cit.; Rasch and Mullin, "Dim Trails—The Pursuit of the McCarty Family," op. cit.; Rasch, "The Twenty-One Men He Put Bullets Through," op. cit.; Rasch, "A Man Named Antrim," op. cit.; Rasch, "More on the McCartys," op. cit.; Rasch, "Clues to the Puzzle of Billy the Kid," op. cit. [All are included in *Trailing Billy the Kid*.]

4 The life of this man has been related in Rasch, "A Note on Henry Newton Brown," op. cit.

5 Special Orders No. 156, Fort Stanton, N.M., December 13, 1878.

Exhibit No. 28, Volume No. 1, Court of Inquiry Convened by S.O. 59, Headquarters, Department of the Missouri, March 28, 1879. In National Archives.

[6] The conversations in this article are compiled from various court records and newspaper reports, but are not to be understood as necessarily being verbatim.

[7] J.H. French to Recorder, Board of Officers, Dec. 19, 1878. Proceedings of a Board of Officers Convened at Fort Stanton by Virtue of Special Orders No. 157, December 14, 1878. Exhibit No. 28J, Volume No. 1, Court of Inquiry Convened by S.O. 59.

[8] Mace recovered from his wounds and took up horse stealing. He was killed by a posse led by Deputy Sheriff Longworth about the middle of March, 1880, while—ungratefully enough—attempting to rob Hudgens' store. See Cimarron *News & Press*, March 11, 1880. Deputy Sheriff John Hurley was fatally wounded on January 28, 1885, while attempting to arrest Nicholas Aragon, who had killed Deputy Sheriff Jasper Corn, of Lincoln County, on October 29, 1884. See Santa Fe *New Mexican Review*, January 30, 1885.

[9] N.A.M. Dudley to Acting Assistant Adjutant General, District of New Mexico, December 17, 1878. Exhibit No. 13, Volume No. 3, Court of Inquiry Convened by S.O. 59.

[10] French to Recorder, Dec. 19, 1878, op cit.

[11] Lew Wallace to C. Schurz, December 21, 1878. In the William Henry Smith Memorial Library of the Indiana Historical Society.

[12] James J. Dolan to Governor Lew Wallace, December 31, 1878. In William Henry Smith Memorial Library.

[13] Rasch, "Prelude to War," op. cit. [See Chapter 5.]

[14] George Kimball, or Kimbrell, was born in Huntsville, Arkansas, March 31, 1842. He accompanied Pike's column to Colorado in 1859 and settled in Lincoln County in 1863. Kimball died at Picacho, Lincoln County, on March 25, 1924. Carrizozo *News*, March 28, 1924.

[15] Las Vegas *Gazette*, March 1, 1879.

[16] E.D. Townsend to Commanding General, Department of the Missouri, March 15, 1879. Exhibit No. 62, Volume 3, Court of Inquiry Convened by S.O. 59.

[17] Rasch, "Exit Axtell: Enter Wallace." op. cit.

[18] N.A.M. Dudley to Acting Asst. Adjutant General, District of New Mex., February 15, 1879. Exhibit No. 35, Volume No. 3, Court of Inquiry Convened by S.O. 59.

[19] Henry Carroll to Post Adjutant, Fort Stanton, February 25, 1879. Records of the War Department, 1405 AGO 1878, Consolidated File Relating to the Lincoln County War, New Mexico. In National Archives.

[20] N.A.M. Dudley to Acting Asst. Adjutant General, District of New Mex., February 19, 1879. In 1405 AGO 1878.

[21] One Peppert, alias Joe Bowers, was a notorious gunfighter at Fort Griffin in 1872. See Carl Coke Rister, *Fort Griffin on the Texas Frontier*. Norman: University of Oklahoma Press, 1956, pp. 129–130. It is not clear whether this was the same individual. In some records, the name is given as Powers rather than Bowers.

[22] Walz, Edgar A., *Retrospection*, op. cit.

[23] Mesilla *Independent*, July 5, 1879; Autobiography of Charles L. Ballard. Roswell *Record*, December 26, 1955.

[24] N.A.M. Dudley to Acting Asst. Adjutant Genl., Dist. of New Mexico, Feb. 21, 1879. Exhibit No. 43, Volume No. 3, Court of Inquiry Convened by S.O. 59.

[25] Walz, *Introspection*, op cit.

[26] George Taylor to R.B. Hayes, April 4, 1879. In Hayes Memorial Library.

[27] Indianapolis *The World*, June 8, 1902.

[28] T. Smith to Dear Governor [Lew Wallace], March 13, 1879. In William Henry Smith Memorial Library.

[29] W.H. Bonney to Lew Wallace, March 20, 1879. In William Henry Smith Memorial Library.

[30] Walter Noble Burns, *The Saga of Billy the Kid*. New York: Doubleday, Page & Company, 1926, p. 163.

[31] Carl W. Breihan, *The Complete and Authentic Life of Jesse James*. New York: Frederick Fell, Inc., n.d., p. 125.

[32] Carl Breihan to Phil Rasch, December 24, 1954.

[33] Dudley to Acting Asst. Adjutant Genl., Dist. of N.M., Feb. 21, 1879, op cit.

[34] John S. Loud to Comdg. Officer, Fort Stanton, N.M., February 24, 1879. Exhibit No. 48, Volume 3, Court of Inquiry Convened by S.O. 59.

[35] On October 5, 1957, David Lawrence alleged in his syndicated column that the use of the Army in the Little Rock desegregation case was a violation of the Posse Comitatus Act originally passed in 1878. This act is the one which governed the actions of the troops in Lincoln County. Background material on the use of troops in civil disorders is contained in "Memorandum as to use of troops in executing the laws, since the issue of G.O. 49 of 1878, amended by G.O. 71 of '78," Records of the Adjutant General, Consolidated File Relating to the Lincoln County War, New Mexico, 1405 AGO 1878, in the National Archives, and in *Federal Aid in Domestic Disturbances*, Senate Document No. 263, 67th Congress, 2d Session. Washington: Government Printing Office, 1922.

[36] N.A.M. Dudley [to John S. Loud], March 1, 1879. Exhibit No. 48,

Volume No. 3, Court of Inquiry Convened by S.O. 59.

[37] Lew Wallace to C. Schurz, February 27, 1879. In William Henry Smith Memorial Library.

[38] Edward Hatch [to Assistant Adjutant General, Department of the Missouri], March 1, 1879. In 1405 AGO 1878.

[39] W.T. Sherman [to Secretary of War], March 15, 1879. In 1405 AGO, 1878.

19.
The Would-Be Judge: Ira E. Leonard

The Denver Westerners Monthly Roundup, July 1964

By Lincoln County War buffs, Ira E. Leonard is remembered as the man who (unsuccessfully) assisted in the prosecution at the Court of Inquiry of Lieutenant Colonel Nathan Augustus Monroe Dudley, Ninth Cavalry, and later (successfully) defended Billy, the Kid, when the latter was tried for the murder of Andrew L. "Buckshot" Roberts. By most others, he is forgotten. Perhaps this is as it should be. His failure to be remembered today is at least of a piece with his failure to achieve the constant goal of his adult life—the prestige, authority, and security of a federal judgeship.

Leonard was born on March 25, 1832, probably in the state of New York, and seems to have grown up in the village of Batavia, New York. As a young man, he worked as a printer in the office of the *Advocate* and later studied law with Judge Moses Taggart. About 1860, he was living in Watertown, Wisconsin, where he was in partnership with Myron B. Williams. Ten years later found him domiciled in Jefferson, Missouri, and a judge of the Twenty-third Judicial Circuit in the southeast portion of that state. He had previously served as prosecuting attorney and district judge. Leonard was an active Republican and was rewarded by the party with the nomination for judge of the supreme court in the elections of 1872. When the ticket went down to defeat, the disappointed attorney left the state, opening a law office in Boulder, Colorado, in 1874, in connection with W.E. Beck. The move may in part have been dictated by reasons of health, as Leonard suffered from severe asthmatic attacks which left him unable to talk. He seems to have been accompanied by his wife, Mariah, born in New York c. 1832, two daughters, Edith, born in New York c. 1857, and Ella, born in Wisconsin c. 1859, and a son, Ira E., Jr.

The following year, Leonard applied for an appointment as a federal judge. When the anticipated vacancy did not occur, he moved to Las Vegas, New Mexico, arriving there in 1878.

The lawyer first enters Lincoln County history on February 24, 1879, when he wrote Governor Lew Wallace, informing him that another lawyer, Huston I. Chapman, had been assassinated in Lincoln, and commenting that he had warned the victim to be more discreet in his conduct or he might have trouble. On March 4, 1879, he wrote to the secretary of war, formally accusing Dudley, then commanding Fort Stanton, of having abetted in the murder of Alexander A. McSween and the burning of his home, of threatening Justice of the Peace John B. Wilson, of permitting the Tunstall store to be robbed, and of making slanderous charges against Mrs. McSween. He also accused Lieutenant James Hansell French, Ninth Cavalry, of drunkenness on duty, of forcing his way into Mrs. McSween's house and insulting her, and of threatening and falsely arresting Chapman. Dudley promptly demanded, and was granted, a Court of Inquiry.

Leonard made his first visit to the county a month later, when he attended the April term of court there. For an individual who had no connection with affairs there and who repeatedly suffered from severe asthmatic attacks, he was wonderfully busy meddling with matters which did not concern him. Wallace appears to have reposed a great deal of confidence in the lawyer and the latter functioned as though he were the governor's deputy. His correspondence with that functionary shows him advising the sheriff and insisting upon his arresting malefactors, testifying before the grand jury, developing a decided antipathy for the officers at Fort Stanton and an equally warm attachment for the McSween cause, demanding that the officers enforce the vagrant act and the law prohibiting the carrying of arms, and in general assisting "in prosecuting and bringing to Justice the Outlaws then under arrest and who might be arrested."[1] These actions did not guarantee his universal popularity. District Attorney William L. Rynerson, suffering from a galloping case of badly bruised feelings, told all who would listen that he was simply a figurehead and that Leonard was the governor's prosecutor, the man who had been selected to see the defendants punished. The outlaws promptly posted a notice on a tree to which Leonard's horse was hitched advising him that if he did not leave the country, they would take his scalp and send him to hell. A few nights later, two desperadoes passed his office at a full gallop and fired two shots at Leonard. A deputy sheriff named McPherson, whom Leonard had brought to Lincoln with him, was also fired upon, the bullet grazing his forehead.

Leonard promptly reached for his pen. He wrote Wallace that Judge Warren Bristol "had the timidity of a child" and was "unable to stay the lawlessness, his own misdirected action had produced"; Rynerson's actions were "contemptible"; Dudley's conduct was "most wicked and vile," and busied himself helping the judge advocate at Dudley's Court of Inquiry. Appearing before the court as a witness, he testified under oath that he "had no malice or ill will against [the defendant] then or now" and that the only motive actuating him was a zeal for the public good.[2] These pious protestations [do not accord (ed.)] with the fact that, practically simultaneously, he informed Wallace that Dudley "is the most unmitigated old scoundrel that ever had an existence" and a few months later described him to the territorial press as "impetuous, vindictive, overbearing, self-conceited and meddlesome."

Within a fortnight, Leonard saw the handwriting on the wall. He warned the governor that it was clear the court intended to whitewash Dudley and that he had a good notion to show his disgust by abandoning the case. When the court quite correctly found in favor of the defendant, Leonard's fury was unbounded. The kindest thing he found to say of the officers composing it was that they were a set of "egotistical damned fools" and that military courts were "an expensive and stupendous farce." Apparently, Leonard's own self-conceit was never troubled by the slightest suspicion that he might be wrong about anything.

The surviving correspondence between the governor and the lawyer arouses suspicions that a deal of some kind had been consummated between the two. The reader is led to suspect that the price for the latter's services was a promise of the executive's aid in securing a federal judgeship. On November 13, 1878, Wallace sent Secretary of the Interior Carl Schurz a petition signed by five prominent lawyers of Santa Fe recommending his appointment to the judgeship of the First Judicial District. President Rutherford B. Hayes, however, selected Lebaron Bradford Prince for the post, and both the territory and Lincoln County ignored the governor's recommendation that Leonard be recompensed for his work.

That worthy was occupied in representing Mrs. McSween in prosecuting a criminal charge of arson[3] against Dudley, alleging that he was responsible for the burning of the McSween home during the Five Days' Battle,[4] and a civil one of libel, accusing the officer of having written letters to Wallace designed to bring her into public scandal. The lawyer made a trip to Colorado and failed to return in time to escort his client to court at Mesilla, whereupon Judge Bristol ordered her arrest for contempt. When she did appear, she requested a continuance to the next term so that Leonard might represent her. This the judge denied, and Dudley refused to consent to the charge being dismissed. The case went to trial before a jury who deliberated less than two minutes before returning a verdict of "Not guilty." The courtroom thereupon burst into applause, which was suppressed with difficulty by the sheriff and the court. So far as the writer has been able to determine, the libel case never came to trial.

In 1880, Leonard was living in White Oaks. The following year, he accompanied Billy the Kid to Mesilla to act as his attorney on a charge of murdering Roberts, and succeeded in obtaining a ruling that the United States court was without jurisdiction in the case. The Kid was then promptly turned over to the territorial court to answer a charge of murdering Sheriff William Brady, found guilty, and sentenced by Judge Bristol to be hanged.

Leonard returned to Lincoln, where he was injudicious enough to champion the cause of a Mrs. Ella F. Murphy. Mrs. Murphy had been employed as a teacher for the Mescalero agency commencing May 6, 1881. Conditions there were far from desirable. Since no suitable accommodations were available, she had to sleep, cook, and live in the schoolhouse itself. The final straw seems to have come when Agent William H.H. Llewellyn informed her that she could not use articles purchased for the Indians and that all blankets and other Indian goods in her possession must be returned. On July 13, she left the agency. That same day, Llewellyn requested that she be removed, on the grounds that she was "incompetent, untruthful, and has been twice intoxicated since I have been here. She is insolent and presumptuous." She had, he alleged, written him an insulting letter when he had informed her that she could not use supplies furnished for the Indians, was an "intolerable nuisance," sought "extraordinary favors," made up incorrect reports, and had had a "questionable career in Washington, prior to her coming here."[5] His request was promptly granted by Acting Commissioner E.L. Stevens.

Mrs. Murphy had let it be known in Lincoln that she had come to the county seeking reimbursement for some cattle which had been stolen by the Mescaleros. A few days after leaving the agency, she obtained a position as a teacher for the school in Lincoln. A few days more and she had told Leonard a sad story of how she had been mistreated by the Indian agent. Leonard promptly wrote the commissioner of Indian affairs that Llewellyn was "devoid of every principle of manhood and entirely unfit to occupy a position of trust," had treated Mrs. Murphy worse than a brute, and had circulated reports that she was a lewd woman. The agent had, he alleged, sought her discharge so that she might be replaced with a teacher of his own choosing, and was secretly planning to have the reservation reduced in size so that he might obtain control of some potential mining property. The teacher also induced a Luther M. Clements to take up the cudgels on her behalf, but his letter does not seem to have survived.

A special agent was sent to investigate, sifted the affair to the bottom, and informed Leonard that he had been duped by a woman who had been treated better than her conduct deserved. No whit daunted, the lawyer took his protege into his home. His guest promptly returned thanks by stirring up trouble between her host and one of his business associates, County Clerk Ben Ellis, culminating in her buying property jointly owned by the two and ordering Leonard to vacate his office therein. He retaliated by beginning an investigation into Ellis's official records. In spite of various warnings, he uncovered enough evidence of misconduct to lead him to threaten to send Ellis to the penitentiary. Meanwhile, however, his erstwhile partner and the cause of the trouble had departed together for parts unknown.

Shortly thereafter, Leonard removed to Socorro and opened a law office. In the winter of that year, P.A. Simpson was removed as postmaster of the village and the newcomer appointed in his stead at a salary of $600 per year. Later, he complained that his expenses totaled $151.50 more than his income.[6] Once settled, the attorney formed a law partnership with G.W. Fox, obtained a financial interest in the *Socorro Sun*, acquired a ranch near the town and interests in mining properties near Kingston, and pursued the almighty dollar in various other ways. All of this seems to have profited him but little. Parish [Joe Parrish? (ed.)] mentions that Pat Garrett helped the Charles Ilfeld Company to collect an "all-but-hopeless account" from Judge Leonard who must surely have been our subject. In 1885, he sold the ranch to H.C. Shipp for an undisclosed sum.

Leonard's health continued bad and in June, 1887, he sold out and, accompanied by his son, moved to San Bernardino, California, in hopes that his asthmatic condition would improve. These were in vain. On November 26, 1888, he wrote Wallace, now living at Crawfordsville, Indiana, that he could see no improvement in his health. He added that he planned to return to New Mexico, and besought his old friend's aid in securing appointment as judge of the Second District. Wallace wrote Attorney General W.H.H. Miller several letters strongly supporting the candidacy of his former comrade in arms in the Lincoln County Troubles. Other old acquaintances also rallied to his support. Even Llewellyn wired Miller that Leonard was "an able attorney and an honest man."

However, dissenting voices were raised. William Watson, a White Oaks attorney, complained that Leonard was physically unable to perform the duties of the office and alleged that in 1880, he had attempted to defraud John E. Wilson of that town out of a mine. Sheriff C.A. Robinson, of Socorro County, alleged that the applicant was in poor health and had been guilty of unethical conduct in a dispute between Benjamin McLain and John W. Terry in 1886–87. Leonard vigorously denied the charges and furnished affidavits from Drs. Joseph S. Martin and Charles F. Blackington to the effect that his affliction would in no way interfere with his performance of the desired duties. These took on a rather hollow sound when the *Rio Grande Republican* announced that Leonard had died on July 6, 1889, and added, "He had been ailing for some time and his death was not unexpected." His survivors could take just pride in the fact that Wallace had characterized the head of their family as "A good lawyer, and an honest man, he is one of the bravest I ever knew."

ACKNOWLEDGMENTS

The writer is indebted to Miss Jane F. Smith, National Archives; Miss Margaret Gleason, State Historical Society of Wisconsin; Mrs. Elizabeth Comfort, State Historical Society of Missouri; Charlotte Marcy Read, Holland Purchase Historical Society; and the Public Library, Batavia, N.Y., for their assistance in collecting the material for this paper.

NOTES

[1] Ira E. Leonard to Lew Wallace, May 20, 1879. In the William Henry Smith Memorial Library of the Indiana Historical Society.

[2] In Proceedings of a Court of Inquiry in the Case of Lt. Col. N.A.M. Dudley. Records of the War Department, QQ 1284. In National Archives.

[3] Cause No. 298, Lincoln County, renumbered Cause No. 533, Doña Ana County, New Mexico.

[4] Rasch, "Five Days of Battle," op. cit. [See Chapter 9.]

[5] Wm. H.H. Llewellyn to Hon. Commissioner, Indian Affairs, July 13, 1881. Records of the Bureau of Indian Affairs. In National Archives.

[6] Ira E. Leonard to Lewis Wallace, November 26, 1888, RG 60. Records of the Department of Justice, Appointment Records. Ira E. Leonard. In National Archives.

20.
THE TULAROSA DITCH WAR

NEW MEXICO HISTORICAL REVIEW, JULY 1968

About six in the afternoon on Thursday, April 28, 1881, Deputy Sheriff Bob Olinger escorted some prisoners from the county courthouse at Lincoln, New Mexico, across the street to Lilly's restaurant for dinner. They had barely been seated when shots were heard. "The Kid has tried to escape and Bell has shot him!" exclaimed the officer. He sprang up and ran back across the street. As he entered the courthouse yard, Billy the Kid discharged a double-barreled shotgun into his head and breast, killing him almost instantly. So much every school boy knows. But who were these prisoners and why were they in custody at the time? Although these men have been neglected in the numerous descriptions of the Kid's famous escape, they are of considerable interest.

The roots of their trouble lay deep in the soil of the territory. In his perceptive *Sky Determines*, Ross Calvin argues that in New Mexico until recently, climate controlled the direction of man's activities and pursuits.[1] Nowhere has this been better exemplified than in the region of the White Sands and the small towns which border their eastern marches. One of these is the now quiet village of Tularosa. Mexicans settled the site in 1858, but were driven back by the Indians. They returned permanently in 1860 and the locale was platted by U.S. government surveyors in 1862. The only water supply was the Tularosa River, which originated from several large springs near the settlement. The colonists immediately began the construction of canals, ditches, and dams to collect the water and distribute it.[2] This brought on clashes with the Mescalero Apaches.

In 1866, the legislature passed an act providing that the settlers' rights to the land and water should be protected against the Indians and all other claimants. When Dr. Joseph H. Blazer, George W. Nesmith, and George H. Abbott purchased the old sawmill in Tularosa Canyon, known as La Maquina, in 1868, they had to agree that all water taken to run the mill would be turned back into the stream.

The first serious trouble seems to have occurred in May 1873. Andrew J. Wilson and some other farmers built several dams across the river. These were destroyed by a party from Tularosa led by Felipe Bernal and José Marcos. Wilson and his friends attempted to repair the dams and were again assaulted by the villagers. Lawrence G. Murphy and Company, Dr. Blazer, "Representing the People of Tularosa Valley," and U.S. Commissioner William Brady petitioned Captain C.H. McKibbin, 15th Infantry, commanding Fort Stanton, for aid and protection. The captain immediately informed Alcalde Perfecto Armijo that he held him personally responsible for not preventing these outbreaks, and warned that he would not tolerate mob action against quiet, law-abiding citizens, many of whom had faithfully served their government as soldiers. He added that he was dispatching Second Lieutenant John W. Wilkinson, 8th Cavalry, and five men to the scene to uphold the civil law, and if necessary would send every available man at the post to support him.

Wilkinson dispersed several small groups of dam-breakers on May 29, but was then attacked by a large gang, who killed one of his horses and wounded the one he was riding. The troopers returned the fire, killing one Mexican. Badly outnumbered, they then fell back to Blazer's Mill, where they were joined by twelve or fourteen Americans. The combined party took up defensive positions and sent a courier to Fort Stanton for reinforcements. Shortly, the building was surrounded by a mob of Mexicans. When the defenders refused to surrender, the Mexicans began firing. About half a hour later, Captain McKibbin and Captain James F. Randlett, 8th Cavalry, were seen approaching with D Troop, 8th Cavalry. The besiegers then dispersed.[3]

Captain McKibbin proceeded to Tularosa, where the parish priest forbade him to enter the town. When the officer observed that something like forty men were posted to defend it, he warned the priest to remove the non-combatants, as he intended to enter by force if necessary. He threatened to hang the priest if fired upon. When they saw a piece of artillery being wheeled into position, the people thought better of the matter and the troops spent the night in the village without incident. Later, McKibbin admitted that his threat had probably been a breach of law, but justified it on the grounds that only the fear of personal punishment had kept the priest from inciting another riot.[4] The grand jury took a less charitable view of his action. After an investigation of the affair, they charged that the captain's conduct was "wholly unwarranted, not to say outrageous," accused him of interfering with purely civil matters with which the Army had no proper concern, and demanded that there be no repetitions of his "unwarranted and tyrannical conduct."[5] There is no evidence that McKibbin's superiors took any notice of their report.

More trouble occurred in 1879, when new settlers took so much water from the river that not even a quantity sufficient for drinking purposes reached the village. The situation was tense for a time, but appears to have quieted down without another armed conflict.[6]

That came in 1881, when employees on the James West ranch, about five miles from Tularosa, began using more water than the villagers were willing to allow. On April 18, they sent Deputy Sheriff Cruz Padilla to serve papers on the men working there. The deputy found John Copeland[7] and a Mexican boy in the fields. Backed by some co-workers, they refused to submit to arrest, contending that since they were in Lincoln County and the deputy was from Doña Ana County, he had no jurisdiction. Padilla had little respect for such legal niceties. He returned to Tularosa, obtained the assistance of Martin Gonzales, Olojino Alijo, and Ruperto Pais, and again went to the ranch. The posse found Charles Wall and Alexander Nunnelly working near the acequia, informed them that they were under arrest and would be taken, dead or alive. When Wall turned to flee, they opened fire, inflicting two flesh wounds. Wall and Nunnelly returned the fire. Copeland, Marejildo Torres, and Augustin A. Balos came to their assistance, with the result that the posse was liquidated in their tracks.[8]

When news of the massacre reached Tularosa, a party of over twenty men set out for the scene. Justice of the Peace Victor Duran was said to have ordered that no arrests be made, but that the men using the water were to be shot down.[9] On the morning of April 19, forty or fifty Mexicans came up to Dr. Blazer's and demanded the surrender of the Nunnelly party. Blazer informed them that the men had already surrendered to Deputy Sheriff William L. Goodlett [Goodlet], of Lincoln County, and that they would be examined the following day. Threats were uttered against the mill owner, but the mob finally contented itself with going to West's ranch, destroying his flood gates, and breaking into and robbing his house. Duran notified Blazer that he would be held in the sum of $200,000 for his actions, as he "had resisted the arm of the law." The justice also proclaimed that he would arrest Second Lieutenant M.W. Day, 9th Cavalry, and some of his men for having violated a city ordinance by entering Tularosa under arms. Day was standing by to defend the post office at South Fork—which he described as "a pair of letter scales and a key." In view of the feeling against all Americans, he declined to be arrested or to permit any of his men to be.[10]

Goodlett [Goodlet] took his prisoners to Las Cruces, where Judge Warren Bristol fixed bail at $1,000 each.[11] That same day, they departed for Lincoln. According to Siringo, their confinement there was little more than nominal.[12] Sheriff Pat Garrett permitted the men to wear their pistols and to use the jail primarily as sleeping quarters. Nunnelly was appointed a trusty and was outside the courthouse when Olinger ran up. He called out to the deputy, "The Kid has killed Bell!" Bob's last words were to answer: "Yes, and he has killed me too."[13]

Among the numerous arms the Kid took was a Winchester. When the trusty complained that it was his gun, the Kid answered, "I don't want your gun, Nunnelly," and selected another. When one of the other prisoners objected that this was his weapon, Billy put it back and took a third rifle.[14]

The Kid ordered Godfrey Gauss and Nunnelly to saddle a horse for him. The latter objected, saying, "Don't you think that will have something to do with my trial next month—I am up for murder." The outlaw answered, "Well, you can tell them that I made you do it."[15]

After the Kid's sensational escape, the prisoners apparently were transferred to the Fort Stanton guardhouse, for Acting Assistant Surgeon Francis H. Atkins protested to the post adjutant that the civilian prisoners had not been given a chance to bathe and change clothes, and had become infected with lice, which he feared might spread to the military prisoners.[16] The men were then turned back to the county authorities.

At the August term of court, the grand jury, under foreman James

J. Dolan, found true bills charging the accused with murder in the fifth degree.[17] The outcome is not known, because the district court record books were taken from Carrizozo a few years ago and have not been returned. The fact that there is no entry in the court register and cost book suggests that the charges may have been dismissed. Moreover, we can follow Wall's activities during the next few years as boss herder for John Poe, John H. Riley, and Max Goldenberg.[18]

The same grand jury found true bills against Dionicio Guiles, Theodosio Carrillo, Juan Isidro Galvan, Juan Sanches, Epifanio Padillo, Ysabel López, Julian Guerra, Bencislado Dominguez, Jose Maria López, Sedero Bargas, Toribio Bargas, Calletano Carrillo, Jose Morales, Juan López, Gregorio Veras, Marcus Chavez, Cruz Viagran, Perfecto Tellis, Juan Miraval, Jose Zamora, and Jose Delfin on charges of assault with intent to commit murder, larceny from a dwelling house, housebreaking, riot, and malicious mischief.[19] These cases were transferred to Doña Ana County on a change of venue. Delfin died, but the others were tried at the April 1882 term of court. Albert J. Fountain appeared as counsel for the defense and succeeded in getting the charges dismissed. This seems to have been the end of attempts to settle rights to the Tularosa waters by gunfire.

NOTES

[1] Ross Calvin, *Sky Determines*, Revised edition (Albuquerque, 1934), p. 1.

[2] *History of New Mexico, Its Resources and People*, 2 vols. (Los Angeles, 1907), vol. 2, p. 823.

[3] C.M. McKibbin to A.A.A. General, District of New Mexico, May 29, 1873, and accompanying papers. National Archives, Record Group 98 (hereinafter cited as NA-RG), District of New Mexico.

[4] C. McKibbin to A.A.A. General, Dist. of New Mexico, June 13, 1873. NA-RG 98.

[5] Daniel Freitze, Foreman of the Grand Jury, to Warren Bristol. NA-RG 98.

[6] Santa Fe *Weekly New Mexican*, June 14, 1879.

[7] This John Copeland was a negro man who had recently been discharged as a private, Company A, 9th Cavalry. He is not to be confused with the former Lincoln County sheriff of the same name.

[8] Santa Fe *Daily New Mexican*, April 24, 1881; Las Vegas *Daily Optic*, April 26, 1881. The spelling of most of the names in the contemporary accounts varies from document to document. Balos, for instance, appears as

Davalos and Dabodas. The writer despairs of determining which versions are correct.

[9] Santa Fe *Daily New Mexican,* May 15, 1881.

[10] M.W. Day to Post Adjutant, Fort Stanton, April 21, 1881. Record of the United States Army Commands, Fort Stanton, New Mexico. Document File 1881–1882, National Archives.

[11] Santa Fe *Daily New Mexican*, June 3, 1881.

[12] Charles Siringo, *Riata and Spurs* (New York, 1927), pp. 103–05.

[13] Alamogordo *News*, June 11, 1936.

[14] Los Angeles Westerners *Branding Iron*, No. 55, December 1960.

[15] Alamogordo *News*, June 25, 1936.

[16] Francis H. Atkins to Post Adjutant, Fort Stanton. Record of the U.S. Army Commands, Fort Stanton.

[17] Causes 385–388, inclusive, Lincoln County. [With regard to "murder in the fifth degree," the Editor consulted the Research Librarian at UNM Law School, who found in the *Revised Statutes of New Mexico, 1865*, chapter 51, section 3, p. 318: "The killing of another human being, by the act, procurement or omission or another, when such killing shall not be made according to the provisions of this chapter, is either justifiable or excusable homicide, or murder in the third, fourth, or fifth degree."]

[18] Albuquerque *Morning Journal*, Feb. 27, 1883; Las Cruces *Rio Grande Republican*, April 18, and May 2, 1885.

[19] Causes 412–422, inclusive, Lincoln County; renumbered 740–749, Doña Ana County.

21.
The Murder of Juan Patrón

Corral Dust, Potomac Corral of the Westerners, July 1960

Historians of pioneer New Mexico have been so preoccupied with Billy the Kid that they have tended to overlook the fact that many of the other participants in the Lincoln County troubles also led exciting and violent careers. In particular, the native New Mexicans have been all but ignored. For example, consider the case of Juan B. Patrón.

Patrón was born about 1855. He is said to have been educated at Notre Dame University,[1] and to have served as lieutenant governor[2] or deputy governor[3] of the territory of New Mexico. These statements are incorrect; there is no record of his matriculating at Notre Dame,[4] and the territory did not have such an office as lieutenant or deputy governor at the time. Nevertheless, his actual accomplishments require no apology. Rendered fatherless by the Horrell's vengeful raid on Lincoln in 1873,[5] Patrón entered politics and distinguished himself at a surprisingly early age. While yet a young man, he became a prominent leader of the Republican Party in Lincoln County, was elected county clerk, and at the time of the Lincoln County War held office as chairman of the county commissioners and speaker of the territorial House of Representatives.

Although he had the reputation of being quarrelsome and dangerous when drinking, Patrón took no active part in the fighting. He was, however, favorably inclined toward the Tunstall-McSween-Chisum faction; not an incomprehensible attitude in view of the fact that he had once been shot in the back by John H. Riley, of the opposing Murphy-Dolan-Riley combination.[6] Unfortunately, the posture of a neutral is not a safe one in a time and place when he who is not with me is assumed to be against me. Convinced that the Dolan forces had delegated Jim Reese to kill him, Patrón sought sanctuary at Fort Stanton. He served as interpreter when the delegation of women from San Patricio called on the post commander, Lieutenant Colonel N.A.M. Dudley, 9th Cavalry, on July 6, 1878, to present a petition imploring his protection. However, Dudley presently found it necessary to warn his guest that he was suspected of being a spy for McSween, and that his life might not be safe even at the fort. On Dudley's advice, Patrón then retired to Las Vegas.

After the Five Days' Battle,[7] Patrón deemed it safe to return to his home. This decision nearly cost him his life. On February 18, 1879, the McSween and Dolan partisans made a peace treaty. After dining together at the Ballard home, the reconciled enemies toured the placita. During the festivities, they visited the residence of Patrón, whereupon William Campbell suddenly announced that he was going to kill their host, and was dissuaded only with difficulty. After Campbell did kill Mrs. McSween's lawyer, Huston I. Chapman, later that evening,[8] Governor Lew Wallace hurried to Lincoln and took personal charge of the situation. To aid him, he organized a militia company, with Patrón as captain, and Billy the Kid and Tom O'Folliard were lodged in Patrón's house after their surrender.

In 1883, Patrón opened a large hotel at Puerto de Luna, where he enjoyed the esteem of both the native New Mexicans and the Anglos. If he had lived, said Otero,[9] he certainly would have been elected to Congress. It is a big "if."

On the night of April 9, 1884, Patrón and his brother-in-law, Cresenciano Gallegos, dropped into Moore's saloon for a glass of beer. There are two very different accounts of what then transpired. According to Patrón's friends, Patrón shortly told his relative that he was sleepy and was going home. A Texas cowboy, Michael Erskine Maney, thereupon walked behind the counter, drew his pistol, wantonly shot Patrón, and then emptied his revolver into the crowd, wounding a Mexican named Gregorio Baros. They attributed the crime to the fact that Maney had been hired to kill Patrón by men who believed that he knew too much about their actions during the Lincoln County War.[10]

Maney spent the night on the Pecos River, the following morning going to the house of George Davidson, where he surrendered to Davidson and Nicholas Griego. After a hearing before Justice of the Peace Pablo Annilla, he was sent to the Las Vegas jail. According to the killer himself, he was born in Seguin, Texas, on June 23, 1857. His father served several terms as district judge and then became editor of the *News*, at Pearsall, Texas. Maney had worked on his father's ranch until the fall of 1883, at which time he had come to New Mexico and obtained a job on the J.J. Cox ranch, under foreman W.S. Peacock.[11] Later, he worked for Charles W. Haynes. In the course of his employment, he had visited Puerto de Luna several times and had become well acquainted with Patrón. On the night of the shooting, the hotel owner had been drinking heavily and had taken violent exception to the fact that Maney was wearing his six-shooter, remarking, according to Maney, that "anyone who would wear a six-shooter was a damned coward," and that "he would get his six-shooter and come back and show me the kind of shooting he could do." The two men separated and Maney went to Moore's saloon. About fifteen minutes later, Patrón entered and started to draw a revolver stuck in his belt. Maney had been warned that Patrón was an ugly customer when drinking; fearing for his life, he promptly shot the New Mexican. Maney specifically denied that he had ever been a member of the Kid's gang or had been hired to kill Patrón.[12]

Then began one of the protracted legal battles so dear to the hearts of New Mexicans. At the district court hearing, Maney pled "not guilty" and gave bail in the sum of $10,000. The case was called for trial on August 22, 1884, but was postponed as witnesses for the defense could not be in attendance. Judge Samuel B. Axtell thereupon remanded him to jail without bond, which, complained the Las Vegas *Daily Optic*, "is, to say the least, very unjust and without precedent....This seems to us to savor more of persecution than a legal prosecution."[13] The murderer again appeared for trial the first week in December. Once more, the defense witnesses failed to appear, owing to the fact they were under indictment for gambling. The case went to trial anyhow, but the jury disagreed.[14] Maney's case came up a third time at the March, 1885, term of court, but his lawyers were successful in obtaining a change of venue to Santa Fe, where trial was set for July.[15]

To the general surprise of the citizenry, Maney's bondsmen suddenly delivered him to the sheriff and withdrew from his bonds, stating only that they had good reasons for their action. The more cynical denizens freely predicted that this meant that Maney would shortly escape from jail. To the astonishment of practically no one, this occurred on May 10, 1885. Early that evening, Maney and a thief named Richard Elliott entered the privy—and failed to return. In the course of time, a guard went to look for them, whereupon it was found that they had escaped through a hole which had been cut in the ceiling. While both prisoners were shackled at the time, it was assumed that friends were waiting on the outside to remove these impediments to rapid transit. It may be significant that Maney's brother was in town and loafing around a livery stable at the time.[16]

Governor Lionel Sheldon promptly offered a reward of $500 for his recapture, and deputies promptly mounted their horses and galloped off in all directions. Such diligence in locking the barn after the disappearance of the horse may have been most commendable but it was also unprofitable. Maney made a clean getaway. Probably, he eventually returned to his home in Texas, for on September 25, 1886, the governor of New Mexico issued a requisition on the governor of Texas for Maney's arrest. Presumably, this was never served, since the Texas Archives contain no record of the case.[17] In 1890, Governor Ross withdrew all offers of rewards outstanding, with the exception of one for Vidal Romero. With the profit motive thus removed, it appears likely that interest in Maney promptly languished. For all the writer knows to the contrary, he may have lived more or less happily ever afterwards.

ACKNOWLEDGMENTS

The writer is indebted to Mrs. Elma A. Medearis, Library of the Museum of New Mexico; William S. Wallace, Rodgers Library; Dorman H. Winfrey, Texas State Library, Archives Division; and Thomas T. McAvoy, University of Notre Dame, for their assistance in compiling this paper.

NOTES

[1] Miguel Antonio Otero, *My Life on the Frontier, 1882–1879.* Albuquerque: University of New Mexico Press, 1939. 11:141.

[2] Ealy, *Water in a Thirsty Land,* op. cit., p. 78.

[3] Frederick W. Nolan, "John H. Tunstall, Merchant." English Westerners *Brand Book*, 4:n.p., March, 1958.

[4] Thomas T. McAvoy, Personal communication, April 30, 1959.

[5] Rasch, "The Horrell War," op. cit. [See Chapter 2.]

[6] Mesilla *News*, September 18, 1875.

[7] Rasch, "Five Days of Battle," op. cit. [See Chapter 9.]

[8] Rasch, "The Murder of Huston I. Chapman," op. cit. [See Chapter 18.]

[9] Otero, op. cit., p. 142.

[10] Las Vegas *Daily Optic*, April 12, 1884.

[11] Peacock himself was assassinated by James C. White on October 16, 1886.

[12] Ibid., April 15, 1884.

[13] Ibid., August 23, 1884.

[14] Ibid., December 6, 1884.

[15] Ibid., March 9, 1885.

[16] Ibid., May 11, 1885.

[17] Winfrey, Dorman H., personal communication, October 16, 1959.

Index